COAL 'MARKETIN

Trade cards were u.
such as G.J. Cocker
Eaton Wharf, Piml.
to the Queen', comb.
guaranteed weight.

RNHILL LONDON.

WHARVES.

PURFLEET WHARF, EARL S^{T.} BLACKFRIARS,
EATON WHARF, LOWER BELGRAVE P^{L.} PIMLICO.

O^r 6 1858

Cockerell & Co.

MERCHANTS.

th Payne & Smiths.

WEIGHING MACHINE

EACH SACK SHOULD CONTAIN 224 lbs.
OF COAL EXCLUSIVE OF THE SACK.

26/ -

£ 3 - 18 -

6

3 - 12

t on Delivery
r Chaldron.

J. Cockerell & Co

E Bay

Oct

The History of
THE WORSHIPFUL COMPANY OF
FUELLERS

THE FUELLER'S TALE

IN CARBONE ROBUR NOSTRUM

The publication of this History has been effected with the co-operation of the Coal Merchants' Federation (Great Britain) and The Society of Coal Factors, and made possible through funding by The Coal Meters Committee and The Worshipful Company of Fuellers.

WOODMONGER SIR ROBERT BROWNE
The Livery's first and only Lord Mayor of London, 1661 (see Chapter II).

The History of
The Worshipful Company of
Fuellers

The Fueller's Tale

The Livery for Energy

From the forests and outcrops of Chaucerian England
to the global fuel economy of the 21st century

Roderick Braithwaite

IN CARBONE ROBUR NOSTRUM

Phillimore

2010

Published by
PHILLIMORE & CO. LTD
Chichester, West Sussex, England
www.phillimore.co.uk

© The Worshipful Company of Fuellers, 2010

ISBN 978-1-86077-578-9

Printed and bound in Great Britain

Contents

List of Illustrations

Frontispiece: Sir Robert Browne

Illustration Acknowledgements

The author and publisher would like to thank the following individuals and organisations for permission to reproduce material. Every effort has been made to contact copyright holders and photographers, but if any errors or omissions have been made, we would be happy to correct them in a later printing.

Numbers refer to illustrations:

4 Adapted from Bazely, M., *Extent of the English Forest in the 13th century*, TRHS, 4 (CUP, 1921); **5** Adapted from Trevelyan, G.M., *English Social History*, Longmans, Reprint Soc. (1944); **6** Adapted from Lobel, M.D., *Historic Towns Atlas* (OUP, 1989); **7** Chaloner & Musson, *Industry & Technology* (1963), *Holkham Bible, 1325-30*; **9** Chaloner & Musson, *Industry & Technology*: Decretals of Gregory, BL, Royal MS 10, E IV, fol. 145v; **10** Reconstruction by Christopher Hughes: Birch, C., *Carr and Carman*; **12** Extract from 'Crafts and Companies in some Civic Lists 1328-1518': Table 9.1, Barron, C.M., *London in the Later Middle Ages: Government and People, 1200-1500* (OUP, 2004), pp.218-23; **13** Adapted from: 'Theoretical extent of London's faggot supply zone, *c.*1300 & *c.*1400': *EconHR*: 'Fuelling the City': Galloway, J., Keene, D. & Murphy, M.; **14** GH; **15** Museum of London; **16** (From left to right, left:) Hazlitt, W.C., *Livery Companies of the City of London* (1892), Hylton Dale, *The Fellowship of the Woodmongers* (1922), Brown, R., *Digging for History* (1988); **17** Rowlandson MS, Bodleian Library, University of Oxford: MS.Rawl.D.725b, fols. 1v, 2r: transcription by Dr Pamela Taylor; **18** Sudbury Town Hall, Suffolk and Mayor's Secretary, Teresa Elford; **19** Holmes, *Elizabethan London*: Braun & Hogenberg, *Civitates Orbis Terrarum*, Museum of London; **20** *History of the British Coal Industry*, v.1 (OUP); **21** Rowlandson MS, Bodleian Library, Oxford; **22** Dale, *Woodmongers*, Guildhall Library, City of London, & Marquess of Salisbury; Prockter & Taylor, *A to Z – Elizabethan London*. See text and Endnote 43; **23** Prockter & Taylor, LTS 122, *A to Z – Elizabethan London*, Colvin & Foister, LTS 151, *Wyngaerde's Panorama of London, c.1544**; *Rocque's Plan of ... London* (1746), Guildhall Library, City of London. *See* Endnote 43 ref date; **24** Museum of London; **25** Guildhall Library, City of London; **26** The National Archives, Kew, London: State Papers for 1667 (*see* Endnotes); **27** Wellcome Library, London; **28** Museum of London; **29** Adapted from Hearsey, *The Great Fire* (1965), also Museum of London; **30** Adapted from a sketch copied from a contemporary plan of London: Dale, *Woodmongers*, Guildhall Library, City of London; **31** Museum of London; **32** Guildhall Library, City of London and

Office of the Mayor of Westminster; **33** *History of the British Coal Industry* (OUP), v.1 'From abundance to scarcity'; **34** McCombe, C., *Museum in Docklands;* **35** From *History of the British Coal Industry*, v.2, Table 8.1: 'Shares of the London market in British & North-east output' (OUP); **36** Guildhall Library, City of London; **37** Science & Society Picture Library; **38** Adapted from Map 1.1., 'Coalfields, principal towns, and navigable rivers, *c.*1700', *History of the British Coal Industry*, v.1 (OUP); **39** 'Extracts from the Diary of Ralph Jackson, Apprentice Hostman', Thornton, J., *Bound for the Tyne*, published as a quartercentenary celebration by the Society of Hostmen, Newcastle upon Tyne, courtesy of J. Petty, correspondent and friend of The Fuellers; **40** C. McCombe; **41** Guildhall Library, City of London; **42** Mayhew, H., *London Labour and the London Poor;* **43** Photograph by M. Barron; **44** Marcellus Laroon, 1688, Dale, *Woodmongers*, F31, November, 2008; **45** Guildhall Library, City of London; **46** Adapted from Pudney, J., *London's Docks* (Thames & Hudson); **47** Mayhew, H., *London Labour and the London Poor;* **48** PM Richard Horne; **49** Dale, *Woodmongers*, courtesy of City of London Surveyor; **50** 1808 print by Rowlandson & Pugin for Ackermann: Guildhall Library, City of London; **51** *ILN*, Guildhall Library, City of London; **53** *ILN*, 8.xi.1849: Eden Hooper, W., *The London Coal Exchange*, Guildhall Library, City of London; **54** Guildhall Library, City of London; **55** John Crowther (1837?-1902?): Guildhall Library, City of London; **56** *Industry & Technology*, Tomlinson, C., *The Useful Arts and Manufactures of Great Britain* (1848); **57** Guildhall Library, City of London; **58** Nail, M., *Coal Duties ...* (1972), also thanks to PM C. McCombe; **59** PM R. Horne and Guildhall Library, City of London; **60** Guildhall Library, City of London; and photograph, George Davison, 1887; National Media Museum, Bradford: Science & Society Picture Library, former Kodak Museum. 'Coal Heavers'; **61** Ayle, 1999: PM C. McCombe, *Mining Magazine* competition; **62** Guildhall Library, City of London, 'PIP'; **64** 'PIP': Guildhall Library, City of London; 'Women at War', Horace Nicholls, National Media Museum, Bradford; **65** *History of the British Coal Industry* (OUP), Illingworth cartoon from author's cartoon collection; **66** Goodall, F., *Burning to Serve*; **67** P. Stafford, SCM and Fuellers' Archive; **68** Smith, *Seacoal*: Museum in Docklands; **70** *History of the British Coal Industry*, V.5: **71** Thérèse Stephenson Clarke.

Roman numerals refer to Chapter V: To the Twenty-First Century – Corporate Life: A Pictorial Review:

Eleni Abbott, XXXVII (left); John Bainbridge, XXXVIII, XXXIX (left); Mrs Marianne Bainbridge, XIV; Doug Barrow, XVII; Jim Bellew, XXXII; The British Parachute Association, XXV (right); Crown Copyright (LS/87/3399/5), IV, (93/6163/12), VII; James Hill, XI, XV, XVIII, XX, XXXI, XXXIV, XXVIII, XXXI, XXXIV; Richard Horne, V; Lewis Photos, XXIII, XXIV; 'Mac' McCombe, X, XI, XII, XIII, XIX, XXI, XXII, XXVI, XXVII, XXIX; Mansion House Photographers, XXX (right); Photoshot, XXXVI, XXXVII (right); Gerald Sharp Photography, XVIII, XXV (centre); The Worshipful Company of Fuellers, 'Presentation of the Grant of Letters Patent, 17 October 1984, Commemorative Booklet', III.

Acknowledgements

I record my gratitude to the many people who have assisted me in researching, improving and producing this first authorised History of the Worshipful Company of Fuellers, and to Noel Osborne, Andrew Illes, Sarah Pavey and the Phillimore team. I apologise if, inadvertently, despite my best efforts, credit and acknowledgement have not been given where they were due.

Fuellers Past and Present:

Frances Algar; John Bainbridge; Doug Barrow; David Bell; Colin Brinkman; Michael Bryer Ash; Mary Chandler; Thérèse, Edmund and Richard Stephenson Clarke; Roger Cloke; Lord Ezra of Horsham; Jane Heginbotham; Richard Horne; John Josling; Chris Le Fevre; Cyril McCombe; David Port; Joy Puttock; Rex Rose; Sir Antony Reardon Smith; Peter Stafford; David Waring; Brig. Edward Wilkinson; Vaughan Williams.

Historians:

Dr Roger Axworthy; Prof. Caroline Barron; Dr Francis Goodall; Dr Clare Martin; Derek Morris; Jim Sewell, former City Archivist, Corporation of London; Dr Pamela Taylor, Archivist, Girdlers' Company; David Wedderburn.

Mayors' Offices:

City of London: Murray Craig, Clerk of the Chamberlain's Court
City of Westminster: Kevin Taylor
Sudbury Town Hall: Mrs Teresa Elford, Mayor's Secretary

Members of Other Liveries:

Keith Court; Gordon Hawes; Barry Isted; Colin Middlemiss; Alan Woollaston.

Archives, Libraries, Institutions, Churches

The Bodleian Library, University of Oxford
Cambridge University Library
City of London, Guildhall Library:
    Stephen Freeth, former Keeper of Manuscripts
    John Fisher, Jeremy Smith, Prints & Maps
    Principal Archivist: Charlie Turpie
    Senior Archivist: Wendy Hawke
Guards Museum: Archivist Maj. Wright, L/Sgt J.E. Tack
Hostmen of Newcastle upon Tyne: J. Petty
House of Lords Library
Institute of Historical Research, University of London
The London Library
London Metropolitan Archives
Museum of London: John Clark, Deputy Head of Department, Early London
    History and Collections, and Nikki Braunton
Museum in Docklands: Dr Tom Wareham, Curator & Claire Frankland,
    Archivist
National Archives, Kew
National Media Museum, Bradford: Brian Liddy
Reform Club: Simon Blundell, Librarian
Royal Society of Arts: Bob Baker, Archivist
St Martin-in-the-Fields: Rev. N.R. Holtham, Chris Brooker
Wellcome Library, Wellcome Trust
Westminster City Archive
Whitworth Art Gallery, University of Manchester

Photography

Marcus Barron
Roger Cloke

List of Subscribers

Brigadier Ian Abbott OBE
J.P. Allen
Air Commodore Paul Atherton OBE RAF
Richard Austen AO
Jane Ayre
Andrew Bainbridge
Daniel Bainbridge
James Bainbridge
John & Marilynne Bainbridge
Ronald C. Baker
Dr Paul W. Banks
Deputy & Mrs Doug Barrow
Anthony James Bellew
James Aloysius Bellew
Jordan Samuel Bellew
J. Ann Bonathan
Colin Brinkman
Neville A. Brown JP
Rodney G. Brown
Michael R.T. Bryer Ash
Richard Budge
Geoffrey Cooke Bunting
W.J. Burke
John P. Byrne
Michael Byrne
Sarah Pauline Carr
Alan Chalmers
Neville Chamberlain CBE
Roger Cloke

F. Don Cox
Niall C. Crabb
Paul A. Cuttill OBE
John Daniel
Robert G. Davy
Nigel Draffin
Mark Evans
Mark Fairbairn OBE
William F. Fortescue
Peter Gaffney
Dr Paul W. Glover MA
Stuart Goldsmith
Peter Grabowski
Dr Michael Green
F. Brian Harrison CBE
Janet & Peter Harrison
Patrick J. Helly
Charles Edward Hewitt
James V.G. Hill
Steve Hodges
John M. Holt
Richard N. Horne
Michael & Paula Husband
Phillip, Sophie & Adam Husband
John Edward Ingham
Adam A. Janikowski
Stefan Judisch
Donald M. Kinnersley MEI
Christopher Nelson Le Fevre

Dallas Lewis
David John Lewis
Tim Lines
J. Brian Lott OBE
John F.P. Lush
Professor Averil Macdonald
Kay MacLeod
Cyril Bernard Mandry
Peter Marshall
Gerry McCann
Bryony McCombe
Cyril 'Mac' McCombe MBE
Ewan McCombe
Doreen McGechan
M.J. Meyer
Paul K. Mott
Nick Moulton MBE
Revd Dr Peter Mullen
Antony Nicholls
Chris Nowakowski
Dr Charles L. Panayides
Katie & Daniel Pantaney
Sir John Parker
David Port
Lynn Port

Claire Poulton
William S. Pretswell
Margaret Pugh
Sir Antony Reardon Smith Bt
Rex Rose
Terrence Shapland
John E. Sharp
Revd Canon John H. Sheen MA
Anthony Shillingford
Archie Smith
John M. Spence
Peter M. Stafford
Richard Stephenson Clarke
Thérèse Stephenson Clarke
G.B. Strahan
P.J. Tottman
Russel Warburton
June Waring
Graham C. Watson
Graham R. Westcott
Brigadier Edward Wilkinson CBE TD DL
Vaughan Williams
Dennis Woods
Gerry Yockney
Ellin Nina Zomaya

THE RIGHT HONOURABLE THE LORD MAYOR
ALDERMAN NICK ANSTEE

I am delighted to have been invited by the Master and the Court of the Worshipful Company of Fuellers to provide this preface to the history of the organisation.

Although today, it is one of the City of London's Modern Companies, ranking 95th in precedence, the history of the Fuellers, in its guise as the Fellowship of Woodmongers, reaches back down the centuries to its original roots in medieval times. The book is the result of painstaking research into the fascinating story of the two companies, the ancestral Woodmongers and today's Fuellers. It is sad to reflect on the unfortunate demise of the former company, but very pleasing to follow the path leading to its rebirth. It is most fitting that this erudite work has been produced as part of a celebration of the Fuellers' 25th anniversary year.

I believe that this book will be of great interest, not only to present and future Fuellers, but also to those who are interested in the history and traditions of the livery companies of London.

My best wishes to the Company in this, its anniversary year – The Worshipful Company of Fuellers, root and branch, may it flourish for ever.

Foreword

It gives me great pleasure to write this foreword to the history of the Fuellers for two reasons. First, it is an intriguing and tangled tale going back to the 12th century; and secondly, it has been researched and recounted with great skill by Roderick Braithwaite, who is highly experienced in this field.

When I joined the newly-formed National Coal Board in 1948, having studied history before the War, I tried to find a history of the coal industry. I was amazed to learn that there was none in existence apart from Nef's great work on the coal industry, particularly in the 16th and 17th centuries. Over 20 years later, when I was chairman of the NCB, I put in hand a five-volume history of the industry which was in due course published.

I regard the history of the Fuellers as a worthy complement to the history of the coal industry as a whole.

In this book we learn about the early and humble beginnings of the Woodmongers and that their guild was first mentioned in 1376. During the following centuries they grew in strength, handling coal as well as wood. But by the middle of the 17th century, trade wars occurred with other guilds, especially the Carmen, and in 1667 the Woodmongers' Charter was surrendered. From then until 1984, there was no Livery Company to represent the fuel distributive trade.

Meanwhile, as the coal industry expanded, so did the coal trade. When coal mining was nationalised after the last war, coal distribution was left in private hands. It was one of my principal tasks during my many years in the NCB to develop effective working relations with the coal trade which, with help on all sides, I believe was achieved.

I gladly gave my support to the project for reviving the old Woodmongers Guild. However, it soon became clear that there would be strong objections to this name from the Companies involved in the disputes in the 17th century and I am very pleased that as a result the name was changed to Fuellers, which now covers the full range of energy activities.

From ancient Woodmonger to modern Fueller has been a long, arduous and fascinating journey, vividly narrated by the author. Energy has once again become a crucial element in the world economy. I am glad Fuellers contributed effective and constructive comments on the Government's Energy White Paper and that the annual Energy Lecture is now an established and important event in the energy calendar. The Fuellers are playing an important contributory role in the formulation of energy policy.

May this last for many years.

Lord Ezra
March 2009

Introduction

Faces in the Fire

In what many claim to be an ominously overheating world, it is clear that the Fuellers' Livery Company – as evidenced in its submissions to the Department of Trade and Industry and in its annual Energy Lectures – is wholly committed to the 21st-century causes of fuel economy and the investigation and control of the effects of carbon emissions.[1]

One item of 'carbon-based' nostalgia may nevertheless still be in order, as a starting point for this first History of a Company that is in fact unique in the world of Liveries.

For children born prior to the age of smokeless fuels, when new houses still had chimneys, 'Faces in the Fire' was a favourite childhood pastime. Fortunate owners of woodburning stoves or inglenook fireplaces can still enjoy that ancient indulgence; the flickering flames of what was once proudly proclaimed by a great national industry as 'the living fire' reveal magical glimpses of strange faces and outlines, some good and firm, others shadowy and evanescent.

It is appropriate that the Company of Fuellers, with origins rooted in man's need for the staple requisites of heat and shelter against the cold, may be characterised here and later in this History through images created by their own products. Over the millennium of his known existence the trades now embraceable with hindsight under the term 'Fueller' move briefly into focus and as quickly fade away again, with gaps of darkness and moments of clarity, like the open fires of old. The 'Fueller' evolves under two dozen different, sometimes concurrent hats: *Lignarius*, *Focarius*, *Buscarius*, Buscher, Wood- or Timber-monger, Coal Meter, Carman, Merchant Adventurer/Hostman/Fitter, Coal Factor/Broker, Crimp, Coal Craft Owner, Wharfinger, Lighterman/Coal Buyer, Undertaker, Coal Merchant, Chandler/Chapman, Small-Coal Man and even 'Coal-Seller'.[2]

From the time of Chaucer's later Middle Ages and even earlier, through to the Livery's revival in the 1980s, these 'Fuellers' have now been coaxed out of the woodwork of history: Robert Wudemongere, Peter le Wodemongere and William

Wodemongere; sheriffs Thomas and Henry Box; Coal Meters John Wirhale, Roger Cook, Henry Cornewaille and Geoffrey Prudhomme; four merchants in the wider tradition of Lord Mayors of Greater London: of the City, Richard Lovekin, Henry le Waleys, and Sir Richard Browne; and as their equivalent, first citizen of the City of Westminster, Pepys' friend, Sir Edmund Berry Godfrey; first Masters John Talworth, John Rephawe; joint-founder of the Carmen, Robert Hammond; first Masters of the combined Woodmongers and Carmen – Thomas Hunt, and then George Heall and his Wardens John Harrison and Henry Williams; or another Pepysian friend, the timber merchant Sir William Warren.[3] A contemporary list would include such legendary trade names or surnames as Horne, Cory, Puttock, Clarke, Charrington and Ezra. An array of over 200 men and women in the text and also in the Endnotes has to represent the thousands who from origins in the London-based distributive trades of wood and coal can be seen to have taken part in the world of today's 'Fueller'.

The Focus

Behind such citizens, the legal imprints of many monarchs – Edwards I, II, III and VI, Henrys II and VIII, James I, Charles I and II, Victoria and both Queen Elizabeths – have a legitimate place, too, in the story's margins. Indeed, if the focus had been on coal alone, then the pantheon of names might even have been extended to include, as did the recent American best-seller, *Coal, A Human History*, such names as Friedrich Engels and Winston Churchill.

However, although ultimately this is not a narrative about any one industry's products or end-use, carbon fuels do run like a rich black thread through the story as whole.[4] The Fuellers' history, like the present-day membership of the Livery itself, is broad church: it certainly touches on such related topics as fuel policy, energy conservation, transport and shipping. Its epicentre, however, is not production, but the selling and utilisation of the resultant product; not politico-technical, but socio-economic, focused on the people who can now be seen as Fuellers.

The Mystery of Fuel

The opening page of the History of a Livery with close associations with the Fuellers – that of The Carmen – carries a quotation from its one-time Master, HRH the Princess Royal, Princess Anne: 'If you know where you have been, it is easier to know where to go to next.'[5] In the case of the Fuellers, that assumption of certainty could mislead; the main thrust of their 21st-century History could as well have been entitled 'The Mystery of Fuel'.

That story is also a mystery in itself. Thanks to the ravages of the Great Fire of London in the *annus horribilis* of the Fuellers' predecessors, the merchant-Woodmongers, 1666-7, they have no surviving records. Much of their past is mysterious, even today. The disentangling of its many myths and formats before emerging as 'The Fuellers' in the late 20th century is therefore a challenge to the social historian.[6]

The process has to assume the character of a detective investigation, with imaginative inference from recent research coming to the aid of the bare facts as they emerge: 'almost all that is worth knowing has to be mined like precious metals out of a rock'. Inevitably, the emphasis of the History evolves from that detailed medieval research to a broader contemporary canvas.[7]

The Chaucerian flavour of the sub-title highlights the broad-brush medieval starting point for much social history, not least that of Trevelyan, and the evolution of the Liveries.[8] It also underlines a key theme – the need to discover a continuity in those who, with the historian's gift of 20:20 hindsight, now merit the title of 'Fueller'.[9]

Their business in fuel is treated as a constant across time, Fig. 1, whatever the trade titles of its practitioners. Typically, the objectives of that trade, such as wood and coal, have fluctuated over the course of history, from being taken for granted, often marginalised or not even mentioned by the historians, to becoming recurrently – and now foreseeably into the future – a focus for high national interest by reason of their decreasing availability.

The Setting: A World of Contrasts

The world of such Livery Companies is a world of contrasts. It is one based today primarily in the City of London, yet its perspective is global. The titles of almost half of its constituent Companies bespeak trades or activities that no longer describe the callings of its members – the 'Livery'. It is still a proud and, indeed, patriotic entity in the life of 'the City', yet it has no overarching corporate mechanism.

The characteristic mode of its aficionados has long been social, collegiate, convivial, seemingly inward-looking – yet the main calls upon the funds of that membership are outgoing, altruistic and above all charitable. The end-purpose of what now accounts for some £40 million of charitable giving has been largely subsumed by the State over the past century, yet that community interaction remains as strong and sincere as ever.

A superficial glance suggests an anachronistic mini-world, secluded from the mainstream, long-since shorn of the regulatory powers that the Liveries' previous existence as Guilds once exercised over their trades. In reality, however, Fuellers are seen to include 'expert specialists in all areas of the energy industry' and significant figures in the nation's financial and industrial 'Networks': although they do not feature in Tim Heald's insightful book of that name, it is not for nothing that the Livery Companies are worthy of mention in Anthony Sampson's more seminal analysis of the country's power structures, *The Anatomy of Britain*.

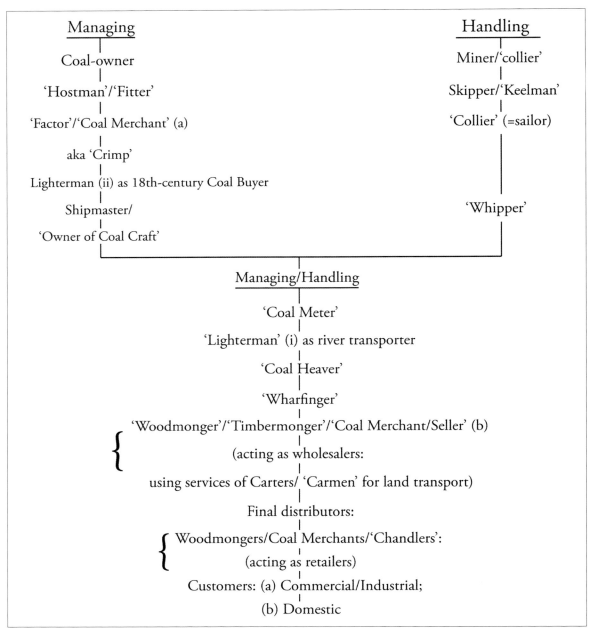

Managing   Handling

Coal-owner   Miner/'collier'

'Hostman'/'Fitter'   Skipper/'Keelman'

'Factor'/'Coal Merchant' (a)   'Collier' (=sailor)

aka 'Crimp'

Lighterman (ii) as 18th-century Coal Buyer

Shipmaster/   'Whipper'

'Owner of Coal Craft'

Managing/Handling

'Coal Meter'

'Lighterman' (i) as river transporter

'Coal Heaver'

'Wharfinger'

'Woodmonger'/'Timbermonger'/'Coal Merchant/Seller' (b)

(acting as wholesalers:

using services of Carters/ 'Carmen' for land transport)

Final distributors:

Woodmongers/Coal Merchants/'Chandlers':

(acting as retailers)

Customers: (a) Commercial/Industrial;

(b) Domestic

1   THE MULTI-STAGE PROCESS IN THE MARKETING OF SOLID FUEL

Although one of the abiding themes of the Fuellers' story will be the final utilisation of all fuels, the greater part of the text will be occupied with the preceding process of distribution. It will also need to unravel the complex of overlapping trades and functions that, over time, became involved in that total process, reaching forward from the producer, through to the final consumer. Solid fuel is inevitably the predominant objective of that narrative. This simplified diagram sets out two sequential streams of human activity – broadly distinguished between 'Managing' and 'Handling' – which formed sections of the role of what can now be seen as the evolving 'Fueller'. They come together under the still familiar label, 'Coal Merchant': (the trade's different ways of working [(i) and (ii)] are explored in Chapter IV). For terms in inverted commas, see Glossary.

Whilst some of the Companies have become household names through their links with the eponymous independent schools founded for their members, such as the Merchant Taylors, the majority of former titles, such as the Woodmongers of London or the Skinners, are no longer current usage. Most of the Liveries are preceded by the designation 'Worshipful', redolent not only of the religious fraternity origins of their ancient predecessors, but also of its medieval sense of 'worship' as obligation and allegiance to a superior; in any case, the practice of the established religion is only formally observed in the annual calendars of events, and is not made a prerequisite of becoming a member of a 'Livery'.[10]

A Context for The Fuellers

Where then does The Worshipful Company of Fuellers fit into this complex picture – is it yet one more of those facets of British national life, so idiosyncratic as to defy comprehension by anyone trying to bring British institutions into line with other 21st-century trans-national organisations?

Or is this small but articulate body, already proudly alone in the global canon of guilds and liveries in embracing fuel and energy as its core interest, also topically unique in another way too?

Looking way beyond their historic origins, the Fuellers have in fact a vital message for their time – and for a world village where resources appear finite. It may be that this is indeed a rather special group of people – a community where experience and insight have at the very least a key consultative role in the devising of policies for the best utilisation of the planet's energy.

The first authorised account of what, in its branches, is one of the youngest – yet in its roots one of the oldest – Livery Companies sets out to answer these central questions. It thereby puts in place one more piece of that vast jigsaw constituting the continuous sweep of British life and history, so finely represented by the City of London. It also exemplifies the evolutionary path of the Liveries: in texture – from the corporate to the personal; in mode – from the economic through the political, and finally to the symbolic and social.

It is timely to highlight one particular problem facing the historian of a group of trades that started out under the now obscure title of woodmongers – so obscure that in an ostensibly authoritative London encyclopaedia, the sole index reference to Woodmongers turns out to relate to a quite different though related Livery.[11] All recent writing has used as its base a slim fuel-oriented volume that appeared in 1922, H.B. Dale's *The Fellowship of Woodmongers*: none of the later coal-related historians – J. Nef, Raymond Smith or the authors of the epic five-volume British Coal Industry series – has felt the need to dig beyond that early, estimable but largely unauthenticated work to extend the enquiry into the early wholesaling Woodmongers themselves.

This History aims to remedy that deficiency: the research has explored many new avenues, including much original but so far unconnected work by academic historians, to verify and, if possible, get behind Dale's articles (and his lecture to the Royal Society of Arts); this work incidentally also ignored the woodmongers' sale of 'timber'. In that process, many background themes of current relevance are identified too: the legal framework for 'true price' against monopolies, closed-shops and trade practices, pricing and the public interest, and the early practice of lobbying.[12]

The narrative also tries to illuminate many forgotten corners which were in their time entirely familiar to the wood and coal trade, but which today demand maps and a Glossary. Just as there is a case for linguistic guidance on terms such as 'bavins', 'talwode', 'crimping', 'jumping' and 'whipping', 'cats', 'hags', 'turn' and 'tret', so there is need to re-visit several historic locations in and out of London, including sites for the Woodmongers' Halls, to position the ancient fuel trade in its setting: Sea Coal Lane, Roomland and Woodwharf, Billingsgate, Duke's Place, Castle Baynard, High Timber Street, St Andrew Hubbard and the famous Coal Posts; (*see* Appendices).

At the heart of this tale there is one word, with an honourable but long-neglected past, which not only serves to embrace much of the Livery's earlier activities but, more particularly, the wide range of its potential membership, and its public stance: the 'Fuellers'. The presentation of their History is equally singular. It has the unity of a one-act play; its five separate scenes highlight the five main evolutionary phases of the world of those many citizens, who once grew solely from the microcosm of London but who are now drawn from Britain as a whole.

Chaucer himself, who never formally completed what in due course he called *The Tales of Canterbury*, could well have dubbed this History, 'The Fueller's Tale'.

[13]

IN CARBONE ROBUR NOSTRUM

2 THE FUELLERS' COAT OF ARMS

For the heraldic 'blazon' (description) of what is a 'heater' (as in flat-iron) shield and the full 'achievement' of the Company's Coat of Arms, see Chapter IV, p.109.

I

 ## The Twelfth to Fifteenth Centuries

The Fueller as Woodmonger-Timbermonger;
The Early Coal Meters:

from trade … to Livery: *'A solempne and a great fraternitee'*

Introducing the World of the Medieval Fueller – Clarifying the Language – Enter a Woodmonger, Left – Woodmongers in the 'London Vineyard' – 'The Best and most Trustworthy Men' – A 'Clean Air' Movement: First Glimmerings? – The Woodmonger and his London – Wood and the Woodmonger – Developing the 'Fueller' Concept: The Coal Meters – Classifying the Worshipful Companies – The Woodmongers in relation to Other Guilds – Coals from Newcastle

As The Fuellers' customary toast emphasises, this History grows from their 'roots' to their 'branches' – to the British fuel trade and its related networks. If one may here be allowed to mix metaphors, a vast medieval haystack conceals the scattered needles of those early roots! They comprise The Fuellers' earliest appearances – as *buscarii* – and as the 'woodmongers' of London. The Woodmongers' first researcher, Hylton Dale, in his Royal Society of Arts paper on 20 October 1922, noted that the long history of those Woodmongers, the main predecessors to the Fuellers, eventually ran on into the late 19th century: 'Acts of Parliament for long continued to style Coal Merchants as Woodmongers'.[1]

Each of this History's four main eras has a striking association with some of Europe's major literary figures. The works of Chaucer, Shakespeare, Pepys and many others all make contributions to the enhancement and imagery of this account of today's energy industry Livery.

 ## *i: Introducing the World of the Medieval Fueller*

In this History, there are many questions to which any Fueller, or indeed anyone with an interest in the City of London and its ancient institutions, will seek answers: What were the origins of the Company – both the 'original' medieval

[1]

3 THE FUELLERS' TOAST
The Livery's traditional toast is called at every formal Court function – here on the occasion of the Election Court lunch at the Mansion House, 9 April 2008: 'The Worshipful Company of Fuellers – root and branch – may it flourish for ever'. Presiding, Master David Bell: to his right, The Rt Hon The Lord Mayor, Alderman David Lewis; to his left, The Lady Mayoress, Mrs David Lewis. In front of the Master are the Company's silver 'Daedalus' trophy and the Master's silver Goblet (see Appendix II, p.166 and Chapter IV, p.135).

origins, as well as the origins of its formal re-birth in the 20th century? Were woodmongers the first representative 'fuellers'? If so, did they actually form a guild, and what kind of guild was it? Did it evolve to have a livery, and can its parochial or 'fraternity' locations be identified? What did those early 'fuellers' trade in – how, where, with and against whom? How relevant are the contemporary terms 'wholesale' and 'retail' and what was the legal framework for their trades?

What documentary evidence is there, in the absence of any Company Minute Books prior to the 20th century, for the existence of a Livery Hall for those early traders? How did their trade rank in the City with other medieval trades, and what relative wealth and influence did they command? What level of authority did they achieve within the City – were there any 'Fueller', let alone Woodmonger, Mayors? If the Livery did rise to such 'grace' within the City, how accurate are the reports of the events that led to their fall from it?

How strict were the medieval restrictions regulating the woodmongers'
everyday trade: could outsiders 'muscle in'? Did the rules change over time?
How did the traders, as opposed to their Livery, survive and evolve? How did
the balance of the products they sold develop through the centuries, and how
were they used? How many trades could be considered to have played a part in
this evolution, and how did they transport their wares? Finally, where do The
Fuellers currently aspire in terms of both membership and outreach: what are
the issues they publicly espouse? Is the theme of 'fuel' still central, and how does
it now relate to the broad field of 'energy'? In short, where does The Worshipful
Company of Fuellers stand today? To answer such questions, the narrative needs
to open in the century just before the City of London's guilds got going, within
the legal framework governing the country as a whole.

Although one historian has observed that 'timber' 'was used almost exclusively
for fuel and extensively for building', for this History 'wood' will serve as the term
for fuel. Timber and wood, as well as 'coal' (meaning charcoal) were a seigneurial
monopoly, and many estates had a wooded
area, or a turbary: the types of fuel used for
different purposes depended on regional
availability. Citizens' hard-won rights to
trade would be no use without a source of
supply: the lords of the manor had to sell
their surplus through intermediaries.

4 MEDIEVAL FORESTS

*Although forests were instituted by the
Normans for royal hunting preserves, and
indeed included woodlands, they were not
primarily for wood, nor an open source
for timber; much of Hertfordshire, Essex
and Hampshire was later appropriated for
this purpose by Henry II – 'The Forest of
Essex'. Nevertheless, an indication of the
abundance of the contiguous wooded land
for medieval London can be inferred from
this map, with the central importance of the
Thames highlighted, showing the extent of
the Royal Forest.*

RIVER
THAMES

Unlike the classic academic histories of Livery Companies with equally long, but happily unbroken, lineages – for example The Grocers, or The Skinners – this history of a Company with a limited archive cannot expect to offer as many new insights into the medieval world as the medievalists recorded. The merchant citizens of that world were seen as 'the people who, uncouth, unlearned, ill-housed, ill-fed and comfortless though they were, still formed England's most important, most wealthy and most influential community throughout the chequered and troublous times of the thirteenth and fourteenth centuries'.[2]

Given such a background, a Fuellers' history needs to draw additional perspectives from the researches of historians such as Caroline Barron and Marc Fitch – and from analogies with comparable guilds as well as from the selected literary sources used by American historian Sylvia Thrupp and others.[3]

Of course, literary references cannot offer more than a modest introduction to the fragmentary, elusive world of the *livrée*. Although Chaucer did not see fit to feature a woodmonger, let alone a 'fueller', in his famous 14th-century pilgrimage to Canterbury, he did include a haberdasher, a carpenter, a webbe (weaver), a dyer and a tapicer (tapestry worker). In depicting these representatives of London's trade guilds as clothed in the livery of one 'solemn and great fraternity', England's first truly national poet was acknowledging the significance of fraternities in the life of late medieval England. The choice of 'the father of the English language' as the first peg on which to hang the hat of the Fueller has resonances for the history of any Livery Company. Not only were London companies in Chaucer's blood – his grandfather was a Mercer and his father a Vintner – but, as Oscar Wilde elegantly put it, he was 'born into the purple of London commerce'.[4]

It is a little surprising that Chaucer did not include a woodmonger – or a timbermonger – among his pilgrims, for these were callings very much within his experiences from an early age. He was born around 1341-4, in the city's Vintry ward, near the Billingsgate wharf where the woodmongers and car(t)men – later to be sundered – were then informally linked in plying their unmissably dirty, noisy and fractious trade. The air Chaucer inhaled from childhood was filled with the smell of woodburning, dung, sewage, and the new fangled 'sea-coal'.[5] Later in life, too, when living over the gate at Aldgate, the horse-drawn 'cars' of that trade became very familiar to him; 'cars' were more often two-wheeled, 12 feet long and narrow enough at three feet wide to negotiate London's streets. Carters suffered many petty restrictions, and in due course rates of carriage were laid down by the city: by 1517 they would range from 2d. to 5d. per load, although for sea-coal the hire-cost was 'as accustomed or agreed':

> No cart serving the City shall be shod in iron … no carman within the
> liberty shall drive his cart more quickly when it is unloaded than when it is
> loaded … no cart shall enter a churchyard … the price of firewood, faggots

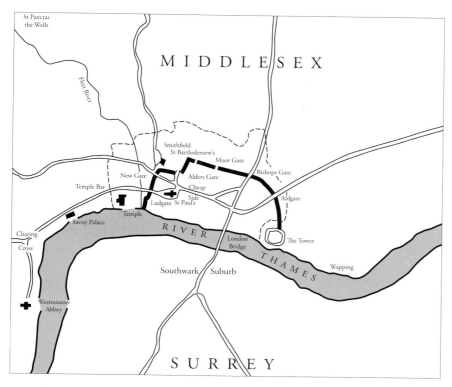

5   THE WOODMONGERS' LONDON IN CONTEXT

A later map of the waterways and roadways from which London's woodmongers would draw their supplies of wood and timber: the key features round the city wall are, from left to right: Ludgate, New Gate, Alders Gate, Moor Gate, Bishops Gate and Aldgate; the two main buildings are (left) Old St Paul's Cathedral, and (right) The Tower of London, by the Thames: the dotted line is the area of the City; the black line is the city wall and ditch. The Strand leads westwards past Temple Bar, the Savoy Palace and Charing Cross, to Westminster and its Abbey. Beyond the City of London, Southwark suburb lies to the south of the sole Thames crossing, old London Bridge; the Fleet Ditch flows down past St Pancras, the Wells (top left), to join the Thames by Ludgate.

and coal [be] assessed by the Mayor and Aldermen … the quarter of coal shall be sold between St Michael and Easter for ten pence; or between Easter and St Michael for eight pence and no more … no carman shall for the future enter the City with wood or charcoal for sale but shall remain outside the gate at Smithefeud or elsewhere as provided except at Cornhulle: (*see* The Fueller's London, Appendix III(A)).[6]

Of the trades serving the woodmongers, carting was still a rural traffic, bringing in along the 'wikked wayes' all kinds of goods including wood and rushes from within a 30-mile radius of the City.

The consumers of fuel embodied great disparities, from rich to poor. In wealthier households, coming to typify large cities such as London, which retained their prosperity, different fuels met different purposes:

[5]

6 CITY OF LONDON, *c.*1270

The focal area for the woodmongers' medieval trade 'below Bridge'. Much detail of the closely related street network is obscure here, but visible are: extreme left: Thames Street (Tamisestrete) meeting the crossing of old London Bridge (located where St Magnus the Martyr church now stands), and its rental-generating buildings and multiple pontoons, and Bishopsgate (Bishopsstrete); the creek forming the Billingsgate wood-wharf lies between three wharves to the west, and four to the east; right, the Tower of London.

Logs heated the hall and chamber, turf was used for cooking in the kitchen, and faggots gave the necessary heat for brewing ... sea-coal, was often bought for industrial [not] domestic, use. Wood was obtained in a variety of sizes, from logs called *astellae* or talwoode, to brushwood bundled into faggots ... London citizens in *c.*1300 burnt each year 40,000 metric tonnes of wood and 600 tonnes of sea-coal, all in a space of about two square miles.[7]

At the Gates, the carters, hired by their woodmonger-clients, or as employees, paid their customary taxes: 'carts that bring wood for sale shall pay one farthing and charcoal for sale one penny';[8] 'a cart that brings ... a hundred of talwode, sixpence at Crepulgate'; twopence on food loads. (Even as early as the time of Henry III, a duty of one farthing per two 'quarters' of sea-coal was payable at Billingsgate.[9])

Chaucer, as a uniquely gifted observer of the woodmongers' medieval City, was 'a Londoner who found a natural audience among rich and influential merchants' in what he referred to spontaneously – in *The Reeve's Tale* – as 'oure citee'.[10] In the year of the earliest record of a Woodmongers' guild – to be confirmed below as 1376 – Chaucer was living at Aldgate, drafting *The Knight's Tale*, the first of what would become *The Canterbury Tales*.[11]

By that time, Woodmongers, although not yet the Carmen, were one such recognised trading group in London – possibly even a Company, although without Livery or Hall.[12] The woodmongers' trade entailed wholesale (gross) as well as retail levels, high and low. That melding of what would only later be called 'classes' in society, is mirrored in Chaucer's pages: 'he brings together "churls" and "gentils"'.[13] Indeed, Chaucer uses the images of two of the fuel trade's familiar products, sea-coal and pitch, to depict a scene in the bawdy *Miller's Tale*: 'Derk was the nyght as pich or as the cole ...'.

Clarifying the Language

As to the names themselves, in the late 20th century the revived Company eventually settled on its sole title – 'the Fuellers' – which itself has a respectable history. A Fueller was 'one who or that which supplies fuel for fires, a fueller or wood carrier', a 'Feweller'. It harked back to the Old French *fouaille* – a 'fire'. Its earliest source is *c*.1400, a 'fewyller/Feweller'; in 1483 there is a further mention. In 1529, the Common Council lists a Fuellers' Master and Wardens. By the time of the first Grant of Letters Patent by James I in 1605 (to be covered fully in Chapter II, p.28), 'ff[F]ueller' is synonymous with 'woodmonger'. Dale quotes Lithgow in 1630: 'divers kind of coale and earth fewell'. Strype's 1754 edition of Stow's *Survey* notes: 'The Carmen ... were incorporated with the people called Fuellers by the name of woodmongers'. The trade of 'woodmonger', in Murray's famous *Dictionary* of 1915, forerunner to the *OED*, is defined solely – an anachronism but a significant one – as 'a dealer in wood, a timber merchant or a seller of wood for fuel'. There is only one reference to a timbermongers' trade, probably in association with the woodmongers, but nowhere any mention of a 'Timbermongers' guild, although a recent book has asserted that the Carpenters 'regulated' all dealing in timber.

The second part of the name has some interesting undertones, given the strong eventual link with the coals of Newcastle and the city's Scandinavian connections: it derives from the Old Norse, *mangari*, rendered as 'a dealer, trader, trafficker'. Only by the 16th century does this noun begin to acquire its more dubious flavour, as in 'rumourmonger', 'swearing like a costermonger', and even the Shakespeare-anointed 'whoremonger' and 'barbermonger'. Although Murray commented that 'it nearly always implies one who carries on a contemptible or discreditable trade', by the 16th century there were enough creditable trades with that same ending to offset that implied meaning, exemplified in unexceptionable City Liveries – the Ironmongers, the Heymongers, or the trade which would initially share the same quay at Billingsgate, the Fishmongers.[14]

Enter a Woodmonger, Left

As with all England's trades, an unrecorded existence long preceded a woodmonger's actual entrance onto the stage of the medieval City, just as

7 MEDIEVAL BLACKSMITH'S FORGE
This early 14th-century drawing shows one of the most traditional uses of 'coal': iron is heated on a hearth, blown by bellows, operated by means of a long handle. Inset: Alchemist's workshop and fire, a wood cut.

the pursuit of his calling anticipated by centuries its eventual emergence into any kind of organised form. Even when those distant figures do at last break surface, the glimpses are few and far between. In the words of Sylvia Thrupp's pioneering research into the later medieval merchants, 'all that one will know of him will be that he ate dinners at his company hall, was sued for debt and died'. Although the carriage aspects of his trade have now been well researched, much of the importing connected with the timber side of his craft, such as the trade in 'sylvan products' from the Baltic, still lies hidden under seemingly unrelated trade labels.[15]

At this point in The Fuellers' story, an obvious but minimised aspect of the former woodmonger's trade must be made clear: he was there to provide wood for all purposes, including wood as working timber for building, not simply as 'a fuel'. Wood and coal for heating were stacked in the same yards (such as Leadenhall) as timber and other building products. Although Timberhythe and Woodwharf evolved as two separate quays 'above Bridge', downstream from Seacoal Lane, it seems that timbermongering was a sub-set of woodmongering.

Woodmongers supplied products for both purposes, even if the various trades using wood – especially the carpenters – might well also buy their stock-in-trade directly at the wharves.[16]

Recent research takes the Fueller's world back to the 12th century:

> In order to satisfy London's demand there emerged in the city before 1200 an identifiable group of specialised traders in wood most often described as *buscarii*, although the vernacular descriptions or bynames *buscher*, *wodemongere* and *tymbermongere* were also used … 90 such individuals involved in London's wood market have been identified. The group includes dealers who appear to have specialised in wood (firewood, charcoal, and [building] timber) and others who dealt in many commodities, including wool, wine and corn.[17]

This project raises vital issues about the woodmongers' early days. The theme of wood as fuel is pursued below. The guild's 'ward and fraternity' locations are still conjectural:

> Castle Baynard Ward, and especially Woodwharf in the parish of St Peter the Less, upstream of London Bridge, was the centre of the London firewood trade, probably from well before 1200. The existence by *c.*1200 of the nearby

8 THE WOODMONGERS' STREETS TODAY

Montage showing the still extant locations of the Woodmongers' medieval days: (i) Old Seacoal Lane, off Farringdon Street, EC4; (ii) Dukes Place, Aldgate, EC3; (iii) High Timber Street, Queenhithe, EC4; (iv) Castle Baynard Ward, EC4.

wharf known as Timberhythe underlines the significance of traffic down the Thames for supplying the city with wood of all sorts ... the name Wood Street suggests that before 1150 there was a market for wood close to the inland commercial heart of the city. Water transport was crucial for the wood trade ... Many woodmongers owned shouts or boats ...[18]

In illustrating the major transport highway for such bulky items as wood – the Thames itself – the 'Feeding the City' project touches on a point of immediate interest, bringing to life some of the earliest individuals who might now be thought of as 'Fuellers':

Londoners who occasionally dealt in wood included prominent citizens such as Henry le Waleys (mayor at various dates between 1273 and 1298), Thomas Box (sheriff 1279-80) and Henry Box (sheriff 1294-5) ... Woodmongers also stored stocks of wood on their wharves; John Ferrour in 1381 had a large pile of faggots and talwood valued at 5 marks lying beside *Pykardislane*, a short distance from Queenhythe.[19]

Identifiable individual woodmongers/fuellers can also now be traced back to the early 13th century. Families then needing to carry no surname other than that of their woodmongering trade merited a will and its public record; as has been authoritatively pointed out, 'since woodmongers were not among the most prosperous Londoners, their wills were largely enrolled in London's Archdeaconry and Commissary Courts.'[20] The improving financial status of the woodmongers will be pursued in detail below, but the authors of the 'Feeding the City' Project also comment that, notwithstanding the three wealthy citizens already mentioned:

9 EARLY USE OF WOOD: 14TH-CENTURY BAKER'S OVEN
Bread loaves are being removed from a wood-fired oven with a longhandled 'peel', and placed in a basket.

Generally ... woodmongers were less wealthy and influential. The 12 identifiable in the 1319 subsidy list had assessments ranging from 10d. to 40s., with a mean of 9s. 8d., just below the overall mean for the city.[21]

Another wonderful source for wills was researched by Marc Fitch among the Commissary Wills, revealing more than 30 'citizen and woodmonger' and 'timbermonger' wills. (This treasure house of names and parishes is recorded in the Endnotes.[22])

Of a further dozen earlier mentions, the first comes in 1260 – Robert Wudemongere – in the Calendar of Wills, at the 'Court of husting', a relic of the City's Danish past.[23] Three years later, in 1263, the gender balance starts to be restored with the appearance of Alice, from a family possibly stemming from Norman ancestry, Peter le Wodemongere, echoing what has been well described as the 'deep-running ... fissure between French speaking lords and English subjects';[24] this was taken by Hylton Dale as the earliest sighting. On 6 November 1371, Thomas Kyngeston, 'Tortebaker', leaves bequests to his godson, Thomas, son of William Woodmongere.[25] Another William Wodemongere drew up his will in 1372.[26]

Historians have described the outreach of London's Woodmongers up the increasingly navigable waters of the Thames, forcing one John Baddeby to renounce 'any right ... to toll on all vessels passing through Baddeby's Lock'.[27] The authors of the 'Feeding the City' Project cast further light on this incident of 1378 and its economic background:

> Because of its bulk in relation to its sale value, wood could profitably be produced only in places close to the market, a conclusion anticipated in More's *Utopia*: 'A whole forest has been uprooted in one place by the hands of the people and planted in another. Herein they were thinking not so much of abundance as of transport, that they might have wood closer to the sea or the rivers or the cities themselves. For it takes less labour to convey grain than timber to a distance by land'.
>
> The need to bring wood to the water as soon as possible ... is likely to have encouraged the use of many smaller landing places, particularly on the middle Thames ... For the south Chiltern area, access to the Thames ... provided entry to London's fuel market, and in 1375 a syndicate of 11 London woodmongers opposed the right of John Baddeby of Taplow, just downstream of Marlow, to charge vessels passing through his lock (identified as the present Boveney Lock).[28]

The economics of the competing fuels hinted at in the 'Feeding London Project' extracts above are referred to on p.18.

Surviving wills are one of the historian's most useful sources. Three particular will-making woodmongers stand out across the years in their shared God-fearing concern for family, chattels, the continuance of their status, and the after-life. David Westbury, died 2 January 1487, makes bequest, among others: 'to Margery Phelip … a platter, a dish, a saucer, a candlestick and 40d. in money'.

Leaping ahead to the Tudor era, Roger Grave, died 16 January 1516, provides striking evidence of the community spirit of his craft. He leaves to his 'bretheren the woodmongers, 20s.': 'to Thomas Kypper, my apprentice, a year of his term, a featherbed, a bolster, a pair of blankets and a pair of sheets, and if he weds Agnes at Master Green's then I give him 20s. towards their marriage, and one of my worsted doublets … to my brother, Thomas Grave, 20s., my second blue gown as it is with the fur, my bow with my quiver'.

The site of a possible 'woodmongers' Ward' arises again with Geoffrey Bell, who died 18 March 1528, wanting his 'body buried in the east end of St Andrew's Eastcheap [= Hubbard], of which parish I am a parishioner'. The problem as to which Ward, parish, and so which 'fraternity' the woodmonger/timbermonger trade might have gathered in and developed from narrows down to the two riverside parishes, St Andrew Eastcheap/Hubbard or, more probably, St Andrew Baynard. (The present-day adopted church of St Michael, Cornhill is shared with seven other Companies.[29])

From the time of Edward I onwards, many aspects of a merchant's dealings would be covered by common law and statute. Around the country,

10 'BILLINGS GATE'

Principal quay where lightermen brought coals, wood and timber ashore to the woodmongers' medieval wharves and 'Room/ Rome-land', for onward transmission by car(t)men for woodmongers – as their employers or their commercial 'clients'.

assize courts provided authority for this regulatory system; London was different, its legal framework shared between the City's Aldermen, and the guilds. Prices, sales and loans were the main objectives, all designed to ensure fairness towards the inhabitants of the City, and a safe context for traders. The Woodmongers' legal wrangles of the 17th century must be seen against this background.[30]

ii: Woodmongers in the 'London Vineyard'

The Fuellers' livery has no continuous set of Minute Books from which to build its story. The onus is thus put on unearthing glimpses of the woodmongers in the rich records of the medieval City, and in the mainstream medievalists' writings. Foremost among such sources must be the recent *London in the Later Middle Ages*.

For the Woodmongers' Company, one of its most illuminating Tables traces the references to 102 crafts and companies in a selection of 21 key civic lists from 1328 to 1518. Of the first 20 of these headings, the Woodmongers only feature seven times, underlining not merely their late emergence, but also their relatively low profile among their fellow trades. Woodmongers were among the crafts which sent representatives to the City's common council in 1376, 1377, and 1381, and are listed under the crafts held by Trinity College, Cambridge in 1485; they contributed to loans – for the king in 1488, and for the Guildhall kitchens in 1504; and later, in 1518, to an important ceremony for those keeping the 'royal watch'.[31]

The ensuing Tudor chapter will explore why the Woodmongers were among the 54 crafts who did not have 'their own Hall by 1540', as compared with 47 who did: before 'sea-coal' increased their prosperity, the woodmongers still ranked economically in a lower-middle position. Small comfort that of two trades that would later cause the Woodmongers much trouble – the Carters or 'Carmen', and the Watermen, the former appears only once in these lists, in 1518, and again had no Hall, and the latter does not appear at all, due to their recent formation in 1514.

In this analysis, the Woodmongers are classified under the generic title 'Wood', alongside the Coopers, Fusters, Joiners, Pattenmakers, Shipwrights, Turners and Wheelwrights, whilst the heading 'Transport', in which George Unwin, the Livery historian of the 19th century, placed the Woodmongers, is reserved solely for the Carters. This ambivalence underlines one of the peculiarities of the Woodmongers' trade – which it shares with 13 'Other' crafts in the Table – that of not fitting conveniently into one clear 'division', such as 'victualling' or 'clothing'.

11 Fuellers' 21st-Century Church, St Michael, Cornhill

Having no existing or provable 'fraternity' origin in a particular City parish, the Livery currently enjoys the benefit of the services of St Michael – and of its vicar – for ceremonial purposes, with seven other Companies.

12 EMERGING INTO THE MEDIEVAL CITY

Increasingly, woodmongers enter into the civic life of the medieval City.

KEY:
Cs = Crafts
GH = Guildhall
bold = Woodmongers

CLRO = Corporation of London Records Office
CPMR = Calendar of Pleas and Memoranda Rolls of the City of London
LBE, G, H, N = Letter Books E, G, H, N

Craft	1328	1364	1376	1377: a	b	1381	1445	1447	1448	1449	1453: a
Vintners	#	#	#	#	#	#		#			#
Wood											
Joiners			#	#	#	#					
Woodmongers			#	#		#					#

Craft	1453: b	1454	1456: a	b	1461	1485	1488	1504	1518	Hall/ 1540
Vintners	#	#			#	#	#	#	#	#
Wood [A above]									#	
Joiners					#	#	#	#	#	#
Woodmongers					#	#	#	#	#	#

Source notes:

- **1328** — Masters of Cs sworn *LBE*, 232–4
- **1364** — Cs contributing to a loan to the king, *LBG*, 171–2
- **1376** — Cs sending representatives to common council, *LBH*, 42–43
- **1377a** — Ditto *CPMR*, 1364–81, 243
- **1377b** — Ditto, 256
- **1381** — Ditto, *CPMR*, 1381–1412, 29
- **1445** — Cs sent to meet queen, CLRO, Jnl 4, fo.72v
- **1447** — Cs contributing to GH chapel, *ibid*, fo.192–9
- **1448** — Cs contributing to peace-keeping, *ibid*, fo.237v
- **1449** — Cs paying for soldiers, CLRO, Jnl 5, fo.11
- **1453a** — Cs going to meet the queen, *ibid*, fo.120
- **1453b** — Cs contributing to peace-keeping, *ibid*, fo.131–131v
- **1454** — Cs patrolling Thames, *ibid*, fo.187v–188
- **1456a** — Cs consulted about a tax, CLRO, Jnl 6, fo.5
- **1456b** — Cs contributing soldiers, *ibid*, fo.106
- **1461** — Cs appointed to guard the city, *ibid*, fo.35
- **1485** — Lists of Cs, Trinity Coll, Cambr, MS 0.3.1, fos 62v–63
- **1488** — Cs contributing to a loan to the king, BODL. OU, Digby Roll 2, fo.28v
- **1504** — Cs contributing, GH kitchens, CLRO, Rep 1, fos.181–182v
- **1518** — Cs appointed to keep the watch, CLRO, LBN, fo.79
- **1540** — Cs with Halls by this date

Also quoted in this work is the research of Anne Lancashire, identifying the London mayors and sheriffs from 1190 to 1558. No woodmonger – or indeed carter – appears in the list, albeit that several individuals who do figure could now be regarded as within the framework of 'Fuellers', given their clear involvement with the business of fuel.[32]

'The Best and Most Trustworthy Men'

On 9 August 1376 two woodmongers, John Asshurst and William Schrympelmersche, make Fuellers' history: as part of 'an immense Commonalty from the underwritten Misteries to the Guildhall … the mistery of Woodmongers sends two members to the Common Council'. It is not certain that there is here any indication of precedence, but these two are shown in the City's *Letter Book* as 46th in a list totalling 47 trades, ahead only of the Pinners.[33]

Shortly afterwards, a will drawn up on 25 March 1387 confirms the corporate organisation of the Woodmongers: John Lot, fishmonger, asked to 'be buried in the church of S. Andrew at Castle Baynard, to which church and to certain parishioners thereof – the best and most trustworthy men of the crafts of Woodmongers and Brewers, he leaves … a brewery'.

Three topics are worth emphasising: first, woodmongers had by now realised the importance of organising themselves, to ensure commercial survival. Second, brewing was a coal-burning trade. Finally, that some woodmongers at least lived in the ward of Castle Baynard. This will also suggests that, at this date, the woodmongers may have been most closely associated with the parish of St Andrew in Castle Baynard Ward.[34] The year 1412 brings in John Dyer, of whom more anon. On 13 October 1418, John Talworth and John Refhawe were sworn in before the mayor as 'Masters of the mistery of Wodemongers' at the Guildhall.[35]

A 'Clean Air' Movement: First Glimmerings?

The 'monger' particle in the woodmonger title has relevance: its possibly pejorative flavour is a reminder of the level of customer-perception of the fuel trade on London's streets, where industrial activity was now manifesting itself in the fumes created by burning wood and, increasingly, coal.[36]

Successive monarchs would take up the cry, with a surprisingly early concern for health if not for safety, as well as a reference to a concept which would later divide the nation – that of a 'commonwealth'. Sea-coal was being imported by 1235, but was believed to be more poisonous than charcoal ('coal'):

> In 1285 and 1288, the Patent Rolls record complaints of annoyance by limekilns in London, caused by the use of seacoal, whereby the air was infected and corrupted. The City's records of 1298-9 show that in that year the master smiths agreed that none should work at night on account of

the unhealthiness of coal and damage to their neighbours. In 1307, a royal proclamation was ordered to be made in Southwark, Wapping, and East Smithfield forbidding the use of seacoal in kilns under pain of heavy forfeiture, 'as the King learns from the complaint of prelates and magnates of his realm, who frequently come to London for the benefit of the commonwealth by his order, and ... of his citizens and all his people dwelling there ... that the workmen [in kilns] ... now burn them and construct them of sea-coal instead of brushwood or charcoal ... and the air is greatly infected'.[37]

The Woodmonger and his London

Within the wide bounds of the see of London, stretching from Surrey to Essex, 13th-century London was already a metropolis, bearing more resemblance, as to size, to the cities of western Europe, with whom its citizens traded, regularly if highly competitively, than to any English town. Some 95 parishes by 1086, by 1540 the city comprised 113 within the jurisdiction of the mayor and his aldermen – the 'liberty of London'.

The same size as Genoa, but built in wood rather than stone, by the late 13th century the population of London as a whole had grown from an estimated 19,950 at the time of Domesday Book (which, however, did not cover London) to some 80,000 people; it would decline under the recurrent plagues to some 40,000 by 1400, re-building to 50,000 by 1500, to explode to some 200,000, including extramural suburbs, by 1600. However, prosperity did not decline in proportion to population fluctuations: measured in taxable income and property, and built on the wool and cloth trade, it continued to grow. By 1534, it generated two per cent of the national wealth. The next largest towns in population size were York and Bristol at 10,000, Coventry at 7,000, Norwich at 6,000 and 5,000 at Lincoln.[38]

London was a leading overseas port, a comprehensive market. Increasingly, it dominated the country's trade, many parts of which were but a fortnight's ride away.[39] It was a vibrant city of Catholic culture, living both piously and lustily; by the early 14th century the City boasted 99 churches, but 1,334 breweries; estimates of taverns vary between 95 and 354.[40]

The City was constantly building and rebuilding. It was joined to administrative Westminster by suburbs and green fields beside the Strand and Holborn; the suburb of Southwark lay beyond the bridge and the bounds to the south. Although not initially a permanent seat of government, London was spoken of as 'the King's Chamber', as 'a mirror of all England', 'the watchman of the realm'. The City was indeed self-governing, but only by royal permission. Under at least one king, Richard II, the city was described as 'abject before him'.

Because of its devolved system, London, like Norwich, had no need to create a central body in the continental mould – a comprehensive 'Guild Merchant' – to monitor trade. Entry to citizenship, and arbitration in

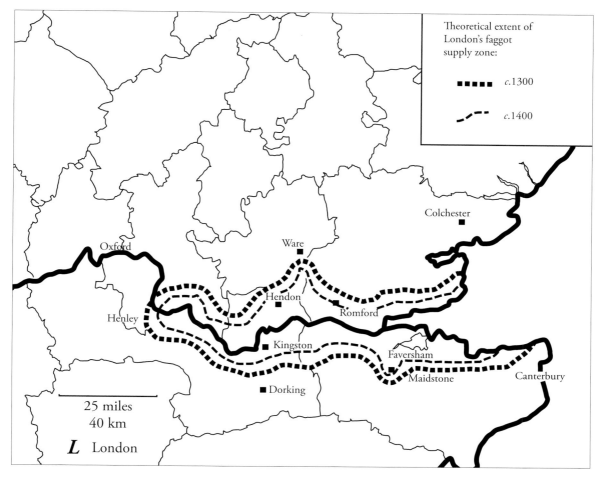

13 'Wood and the Woodmonger'

Adapted from: 'Theoretical extent of London's faggot supply zone, c.1300 & c.1400'. (bold broken line = limit of area studied).

demarcation disputes, could be usually controlled through the various guilds that were emerging: 'tax to the Crown was mediated through assemblies of merchants and then through the Crown in Parliament'.[45] In the 14th century, from the City Courts (Husting, Aldermen, Common Council), craft organisations took over some of the responsibilities earlier exercised by the Mayor and Aldermen.

These bodies were founded originally on religious fraternity and indeed parochial lines. In order to have a proper voice in the conduct of their market – and their workforce – both exporters and importers needed to identify themselves with a particular trade entity, known initially under the continental name of a 'mistery' or 'mysterie'. Under Edward III and Richard II, London's early woodmongers were an integral part of a noisy, rough, dangerous, unstable, linguistically many-sided world.

Wood and the Woodmonger

The evolving economics of the woodmongers' original product, wood, in its capacity not as timber but as a fuel vis-a-vis 'sea-coal' are outlined in the 'Feeding London Project':[50]

> A high proportion of its final price was represented by the cost of transport. The great cost of shipping coal to London is reflected in the fact that the London price in 1259 was at least four times the Durham price in 1300 … striking is the sharp rise in firewood prices during the later thirteenth century … the price rose dramatically in the late 1280s and 1290s reaching a peak of 38d. [per hundred faggots] in 1291/2.

> … Over the same period in London the price of wood fuel appears to have increased more rapidly than that of coal. In 1259 sea coal was purchased in London for 12d. and 14d. a quarter … in *c.*1270 the London price for what may have been the equivalent weight of firewood (27.75 faggots) was 7s. 8d.

> By 1300 the London price for coal was probably less than the 16d. per quarter for which it sold in Northern Hertfordshire, while that for the equivalent weight of faggots was 13s. 3d. This represents a price increase of less than 23 per cent for coal by comparison with 70 per cent for faggots, and presumably a corresponding increase in the propensity to consume coal.

As the 14th century opened, a woodmonger's 'heating product-range' still lay mainly with the fuel from whose name his lowly trade had sprung; wood was 'perhaps the most widely used raw material in the pre-industrial world'.[51] From Domesday Book, it is clear that at least 15 per cent of the available land was still woodland. Of some four million acres of that 15 per cent, there were many coppiced woods, all carefully managed; each person needed on average an acre of woodland for his fuel.[52] Villagers had rights 'to take wood for building, fencing, and fuel from common woodlands', and these had become 'enshrined in "housebote, haibote and fuelbote"'.[53]

At this time, Londoners were burning 140,000 tons of wood, to warm their homes and cook their food.[54] They had developed a 'voracious appetite for kindling'. Up to the 15th century, timber from the surrounding woods and forests (Fig. 13) also served London's other needs: joists and beams for house-building; panelling as wall insulation; wood for fashioning by carpenters and joiners into everyday products – from the log rolls which long served as pillows for the poor, to the wooden platters and utensils which were still normal use. From the 15th century, as fears about deforestation spread, Prussia and even Ireland took over as the woodmonger-merchants' source of timber – 'clapholt', 'weynescote', 'Ryghholt', and wooden articles such as boxes – as well as 'pitch, tar and ashes [often under-rated]'. Coal imports, for example via Bristol from the Forest of Dean, were carefully taxed; from the Tyne, most of the vessels coming away took coal as part of their return cargo, probably amounting by 1377 to 7,000 tons.[55]

Yet wood was still the preferred fuel for domestic heating, anciently venting through the roof, but fashionably in the greater houses – including some of the merchant-woodmongers' – being burned from the mid-14th century in purpose-built wall-fireplaces (called 'chimneys') with brick chimneys ('tunnels'). Above the cellars were a hall, a parlour, a bedchamber, with a chimney and a closet, a kitchen with a pantry, a larder and other offices. The house normally had one main chamber, with small shared unheated rooms for children, servants, and also some resident apprentices or journeymen in the roof. Real warmth, however, at night let alone in winter, had to come from material, not fuel: heavy bedroom drapes and wall-tapestries substituted for any form of upstairs heating. As to the labourer, he was lucky if he had a small cottage of his own, even if this was often a two-room dwelling with an earthen floor with no chimney, and built of thin wood planking.[56]

Furs were worn on practically every occasion and for a wide range of purposes – that is, if the sumptuary rules on clothing sanctioned their use for a particular level of the hierarchy. The merchant-woodmonger satisfied those criteria; initially his lowly underlings did not. The comment of one leading historian has implications for the Woodmongers' later problems with the Carmen: in due course, an Act of 1363 had allowed different furs 'for each class in society'. Despite that extension, 'workmen like *carters* and shepherds, keepers of beasts and threshers of corn, servants of various sorts, and those who had less than forty shillings worth of goods', were not allowed to wear any at all: medieval distinctions were being drawn.[57]

Meanwhile, the frontiers of agriculture were advancing, eating into the woodlands; by the mid-13th century, there had been an incipient awareness of the need to conserve them.[58] Other primitive fuels were still in use: turves of peat from the great turbaries of East Anglia and elsewhere (causes of the future Broads) – albeit with a low calorific value, and expensive to transport overland. The poor used sedge, thack, heath, rushes and other local specialities.

There were already signs of future change, and of the trade interactions that would dog subsequent centuries.[59] By at least 1228, 'sea-coal' for the wharfingers and woodmongers was being brought into the City from the Thames by the lightermen and watermen, in limited quantities. Early on, these shiploads came into Queenhythe 'above Bridge' and later at Billingsgate 'below Bridge'; reclamation there would facilitate a harbour deep enough for larger ships, and also land ('Roomland') for the off-loading and stacking of timber and coal, subsequently to serve also as a market.[60] Billingsgate, 'Timberhythe, and 'Sacoles' Lane, cargoes would be landed from flat-bottomed 'shouts' or freight-boats, owned by the woodmongers.[61] 'Charcoal' continued to be used for 'industrial' purposes; Gray recorded that 'Coales in former times was onely used by smiths and burning of lime'.[62] Apart from brewing, other uses were soap- and glass-making, smelting and ironwork. By the 13th century, coal had 'ousted oak brushwood as the fuel for on-site kilns'.[63] Despite this development, coal had been temporarily banned, as a pollutant, in 1273.[64]

 ## iii: Developing the 'Fueller' Concept: The Coal Meters

The size of the Livery itself was determined by the difficulty of obtaining loans (usury) for the capital needed to afford storage areas in London's crowded spaces, for leasing or owning river-wharves and ships, or owning or hiring carts for distribution.

Of interest here however is the greater scope for the application of the term 'Fueller' to embrace callings that touched upon the fuel distribution trade and made it possible. Magna Carta had established that London should undertake for all England the official measurement of weights and sizes.[65] By 1330, what can be seen as a sub-craft of fuel importation, the ('Land') Coal Meters [measurers, weighers], had been appointed and formed into a fraternity. They were an efficient cadre of public officials employed by the City, albeit in saleable public positions that some accused as mere sinecures.

Their job was to log and check the 'croquets', paper slips recording the unloaded tonnage after every incoming tide up the Thames. Eighteen years later, in 1387, the same device was used for salt, with the appointment of Salt-Meters. Such men, who also supervised the grain and oyster trades, charged for their services.[66] Smith records that 'by the 14th century there was obviously a fair amount of traffic in sea-coal in London, for in 1369 the City appointed four meters for imports':[67]

> … need had arisen for the measuring of coal … it may be reasonably conjectured that this method was devised to ensure fair measure for the consumers, who probably purchased their supplies from the shipmasters at the wharves where cargoes were unloaded. The procedure was then possibly the same as that found to exist in subsequent centuries, viz., the coal was measured out by a vat of standard size. There is no evidence, however, to show that at this early date the London traffic was sufficiently extensive or remunerative to have called for a market, still less that it was organised under guild regulation. The staple fuel was still wood, and that trade was in the hands of the Woodmongers' Company, but little or nothing is known of the organisation or trade methods of that company at this time, or indeed before the 16th century.[68]

Relevant to the Coal Meters, Fig. 1 has offered a simplified guide to the ways in which the various sub-sets of the 'Fueller' concept would come to inter-relate over the course of the centuries, p.xxiv. The evolution of the two kinds of Meters (Land Coal Meters, and Seacoal Meters), carried forward into the framework of the 19th-century fuel trade, is set out in Appendix III(B).

Classifying the Worshipful Companies

Comparison with other merchants can conjure up a first glimpse of the 'life-style' of the merchant-woodmonger of this time. Many woodmongers in full vigour would by now have been emulating 'the stridently colourful dress' that offset London's dark and noisome streets, like any other befurred 'middling person'.[69] Some sense of the modest financial status of this evolving citizen will be traced in the next chapter. Yet, comparatively minor crafts became involved in the City's administrative affairs:

> Election by craft ensured that even the most modest crafts had a say in the city's deliberations; in 1377, for example, the bakers, the cordwainers, the curriers, the pouchmakers, the tanners, the tawyers, the brasiers, the cardmakers, the pinners, the painters, the fusters, the joiners, the woodmongers, the horners, and the tallowchandlers ... all sent representatives to the common council.[70]

A picture of the guild scene in which these early woodmongers played a part is now appropriate. At its heart are the origins of the Livery title 'worshipful'. 'Medieval merchants found nothing strange in opening their account books with the heading "In the name of God and of profit" ... spiritual authority suffused and judged the secular world.'[71] In many cases, craft associations formed in the localities where they worked. The City was honeycombed with what developed naturally as fraternities, usually attached to their only meeting-place, the parish church; as well as being a kind of 'police system' to ensure that their own cohesion remained intact despite the impact of Crown or City, they were also a 'brotherhood'.[72]

From these religious roots also grew the medieval belief in a 'true market price' – equitable, commercial and, increasingly, legally enforceable: as Victorian writer Charles Reade put it, 'Honest trade was small profits, quick returns, and neither to cheat nor be cheated'. London prices were regulated not merely for victuals but also for charcoal and faggots: wood and coal were reported as 'forestalled' in a Court of 1300; in 1379, 6,000 wood billets were similarly forfeited.[73] As Chapter II will demonstrate, in the strictures later levelled against the Woodmongers in their coal trading, the fine line between normal business and unethical practice was blurred: the simplest form of 'regrating' – buying wholesale and selling retail – became censurable.[74] 'Medieval society was structured in a complex system of personal obligation, typically arranged in small hierarchies within the great hierarchy of the realm'.[75]

The first listing of London guilds might be said to have occurred in 1170-80 when 19 guilds were fined 16 marks as 'adulterine' guilds by the Crown: 'coming into existence without its licence'.[76] A parallel distinction has been drawn within those trades that had already formed religious or localised fraternities, and those who had not yet done so. The seniority of the structured guilds that evolved from those fraternities was first measured by their perceived 'greatness', and then latterly by the chronology of their incorporation as companies; the Woodmongers did not bear comparison with those ordained as 'The Great Twelve'. Guilds could also evolve for the lower 'artisan' elements within their own craft. They could be 'yeomen', 'bachelors', 'journeymen' or servants within a given craft, and would be subordinate to the ruling group, composed of masters and employers.[78] The merchanting Woodmongers appeared to be a single entity.

Another kind of classification lay in whether a guild was one of the few 'Greats', like the Skinners, which were then linked with an industry rather than with a trade.[79] The most relevant differentiation for the Woodmongers, however, was highlighted by social historian Asa Briggs: 'Craft guilds did not necessarily share the same interests as merchant guilds'.[80] Even if there was little craft in being a woodmonger, by that era the work of a European merchant, exemplified at its peak in the merchants of Venice, involved many intricate mercantile skills, with complex systems of credit and financial management. An important distinction lay in the epithet 'monger': mongers did not 'make' things, they sold them. The Woodmongers should certainly be seen as a merchant guild, even if their 'wholesaling/retailing' functions were still integrated, and not yet separated out.[81]

Within a particular trade, the City authorities distinguished sharply between two levels of workers: those enfranchised 'freemen' – and those not 'free'. These latter could be of two kinds: 'foreigns' – possibly London-born Englishmen but not (yet) citizens – or 'aliens' – foreigners born overseas. These latter lived in small communities in chosen locations, composed partly of the manifold incoming European population which was being drawn into one of Europe's fastest-growing cities.

One part of the contradictory raison d'être of the guilds was to prevent either of these 'outsider' categories of worker breaking into – let alone breaking down – the hard-won standards and privileges of the known trades, whilst at the same time needing their presence at the lower levels of competence on which those trades depended. A wholesaling woodmonger could well be employing foreigns or aliens to do the unavoidable manual work of his market; some of those employees might well in due course aspire to yeoman status – juniors – within his trade.

There were four routes to freedom: honorary; by inheritance/patrimony (including *in vitro*); or as apprentices, taking seven years 'for the mystery of their craft to be acquired', in order to join that 'freedom', and fourthly, the freedom of the city could be bought ('redemption').[82] Prior freedom of a guild could pave the way for 'Freedom of the City'. By the early 13th century, these methods of admission were generally accepted, but the machinery by which citizenship evolved was only securely built up by the late 13th and 14th centuries, the era when the Woodmongers had certainly become 'incorporated'; (a technical term meaning incorporation as a single body by royal charter: in the 14th-century there is evidence that the woodmongers were already acting together as a group).[83]

Despite their economic importance, the trading freemen had the habit of describing themselves first and foremost legally, by their status as a freeman – a citizen – and only then secondarily by their trade; thus in 1412 the History has encountered a John Dyer – 'citizen and woodmonger'. As the City's population recovered and grew, and trade expanded, by the 15th century the misteries became practicable units for the control of the affairs which the City delegated to them.[84]

Of the 120 misteries named between 1309 and 1312, some, like the Woodmongers, later disappeared, split up, or coalesced with others.[85] A poorer section of a craft might gradually fall into dependence on the most enterprising section. Enterprise was the keyword: City custom decreed that every citizen had the inalienable right to buy and sell wholesale whatever commodity he pleased.

Some guilds in the early 14th century may have been little more than informal groups with some kind of mutual responsibility: woodmongers were in this category. The misteries had been recognised as City entities by the end of the 13th century. As late as 1364, it was decreed that all misteries should elect wardens to supervise the work and behaviour of their members.[87] Several of these misteries may have operated as private associations, others were under the aegis of one of the many parish fraternities supported by the humbler citizens.[88] By 1328, at least 25 misteries were in a position to register the names of their wardens.[89] During the 14th century, many other misteries followed suit, by securing recognition of ordinances which implied some form of association. By the 15th century, there were probably 200 or more religious or parish guilds in London, most of which were not craft guilds.[90] In due course membership of a mistery would become a prerequisite to becoming a freeman.

The Woodmongers in Relation to Other Guilds

There were various other ways of classifying the Woodmongers. The writer Carew Hazlitt in 1892 would simply list Woodmongers, with the Carmen and the Watermen, as 'Voluntary Associations that have disappeared or merged …'. He is also the sole authority for the suggestion that the Woodmongers may once have had some kind of relationship with 'the Clockmakers, through the call for the old-fashioned cases for coffin-clocks'.[91] Unwin classed them differently:

'the gilds of transport entered upon the most active period of their existence at a time when the gilds of handicraft were becoming obsolete.'[92]

By this token, a marker was laid down as to the value placed by the community on the work of the woodmonger, 'vertically linked' as he was to the carman and lighterman. Sylvia Thrupp later offered a further classification:

In some crafts all members carried on the same kind of economic activity. The tilers for example, were all wage-labourers, the fusters were piece-makers for the saddlers, and fellmongers and woodmongers were examples of small trades in raw materials.

14   THE RIVERSIDE BY ST PAUL'S

The woodmonger's much-used Paul's Wharf ('Paulus wharfe') is the last identified wharf, lower left.

One more – even if linguistically confusing – insight into the relative standing of the Woodmongers in the later medieval period had surfaced in the famous list drawn up by the Brewers Company clerk, 'of the names of all the crafts exercised in London from of old and still continuing in this 9th year of King Henry VI' (i.e. 1421/2). Woodmongering is loosely seen as a 'craft', conceived here as equivalent to 'guild'. At this date there is no reference to the Carmen, Watermen or Lightermen – all trades that would later impinge heavily on the Woodmongers. The Woodmongers now figure as 87th in that list of 111 guilds (the source of the total already mentioned above). Below, or at least, after them, were listed such apparently established guilds as: the Writers of Court letters, Limners, Leches, Ferrours, Coppersmiths, Upholders, Carvers, Glasiers, Felmongers, Woolmen, Cornmongers, Blacksmiths, Ropers, Lanternmakers, Haymongers, Bottlemakers, Marblers, Netmakers, Potmakers, Glovers, Hosiers, Orglemakers and Soapmakers.[93]

15 'CARS' FOR THE WOODMONGER

The next chapter in the Woodmongers' story will find them at odds with another guild, the Carmen, despite their mutual reliance, and joint need for 'car-rooms' (licences). The vehicle of their shared trade – the medieval cart – was still a simple design, often two-wheeled: depicted here on a 17th-century 'Trade Token', see Chapter II, pp.62-3.

Coals from Newcastle

Fuel production is not a subject for the Fuellers' History, but as the use of coal started to impinge on the London market, the guild system – and the 'Fueller concept' – also reached out territorially, and back up the long distribution chain, almost to the threshold of the producers, the coal-mine owners in Newcastle upon Tyne and elsewhere. North-East producers had created their own links in the distribution process, the 'Hostmen', the same concept that prevailed in Calais for English wool merchants trading, and thus lodging with 'hosts', at the Wool Staple. The Hostmen, and their associated citizens, the Merchant Adventurers, have been portrayed by a researcher for this History as 'mafia-like', constituting a fourth trade or guild that can now be embraced retrospectively under a 'Fuellers' umbrella;[94] the evolution from their origins, operating also in cities such as York, to their contemporary role, will be pursued in Chapter III (*see* pp.76-81).[95]

"The Arms and Crest of the Woodmongers Company of London (incorporating Fuellers and including Carmen) granted by Patent of Clarenceux King of Arms 1st. October 1605, with Supporters, St. John the Baptist and St. Katherine, as used by the Company." ∞∞

16 VARIANTS ON THE ARMS

Ensuing chapters will trace the evolution of the Arms, Crest and Motto over the centuries.

Another result of the entry of sea-borne coal into an erstwhile woodbased market, and of the closed nature of the medieval guilds, was that the distribution of coals could be – in due course had to be – run by members of the mercantile bourgeoisie who were neither Woodmongers, Ship masters nor Hostmen:

Richard Lovekin, Stockfishmonger, Mayor of London in 1358-9, 'purposed by the grace of God to freight a ship called "la Weselere" of Dordright [near the mining centre, Liège] with seacoal and other merchandise … to carry to … London'.

Within a century the original trade-specific membership of the Liveries would evolve: 'By this time [the late 15th century] the great city companies were no longer confined to persons actually engaged in the trade which each represented'.[96] Retrospectively, such merchants must nevertheless now be seen generically as 'Fuellers'; then and in the ensuing Tudor era this umbrella concept embraced members of the 'Great Twelve':

> John Broke, an unexceptional and apparently typical mercer, in addition to selling cloth to Antwerp from a warehouse in St Bride's parish, was wholesaling cloth through a store in St Mary Le Bow, and was also bringing in coals from Newcastle.[97]

Such merchanting overlaps were a foretaste of the intricate development of trade that would become the norm by the 18th century. The trades that participated in the business of fuel would be a characteristic part of that development.

17 WOODMONGERS' CHARTER OF 1605

Through Letters Patent (patens = open to view), the Charter of King James I granted Livery status to the combined Woodmongers and Carmen: 'James by the Grace of God, Kinge of England, Scotland, France and Ireland … at the humble petition of the Woodmongers and Carrmen of the said Companye within the Cittye of London and the Suburbes therof, for the better governmente rule and order and everye of them shalbe by vertue of theis presentes one bodye Corporate and pollitique in deede and name; by the name of the Master, wardens & Fellowshippe of woodmongers of London …'. Contrary to references elsewhere, this Charter is now part of the shared heritage of the Carmen and the Fuellers.

II

THE SIXTEENTH TO SEVENTEENTH CENTURIES

The Fueller as Fuel Merchant, Carman and Wharfinger

from liveried monopoly ... to commercial competition

Woodmongering on the Page – Overview – Success or Failure? – The Fault-Lines – The Woodmongers' Environment – Numbers and Finance – A Hall as Status Symbol – The Elizabethan 'Fueller' – First of the Turf Wars: The Carmen and the Wharfingers – Woodmongers as Jacobean Lobbyists – Evidence Old and New – Restoration, Mystification, Deprivation – Woodmongers' Coals and the Plague – Annus horribilis: 'The Malicious Bloody Flame' – The Coal Dues: Rebuilding the City – Token Characters

The Tudor and Stuart eras of the Fuellers' history were to prove momentous for the increasingly politicised Company of Woodmongers, balancing its interests between the communal City of London, and the royal City of Westminster. This relationship would clarify over the century of the Livery's *annus horribilis*, from late 1666 through to 1667, sharpened by the Crown's increasing need for taxation. In no other era would the Head of Government, monarchical or Protectorate, impact more markedly on the public standing of the Woodmongers.

i: *Woodmongering on the Page*

The double century would also be notable in other ways: in an apparent mystery over 'the surrender'; in the spread, now to the Wharfingers, of trades that could be embraced by the 'Fueller' concept; in the revelation that a member of what was now a Woodmongers' guild helped to found their then arch rival, the Carmen (*see* Endnote 1); and in the fact that a Woodmongers' Hall existed longer than previously believed. Notable, too, was a richness of visual references, on paper as on vellum, to the Woodmongers' Livery

18 MESSAGES ON THE GODFREY CUP

A celebrated item in the history of silverware commemorates in its engraved cameos two of the worst natural disasters to befall the City of London – the Plague of 1665, and (here) also casting a shadow over the now solo Company of Woodmongers, the Great Fire of 1666. It also thereby evokes a scandalous 'whodunnit', the murder of the most famous Master Woodmonger Sir Edmund Berry Godfrey. (He stars alone in the Museum of London, although the exhibit only refers to his dealings in 'wood and coal': see Fig. 32, p.62.)

(though with no traceable documentary uses yet of the term 'Coal-Sellers').[1] That richness is seen foremost in the Bodleian manuscript about the Livery, constituting today some of the Company's most beautiful and historically meaningful archival records.

The literature of the day contains a quartet of instances, ranging from the negative to the positive: from the pages of the Diarist John Evelyn's polemic *Fumifugium*, a diatribe against the effects of London's coal-smoke (he also invented one of the first briquettes),[2] to Daniel Defoe's *Journal of the Plague*, his retrospective comment on the uses of smoke to combat the City's first great 17th-century disaster, the countrywide Plague of 1665.[3] In parallel must be seen the ambivalent references in Samuel Pepys' *Diaries* to the woodmongers' products, in being first the prime cause – as timber – and then, as a source of taxation – to coal. Coal would ensure the recovery of the City, from its second major crisis, the Great Fire of 1666. Both events were depicted in tableaux on the famous Godfrey Cup, shown left.[4]

The printed word would also enhance the Fuellers' story at a different level: the introduction into popular parlance of the most enduring metaphor about the woodmongers' now predominant fuel product: Thomas Fuller's coinage in 1622, in his *Worthies of England*, of the sardonic phrase, 'carrying coals to Newcastle', said at the time to equate to 'bringing owls to Athens'.[5] Less enduring was the saying that arose earlier, by 1606, 'as common as coals from Newcastle'.[6]

However, in global terms, the most noteworthy citations of the woodmongers and their trade in wood and coal at this time come from the hand of the world's greatest dramatist, William Shakespeare – though his low opinion of the trade's products was merely a reflection of common usage. Both instances, in *King Henry V*, are placed in the mouths of everyday characters – Fluellen, Bardolph and their Boy – to provide light relief. However, their significance here derives from the insight they offer into the way the woodmonger's trade was then perceived, 'carrying coals' being defined in a Shakespearean Glossary as 'to perform a degrading service, submit to an indignity', whilst a woodmonger was anachronistically defined as still just 'a dealer in wood':

[Boy] Nym and Bardolph are sworn brothers in filching – I know by that piece of service that the men would carry coals, They would have me as familiar with men's pockets as their gloves or their handkerchiefs … their villainy goes against my weak stomach; [Fluellen to Pistol] If I owe you any thing, I will pay you in cudgels: you shall be a woodmonger, and buy nothing of me but cudgels.[7]

Overview

These on-stage appearances of 1597 provide a pause 'off-stage', both to look back and to look ahead, to sketch in an overview of the evolution of 'The Fueller' as he is now starting to appear.[8] A dozen phases can be identified. Viewed in terms of the Woodmongers' Livery itself, the story has been traditionally seen as one of eventual decline; in the framework of the wider theme of 'the Fueller', that idea now needs to be questioned.

The emerging picture in the early middle ages is of woodmongers initially pursuing their triple trade as a single wholesaling-retailing entity, buying and selling plant or 'sylvan' fuels, timber, and all kinds of 'coal'. ('Retailing' appeared in 17th-century usage, but it clearly embraced wholesaling functions.) With the coming of coal, the need for capital was increasing; although a split later developed between the two trade-levels, the Woodmongers' fraternity must still have included both.[9]

The third phase was their appearance as an organised guild, a Mystery, by 1376. The gap in medieval records, known by some as 'the silent years of the London Guild story', then ensued: it might have yielded a 'Coal-Sellers' mention. A fourth phase would be reached when the Mystery of Woodmongers started to be included in the various corporate ceremonies of the City.[10]

The 16th-century emergence of both the Carmen and the Wharfingers is traced below; it would raise the first of the two major competitive blips in the Company's progress. Yet by the time of James I, in 1605, Woodmongers were achieving their fifth phase and, as it transpired, their formal high point, the granting of a Royal Charter to the temporarily unified Company of Woodmongers and Carmen.[11]

Reciprocity between the Crown and the guilds had long been a feature of their relationship: City companies were important enough for Elizabeth to ask that her proclamations be read out to them direct, as the bishops did to the clergy. Privileges in the form of charters were sold to Londoners as a further means of raising revenue. London crafts began increasingly to seek the security of a royal charter. However, this was not a universal ambition: by no means all crafts or trade associations felt they had to gain a royal charter of incorporation. Some continued simply to seek the approval of the mayor and aldermen. In the first 40 years of the 15th century more than 16 crafts had their ordinances enrolled in the City's *Letter Book*.[13]

The fuel trade was already splitting along product boundaries. Chapter IV will trace the history from 1638 of the Society of Coal Merchants, associating with the Woodmongers in 1639; in the wider 'Fueller' setting, these are the sixth and seventh phases of evolution.[14] In 1667 would come the eighth phase, anticipated, but mysteriously unresolved, in Carolingian hand in the State Papers: failure to 'yield Obedience' to 'His Majestie's Attorny General'. This event, often described as a surrender, was in fact a public humiliation, seen with new evidence to be foreshadowed 30 years earlier – withdrawal of the Woodmongers' and Carmen's Royal Charter.[15] The last four of these phases are covered in Chapter III – starting with a renewed attempt to secure a Woodmongers-Carmen charter under Queen Anne (surprisingly ignored in the Carmen's History).[16]

The next 200 years saw the formation of the Society of Owners of Coal Craft in 1739 (they would eclipse the Woodmongers' coal interests by 1764) and of the Society of Coal Factors (1761). The year 1843 will bring forward by a whole century the last previously known reference to woodmongers in any context.[17]

Success or Failure?

Yet as the 16th century was unfolding, the Woodmongers seemed to have arrived: 'At the Court of Aldermen of 8 June 1518, to settle the number of bowmen each Company should send to follow the Lord Mayor to keep the watch on the vigils of St John and St Peter, it was settled the Woodmongers would send two bowmen, the same number as the Cordwainers and 11 other lesser Companies.'[18] They commanded all the constituent aspects of their trade, without competition; they were achieving their own niche within the City's hierarchy. As to a Hall, although it seems that they did not have one of their own before 1540, two Woodmongers' Halls appeared in the annals over the ensuing years, Fig. 22, Fig. 23 (later confirmed in manuscripts of 23 December 1649 and 17 April 1667).[19] To be at their known degree of participation in the various royal and City rituals, they were by now at least a Company, although again there is no archival date for that stage in their ascent.

By the start of the 16th century, no data on the size of the Company had yet appeared, though their City status seemed secure. By '23 of Henrie VIII' (1531/2) as Stow put it, quoting from the Brewers' famous First Book – the Company of Woodmongers had at least attained such importance within the City ranks as to penetrate the highest level of power – the Mayoralty. The wardens and two 'persons' with one 'messe' (mass) attended the 'May[i]ors feast in the Guild hall', no. 48 in Stow's record of 'president', out of a total of 60 companies represented. Perhaps significantly, they were still 'unclothed' in a Livery at this time (even though in today's City listing it is the norm that several Companies remain 'without' Livery). The phrase 'No Clothing' attached to nine other companies, with no apparent unifying characteristics, the four higher in assumed precedence being the 'U[V]pholders' at 33, 'Turnars' at 37, 'Glasiers' at 46, and 'Linnenedrapers' at 47. Five equally 'unclothed' but established guilds below them at the table were the 'Foysters' at 50, Grey Tanners at 51, Lorimers at 55, Fruterers at 58 and 'Ferrers' at 59. By 1558, the burgeoning coal sector of the fuel trade was said to be in the hands of a mere 14 citizens. On 14 January 1559, those Woodmongers would have been among 'the members of the City Companies in their livery and costly furs' behind special rails watching Elizabeth I's Coronation procession from the Tower to Temple Bar, as once more on Sunday 24 November 1588, at the Armada celebration.[20]

Eight years earlier, in 1580, a will of one William Heron had directed 'his executors to convey his lands and tenements to the *corporation* of Woodmongers or of the clothworkers'.

Of others already in Livery on Stow's list, the 'Bladesmithes' were last at 60th; heading the list were the 'Twelve Ancients' all of course in Livery, such as the Guild that shared the public quay and harbour at Billingsgate, the Fishmongers. Although there were some 26 carters – or rather, 'commercial carts' – in the City by 1502, there was no mention yet of any Livery for the Carmen, nor for any Watermen, Lightermen, Wharfingers, or Coal Merchants: their day was yet to come.[21]

The Woodmongers' trade had to be expanding in line with an ever-more prosperous realm, as standards of living, cooking and heating, rose

19 THE ELIZABETHAN MERCHANT

A typical Elizabethan merchant, his family and retinue: a woodmonger merchant's outer coat would have been edged and lined with fur, with bands of fur framing the two openings in the sleeves. His lady's plain stuff gown would have been worn open, over a bell-shaped 'Spanish farthingale'.

continuously; the Elizabethan merchant, family, and retainers were doing well. This was the case for the wealthier classes, despite the setbacks of recurrent Plagues, with their attendant 'troughs' in the population; it was also true to a lesser extent for general fuel consumption, and for domestic and civic construction.

The industrial uses of London's new wonder fuel, coal, also seemed to grow steadily, and coal production in the North-East, and elsewhere, expanded with every year that passed. The fabled Elizabethan age looked to prove equally fabulous for this pivotal trade, its merchant-traders, and their Company.

However, within a century and a half the prominence of the Woodmongers was to be challenged; their monopolistic position was to be broken, and recently bestowed royal favour was to be dashed from their lips. An implication that this favour had been given in return for funding towards James' Plantations in Ulster is lent credence by an entry (upside down!) at the back of the Minute Book of the Plumbers' Company.[22] It stated:

> In the years 1610 to 1640 the City of London bought of King James I twelve estates or lordships in Ireland with the royalties and the customs of the same and the payment to King Charles II had since bought off the custom of the same, whereof part of the rest remained behind unpaid.

The Vintners made the major contribution at £2,080, but gathered in graded sums from nine other Companies; the mighty Grocers not surprisingly top that list at £540 13s. 4d., but the second largest payers are the Woodmongers, for whatever reason, at £200. Then come the eminent Weavers, at £100, followed by the Plumbers themselves, the Tylers and Bricklayers, and the Poulterers at £80; and lastly the Blacksmiths, Fruiterers and Curriers, at £64. Plumbers' chronicler Anthony Young concluded that the 'Company earlier had a direct interest in the Irish Estates through the Vintners'; however, such a straight commercial motive seems to sit oddly with the Woodmongers.

As a final pointer, despite their signal input to the remedying of one of London's greatest civic disasters – the 'malicious bloody flame', as Pepys would put it – the Woodmongers were to be so execrated as infringers of the country's evolving legal system, as well as of the City's conventions, that their Livery would in due course vanish from the records.

The Fault-Lines

Half a dozen fault-lines can be discerned in the apparently secure medieval structure of the Woodmongers' Company. To start with, fuel distribution was inherently as fissiparous as its own products. It was a composite business, with sequential inputs from other trades – Carmen, Wharfingers, Lightermen – and comprising two main intercompeting fuels.

Potential internal fissures were there from the outset; the coal faction would increasingly seek to break out from, and overtake, the historical trade in wood. Coupled with that was the simple truth that this was no inward-looking craft guild, with an inbuilt pride to make it cohere. In addition, merchant guilds were broadening out, ceasing to be trade-specific; merchant members could favour whichever guild seemed best positioned to advance their commercial interest within the City's networks. The wholesaling strata were themselves separating out into lower and upper levels, according to status: import-export merchants were often having to deal with other intermediate merchants, and making partnerships with men of different 'crafts', such that it was 'often difficult to tell … to which company a merchant belonged'.[23]

Thirdly, it seems inevitable that out of the monopolistic stranglehold that the Woodmongers' Company sought to maintain over London's fuel trade there grew a sense of unchallengeable power, and hence cupidity; opportunities for overreaching greed and corruption would not be far to find. Although reinforcing this, in the fourth place there had developed by the end of the previous century a need to oppose 'the principle of group monopoly and exclusive privileges' with 'the principle of the freedom of the wholesale trade'.[24]

Tendencies towards stricter practices and legal sanctions, and an encouragement of 'the multiplicity of Traders in Victuals and Fuel', were starting to be seen.[26] By the mid-point of the next century, business would be under an ever stronger puritanical spotlight in both City and Parliament; deviations from probity, inherent in a hitherto imperfectly measurable trade such as coal shipments, would become unacceptable and intolerable.

Penultimately, growth in the use of coal, although well within the scope of the merchant-woodmonger, was now fitting uneasily under the 'Woodmongers' title. A merchant was also human and, in an era of outward show, sensitive to his external standing; it could well have irked him to have to continue to operate under an emblem, however ancient, whose relevance was ebbing: 'woodmongering' might well be sounding 'old-fashioned'.

Indeed, for the wood interest alone, the terms 'timber-monger'/'timber merchant' were coming into greater use. In parallel, by the mid-17th century the term 'coal merchant' had articulated itself – however briefly – in a new body already introduced, the Society of Coal Merchants, whose interests were not necessarily or inevitably synonymous with those of its Livery Company.[27]

Last, but by no means least, the restrictive, interventionist influence of the ancient guilds themselves was slowly weakening in the face of the straightforward pressures of a freer commercial market-place.

Such multiple trends did not necessarily have anything to do with the profitability of the expanding fuel trade itself, whoever might be participating in it, but they certainly militated against the healthy survival of the erstwhile medieval format of a merchant guild.

ii: The Woodmongers' Environment

Wood still played its part in the citizens' public life: when Mary Queen of Scots was executed in 1587, bonfires in the streets were the immediate popular response, including one huge fire outside the door of the French ambassador.

By the turn of the 16th century, over 200,000 people would be living within the City walls, out of an estimated wider population in London as a whole of between 422,000 and 485,000.[29] As living standards rose, London continued to be a city of landlords and tenants, burning fuel in grates, but still needing a 'poor man's wharf for coal and wood'.[30]

European trade, Elizabethan privateering, and relative peace, had made London – in F.J. Fisher's apt phrase – 'a centre of conspicuous consumption'.[31] Yet it was still a dirty, untidy city: 'Raw materials and fuel were stacked in various corners or stored in lean-to sheds … Waste products … from furnaces, stables and the crowded tenements either escaped through chimneys into the pall of smoke which hung in the air, or were thrown into the street where they lay until carried away by rainwater along open channels (or 'kennels').'[32]

In his report to King Charles II of 1671, Sir Christopher Wren would reinforce this picture of noxious chaos, much of it to be lain – even literally – at the woodmongers' door: 'Everywhere the area was "inclosed and incumbered with Poles or Brickwalls, irregular houses and buildings, Piles of Timber, Billetts, Faggots and heaps of coles, many boarded sheds and several … Laystalls"'.[33] Despite the wealth amassed by its upper and merchant classes, the judgement of the classic chronicler of the City's rebuilding is damning: 'By modern standards, in fact, much of the old city would have been classed as a slum'.[34]

The woodmongers' thoroughfares differed greatly from today's London, the streets narrow and crowded. Holborn was a broad country road outside the City, just beginning to be built upon, running westwards through open pasture to the church that still carries the name of St Giles-in-the-Fields. It is easy to imagine the hazards caused by the horsemen and trains of pack-mules, and, towards the end of Elizabeth's reign, by the 'Cars, Draies & Coaches' of which Stow would later complain. The other major thoroughfare open to the woodmongers and the trades that served them there, was also very different from today's Thames: it is necessary to think of a wider, shallower river, with a long shelving foreshore at low tide, coming right up to churches like St Magnus the Martyr at high tide, and with stairs running out into the current like a landing stage, which would only be used when the tide was right.[35]

There is much known detail also as to the woodmongers' living patterns within this environment. As later research in the *London Journal* indicates, it is now also possible to identify a number of Wards within Tudor London where the woodmongers – although not yet coal-focused – might have congregated.

Unlike their later fellow Thames-based users, the Fishmongers, in Billingsgate Ward, or another waterbound trade, the Salters, at Queenhithe, the records do reveal that at least four woodmongers lived within Tower Ward, then in the top quartile for prosperity.[36] However, the most likely site, giving a glimpse of a possible although unprovable fraternity origin for the Woodmongers' Company, had already entered the literature:

> Castle Baynard Ward, and especially Woodwharf in the parish of St Peter the Less, upstream of London Bridge, was the centre of the London firewood trade, probably from well before 1200. Later, significant numbers of woodmongers owned houses, wharves and other property there.[37]

One other 16th-century item shows, through the occupations of the fathers of 132 freemen between 1496-1515, how the guilds interacted with each other; one of these was a woodmonger who fathered an apprentice to the Skinners.[38]

Numbers and Finance

Two questions need addressing: how many Woodmongers were by now plying their trade in Tudor London? Indeed, how wealthy did it make them? Before final evidence arises in 1617, Sylvia Thrupp's classic study of London's medieval merchant class offers a broad analysis.[39] There were some 4,400 free citizens in 1501-2, compared with some 4,000 in 1377.

The study provides a first indication of the economic status of the Woodmongers' Company. Its Table 4 gives a total of 784 in the 1501-2 (Livery) List. This details 36 Companies, averaging 22 members each. However, the figure of 784 was thought to be too low: 'the list of companies is not complete. Among those omitted are the broiderers, the clothworkers, the glovers, the hatter merchants, the latteners, the scriveners, the shipwrights, the upholders (upholsterers), and the woodmongers, all of which, with the possible exception of the latteners and the upholders, had members who were substantial citizens … In all, the nine companies could probably have brought the number of the more substantial middling citizens up to about 1,000'.

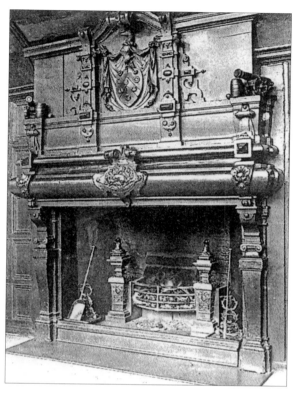

20 THE 17TH-CENTURY FIREPLACE
Domestic fireplaces evolved significantly during the 17th century, allowing draughts to come in from below (although still in the country, even by the end of the 18th century, 'a common cook would not know how to manage a coal fire'). A visit to this dining hall at the old Charterhouse (the arms of Girdler Thomas Sutton, first holder of the Lease of Whickham and Gateshead collieries, are over the fireplace) would feature on the programme of John Bainbridge, Fuellers' Master, in 2009-10.

The names of the Master and Wardens Assistants
& whole Liuerey of the Felowshipe of Woodmongers
as the are placed in An° 1617 :

George Heall Master:

the too Wardens:

John Harrison & Henry Williams:

the Assisttents

Thomas Hunt	Thomas Milles
Richard Wootton	John Eayer
Ephraim Androse	Thomas Bridge
Walter Kighte	Fraunis Sadler
John Atkins	Roger Coleman
John Wainwright	George Moore
Heugh Capen	George Thornton
Edmond Dawson	Thomas Morley

the Liuerey

Anthony Bushop	Thomas Warner
Thomas Sawsby	John Bromfeild
Thomas Cumbers	John Bigges
Richard Blakamoore	John Cutler
Edward Temple	John Warnen
Fraunis Osbolstone	John Beare
Thomas Robinson	John Mouke
George Hubberds	William Chesson
Heugh Baly	George Wainwright
John Combers	Thomas Willimott
George Winkfeild	William Ham
Henry Piggin	John Jackson
Stephen Cox	Richard Bull
Florice Mallard	Heugh Crooke
Thomas Lockwood	William Dauies
Humphre Clarke	John Bush

Thomas Copley Clicus eisdem die
et Anno Supradict

21   THE WOODMONGERS' LIVERY, 1617

'The names of the Master and Wardens [,] Assisstants & whole Liverey of the Felowshipe of Woodmongers as the[y] are placed in An[o] 1617. George Heall [,] Master; the too [sic] Wardens [:] John Harrison & Henry Williams [etc].'

On this evidence Woodmongers might now be regarded as among the 'substantial citizens', the merchant class, at both wholesale and 'retail' levels, but, on the basis of these calculations at least, with possibly no more than 30 members. However, in addition to many wills, there is also an indication of the financial status of these Tudor merchants, during a period of 75 years, in the so-called Amicable Grant Assessment of 1525, which has yielded qualified data about the 'wealth' of 2,089 individuals, out of a list of 2,507. (This was not the total wealth, since it excluded wealth in property, and thus discounted the capital woodmongers needed for investing in wharves and various forms of transport.) It was in effect 'a snapshot of the merchant class and the most successful among the artisan class: from those who were very rich to those who were comfortably off ... there was an enormous disparity of wealth among the freemen of the city'.

Londoners were valued at £1,000 or more, all but one spread across the greater companies. The numbers assessed ranged from 161 (tailors) and 110 (mercers) down to an individual paver, lorimer or glasier: only five woodmongers were brought into the net, too small for analysis to be carried too far. The average 'wealth' ranged from £417 (mercers) and £411 (merchant taylors), down to £9 (founders), or £6 (greytawyers). The average for the woodmongers was £35: 38 trades averaged higher, 60 trades lower, in several cases, for example 'hakneymen', 'poulterers' or 'plaisters', much lower. Three of those woodmongers averaged 'wealth' in the £5-19 bracket, none in the £20-49 bracket, but two with 'wealth' of £50 or more; in that category there were three out of 39 barber-surgeons, 39 out of 208 goldsmiths but all six of the 'merchants of the staple/staplers' with 'wealth'. The woodmongers ranked 43rd by 'wealth', placing them at the lower end of the upper 40 per cent of the City's traders but relatively comfortable. However, at 1501 this research did not show any woodmongers in livery.[40]

For a century later, Dale quoted from the City records for 22 August 1604 a 'Humble Petition of the Wardens of the Poor Company of Woodmongers complaining that as the Company was "very much decayed and hath not above seven persons of the whole Company that trade in wood"', they be allowed to have 12 'mere Woodmongers' ... 'made free of this City by redemption'. However this plea neither confirms the research evidence of relative prosperity, nor does it conform with the conclusive manuscript in the Bodleian, for 1617, Fig, 21. This showed the total of the 'Felowshipe of Woodmongers' as 51, now on their own again, despite the joint Charter of 1605, excluding the Clerk (clicus), Thomas Copley. It was composed of a Master, George Heall, two Wardens, John Harrison and Henry Williams, 16 Assisstants [sic] (including a Roger Coleman) and 32 more in the 'whole Livery'. The supposition must be that here was a case of special pleading with the City Council.[41]

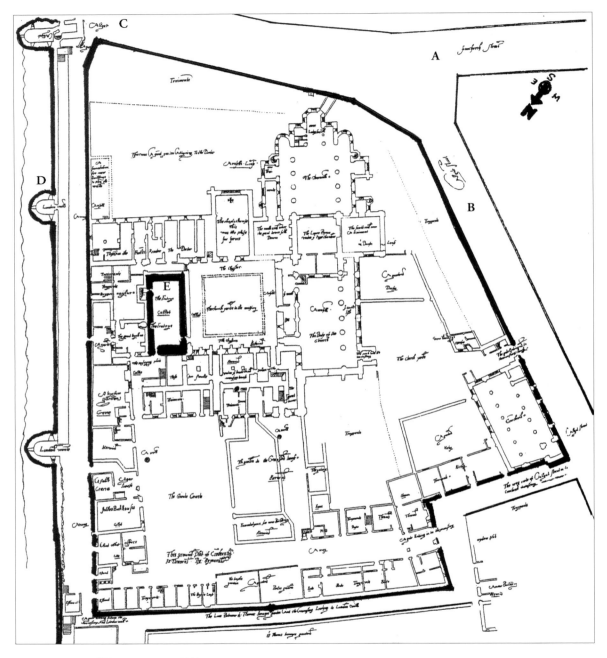

22   A First Woodmongers' Hall?

Drawing shows author's amended version of the speculative 1562 location of a first Woodmongers' Hall within Holy Trinity Priory, Duke's Place, Aldgate, as suggested by Dale. (This idea is questionable: the 'Agas'-attributed woodcut of 1570 + omits any reference to a Hall there). Dale's drawing shows: A = old Fenchurch Street; B = old Aldgate Street; C = the Aldgate itself; D = the old City Wall and battlement; E = the 'Fratery', Dale's authority for the site (middle left). Author's marking of compass points (top right) appears the only way to reconcile the upside-down positioning of the Aldgate, with London Wall to the east; (there is still a Duke's Place, off today's Aldgate Street).

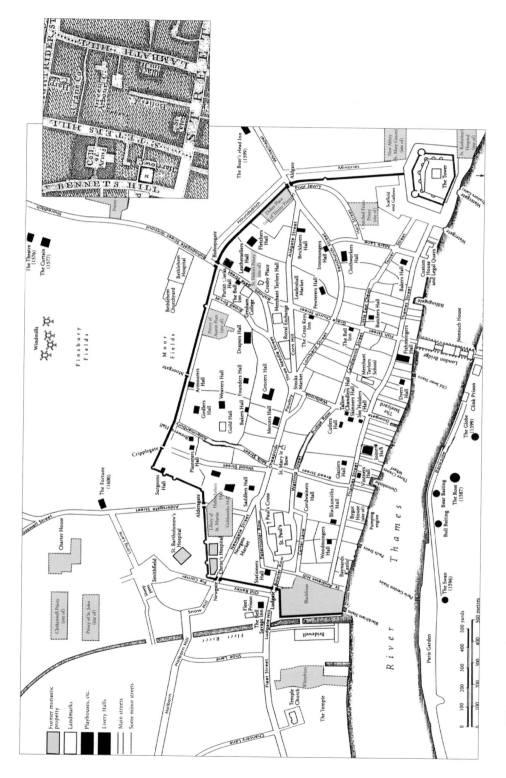

23 WOODMONGERS' HALL, PAUL'S WHARF, 1570?/96–1666

Main map is sole extant illustration of the probable location of a verified Hall, destroyed by the Great Fire, 1666.

Inset: Author's adaptation of Rocque's map indicating a building at west end of Embroiderers' tenements, 'Poor Widows Alley', south of then College of Heralds. The 19th-century Queen Victoria Street now covers the site. Outline of the inverted 'U'-block of today's College of Arms is clear. [L. Picard, Elizabeth's London, Weidenfeld & Nicolson, Orion Publishing Group, p.17; J. Gilkes, 2003; 'Paul's Wharf' at a year full of meaning*, leading up past Woodmongers' Hall site to Old St Paul's. See Endnote 43 'ref date.

A Hall as Status Symbol

By the time of that Charter, the Woodmongers, as well as the Carmen, are each recorded as having acquired a Hall. Birch reports a Carmen's Hall as located, even briefly, at Harpe Lane, by 1562. Tantalisingly, Dale, presumably on the basis of the 'Agas'-attributed Hogenberg map of London, showed a plan of Holy Trinity Priory at the old Aldgate, near what is still today's Duke's Place, in whose Fratery what might have been a first Woodmongers' Hall was asserted to be housed. Close scrutiny of this plan shows no reference to the Woodmongers, nor does the 'Agas' woodcut of the 1570s show one. However, by the time of Stow's Survey of 1598, let alone the Woodmongers' *Remonstrance* of 1649, the existence of a 'second' Woodmongers' Hall is verified. Sadly, unlike the nearby Upholders' Hall, also 'destroyed in the Great Fire', there is (as yet) no blue plaque to record the site of this substantive – possibly the first but certainly the last – Woodmongers' Hall.[42]

Equally, it has proved impossible to verify Dale's assertion that 'this priory formerly had an altar dedicated to St John the Baptist, and as he was the patron saint of the Woodmongers, and for centuries a wood-market had been held outside the Aldgate in Portsoken, it is probable that the altar was given by the Woodmongers … After the death of Lord Audley, who apparently owned the priory following its dissolution in 1531, 'the chapter house was turned into the Church of St James, and the Fratery or Refectory became the Hall of the Woodmongers' (later called Duke's Hall, in Duke's Place). In 1603 the then owner, the Duke of Norfolk, apparently 'sold the whole place to the City of London … who terminated the Woodmongers' tenancy'. Dale wrongly surmised that the Woodmongers then 'took some room near the *Dog Tavern*, facing the Customs House'.

The damage to this whole area in the Great Fire, including the Woodmongers' and 43 other Livery Halls and many woodmongers' woodwharves, will be detailed below, see p.59. By the time of the Privy Council of 1667 a second Woodmongers' Hall was explicitly referred to. Stow wrote: 'touching lanes ascending out of Thames streete, to Knightriders streete, the first is Peters hill … At the upper end of this lane, towards the north, the houses there be called Peters Key … Then is Powles wharfe hill, on the East side thereof is Woodmongers Hall. And next adioyning is Darby house'. Harben clarifies: 'Woodmongers' Hall at the west end of [Poor Widdowes Alley] with the College of Heralds [now 'Arms'] to the north' (*see* Appendix III(A)).[43]

The Elizabethan 'Fueller'

At home, a woodmonger-merchant's household of the 'middling sort' was 'decorously religious', singing 'psalms together as part of their daily family worship'. On their dining table, 'knives and spoons would be the work of

cutlers and pewterers respectively; forks were regarded as peculiar objects used by foreigners abroad, but quite unsuitable for the Englishman's dinner table … Spoons would now be made of silver, while pewter and latten [a mixed yellow metal like brass] would be appearing on the tables of those whose parents had been content with wood'. 'The average London Merchant was accustomed to dine at noon and to sup at six in the evening …'.

In the rest of the house, of interest to today's Fuellers, for comparison with medieval practice, were fast-evolving standards of heating, and the steady replacement of wood by coal, making smaller hearths possible and fashionable. Holmes noted the:

24 THAMESIDE, 1630

The busy north bank of the City, seen from Southwark; this painting gives some idea of the crowding of the ever-growing City, at the time of the Woodmongers' mid-Stuart ascendancy as a Livery Company.

[43]

increase in the number of brick or stone chimneys ... outlines of hearths with chimney flues above them can be seen on the outside wall, showing that they ... were later additions ... The fire would no longer be built in the middle of the main hall, under a central louvre through which the smoke might eventually find its way to the open air, but on a hearth, under the draught provided by a proper flue ... The provision of chimneys made it easier for different rooms to have their own individual sources of warmth. Some of them were still heated by tiled stoves, after the fashion of those used in northern Europe ... Elizabethan oak had come into general use ... in former days it had been used only for shipbuilding and as the framework for churches and the palaces of princes ...

 ## iii: First of the Turf Wars: The Carmen and the Wharfingers

Whilst the evolution of a trade has necessarily to be viewed mainly at the level of social history, in the mid-16th century the reality was that life for every citizen was lived at a higher level – of political and religious awareness, of the fight, often to the death, of the old Catholicism against the new Protestantism. For the capital's fuel trade, that fierce interaction was echoed on the streets of London. Into a scene of improving Elizabethan domestic life-styles now erupted the first of the Woodmonger-merchants' two demarcation disputes – the 'turf wars' that were finally to upstage them.

Two additional trades have now to be included under the retrospective Fuellers' umbrella: the Carmen, and an older Company, the Wharfingers. This tortuous and often petty story has been detailed at length in the histories of the Companies concerned. However, it awaited a recent paper in the *London Journal*, and a new thesis, to investigate what now became a three-cornered contest.[45]

The Carmens' and the Fuellers' interests would clash once more, in the 20th century. A little of the good sense and well-honed nationally-tested negotiating skills which resolved those latter differences would not have come amiss then.[46] At least the 20th-century situation would be a two-part affair, quickly over and done with, to mutual satisfaction.

'Carmen' (or carters or carriers) are known to have been loading imports off the London quays, and onto their 'carrooms' or standings, by 1277, twenty years after the first record of the bringing ashore of coals from the river. The term 'carroom' became synonymous with the licence that enabled the carmen to carry out their vital but intermediary transport role. By 1369 the four Coal Meters had been appointed, bringing some order. Nevertheless, there was inevitably friction on the streets – caused both by their narrowness, and also by the rough nature of the trade itself: in 1479 Common Council acted to stop cars blocking the streets ... the disorders of the carmen were still news.

By 1502, the City had pronounced – understandably – that 26 horsedrawn cars should be enough for the congestion of their streets, and also – more arbitrarily – for London's needs. In 1512, the City ruled that only 40 carts be authorised to ply for hire. In 1516, the Court of Aldermen were announcing their order of guild precedence, and thus fraternities and guilds were reinforced as the flavour of the century. Now appeared the first signs of future problems, for one Thomas Newman, an Innholder, got together 14 other freemen, to offer the City a triple service – first the provision of carts for royal purposes, and then muck and rubbish collection.

The third promise was to move wine, oil, wood and 'other wares and merchaundyses' from wharf to market, including 'colwood, billet ffagot' but – crucially – 'coles only excepted'. The price was a right to organise a Fellowship, open for the first time to members from outside the city walls. Other traders could still own carts. In the following year, 1517, the Fraternity of St Katherine the Virgin and Martyr of Carters was formed, with sole rights to offer carts for 'common carriage'.

The future portent lay partly in the omen that one of the 14 was Robert Hammond, already a Woodmonger, and another, Scott, was on the way to becoming one by 1528; it also lay partly in the fact that there were within this new group members of 11 other guilds – a Tallow Chandler, Skinner, Salter, Tailor, Saddler, Brewer, Brownbaker, Coffermaker, and Fuller, two from the Greytawyers and two more Innholders. All had legitimate but seemingly separate interests in the process of carting, free from royal distraint – the King's corrupt 'cart-takers' – and in regularising the endemic friction with suburban carters.

Already by 1527, ten short years later, the Carmen were accused of failing in their task, and in 1528 new ordinances were introduced, regulating the trade: woodmongers with wharves were restricted to one cart each, and had to join the new Brotherhood. In 1529, the fraternity was incorporated as a Company by act of the Common Council. The second of the Carmen's historians has commented:

> Transport crosses all trades. It is catholic in its intentions … It was too much to hope the new Guild could cover all comers and all contingencies. As trade grew, so did industry, and the carmen's Guild gradually lost control … the Woodmongers outnumbered the Carmen, so they became the principal purveyors to the Crown. In 1536 they were subject to City control, for 'creating a scarcity of wood'.

In 1546, the Court of Aldermen decreed that anyone operating a wharf big enough to use the royally-favoured long carts (14 feet long and four feet wide) should maintain at least one, to be pressed into royal service if required; in return wharfingers, usually Woodmongers by guild, could run two cars – one for fuel, and the other for general carriage:

The Woodmongers virtually ignored the requirements but exploited their advantage, undermining the Carmen's trade and their Fraternity. Now there were two transport guilds, and the Woodmongers were the larger. Their membership overlapped … Things went from bad to worse in 1549 when the Aldermen ordered the Carmen 'to be obedient … and to comen redilly at all times at the lawful somens of the … Woodmongers' … In 1580 the Woodmongers swallowed up the Carmen's fellowship – but it proved an indigestible dish.

The Carmen were subordinated to the Woodmongers; they kicked against the loss of their limited sovereignty. Two years on, so fragile was the whole arrangement, that an honest broker, the Governors of the newly-established local charity school of Christ's Hospital, was asked by the City to accept 'oversight' of all Car activities in the City. Stow records that the Hospital had been founded in the reign of Edward VI, so that 'the innocent and fatherless' might be 'trained up in the knowledge of God'. The income of the Woodmongers would now go to 'the relyefe of the poore children'. All fines went to the school; every carman, carter and woodmonger paid them a quarterly rental of 6s. 8d. too.[47]

The Governors, however, found their new unaccustomed duties of supervision, including the 'sealing' of carrs, 'verie troublesome', and the Woodmongers saw an opportunity to regain the lead. In 1586, they went over the head of the City and asked the Board of Green Cloth, which handled the provision of goods for the royal Household, to redress their grievances vis-a-vis the Hospital, but their attempt was foiled.

By 1596, the Woodmongers and the wharf keepers came before the Court of Christ's Hospital to be reminded to provide their cars according to the new rules now in force, and by 1598 the regime for control became tougher; in no time, by the dawn of the new century, the Carmen and the Woodmongers chose to appear before the court of the King's Bench, and won their suit. *Carr and Carman* records the important principle:

> The details are not recorded, but the gist was in line with other judgments of the time – that unskilled trades should not be restrained.

Christ's Hospital appealed to the Privy Council, who came down on their side; they were trying to please everyone, an impossible task. In 1603, the Woodmongers and the Carmen jointly flouted the authority of the Hospital:

> Given the Court ruling, which suspended the City's authority over transport, the Woodmongers exploited the market. The City had to bow to their demands … until now, ships offloaded coal onto the wharves; as consumption grew, ships grew larger and more numerous. The quays could not accommodate them, so lighters took up the loads. The coal merchants

of the century were fuellers – Woodmongers ... However, just as physical control of coal imports passed from shore-based Woodmongers to Thames-borne Watermen [embracing the Lightermen, the next seed for future demarcation] so timber was being replaced by coal ... The guild system was about to be rocked by a new brand of entrepreneur.

In 1605, by means fair or possibly foul, the Woodmongers obtained James I's agreement to grant them a Royal Charter and recognised Livery status, to end the Hospital's well-meant but inadequate 'oversight', as well as the rivalry between the two interdependent guilds, by giving the Woodmongers overall power.

Woodmongers as Jacobean Lobbyists

At this point, a fresh eye on the Woodmongers is timely, from a modern historian already cited. As a New Zealander he is free of bias; through his account, Fuellers are thereby spared the word-for-word regurgitation of the argument which made earlier accounts both impenetrable and inevitably partisan:[48] 'In 1620-1 a long severe winter caused the Thames to freeze over ... The frozen waterway made the delivery of wood difficult ... the shortage of fuel nearly forced the closure of Parliament and the removal of the Royal Court from London. But the harsh weather was only part of the problem – a private dispute between Wharfingers, Carmen and Woodmongers had resulted in engrossing of fuel, exorbitant prices and a dearth of wood in London.'

> This Company squabble and the monopolistic control over carting from the wharves held by the Woodmongers occupied the time (and the patience) of the Common Council of London, the Privy Council, Star Chamber and, in 1621, Parliament ... Whilst Parliament was often a last resort for battling interest groups, it was one that neither side could afford to ignore ... the supremacy of statute law made it the most dangerous for the potential losers. In 1621 the London Company of Wharfingers exhibited a bill to Parliament for 'the better governing of Carmen and Cars' ... the measure immediately sparked a campaign by the Woodmongers who governed London cars ...
>
> The Woodmongers took the opportunity presented to them by the accession of a new monarch to petition for a revised charter. James granted this in 1605 and the Woodmongers assumed complete control over carriage in London ... The Woodmongers agreed to pay £150 to Christ's ... In 1606 the Court of Aldermen ordered that all carmen plying their trade not of the Woodmongers were to be imprisoned. The following year the Company's ordinances were ratified by the Lord Chancellor, to be confirmed in 1608 by the Privy Council.

TO THE
Worthy Citizens of LONDON,

But especially to the Worshipful the

COMMON-COUNCILMEN

Of the said

CITY.

The Case of the Woodmongers within this City, in relation to Cars, &c.

Hereas by a late Act of Common-Council, made in the Majoralty of Sir *Thomas Davis* Knight, deceased; It was Enacted (amongst other things) That no more than four hundred and twenty Cars of all sorts, both for Fuel and other Carriage, should be used within the City of *London*: And that seventeen shillings and four pence Yearly Rent, and twenty shillings admittance, should be received by Christs Hospital, upon every Car, &c. And that no Wharfinger or Woodmonger (not being duly allowed by Christs Hospital, and within the aforesaid number of four hundred and twenty) should be permitted or allowed to work any Car for the Carrying forth of their Wood and Coals, &c. upon a certain penalty therein named: upon which there was an Action brought, in the name of the Chamberlain of the City of *London*, against Mr. *John Veere*, a Woodmonger, for working his own Cart, in the Carrying forth his own Goods, contrary to the said Act; which Action the said Mr. *Veere* removed into the *Exchequer*, where it was Argued several times before the Barons by Council Learned on both sides: and at last after several Hearings of all that could be said on both sides; the Barons took time and set a certain day to deliver their Judgments in the Case, which accordingly in *Hillary* Term, 1679. they did; when every one successively delivered his Judgment, and *Nemine contradicente* they all agreed; and declared this Act of Common-Council to be unreasonable and illegal, and (as they were pleased to term it) a Monopoly. Notwithstanding which, some persons have undertaken to prepare a Bill, and endeavor to have the same passed into an Act of Common-Council, wherein they still exclude the Woodmonger from the Carriage of his own Goods in his own Cart. Now we who are Traders in Fuel within this City, well knowing what a tender regard (the Case being well understood) every Worthy Common-Council-man will have of the well-fare of his Fellow Citizen, have made bold humbly to offer some Reasons to shew the unreasonableness of this exclusion or prohibition, *viz.*

1. If this Act pass, many poor men, who are imployed by the Woodmongers as their Carmen, and get their Livelyhood by them, must then be discharged, and consequently they and their Families perish, they being uncapable of following any other Imployments.

2. The Woodmongers have most of them laid out great Sums of money in building Houses, Stables, and other Buildings, and the rest have taken Wharfs and Houses at great Rents, and all of them have been at great charges in providing Horses, Carts, and other conveniencies fit for their Trades, in hopes to support their Families thereby, and if this Act pass, must not only Sell their Horses and Carts to great loss, but their Wharfs and Buildings will be in a great measure rendred useless and of little value, and when occasion requires for disposing of them, it must be done to very great loss, many of their Wharfs standing in places fit for no other Trade.

3. The Woodmongers within the City who are Freemen thereof, and are the only persons which will be concerned in this Law, pay all Taxes both for the support of the Government of this City, and bear all Offices relating thereunto, will be in a worse condition than those without, who will be at Liberty to work as many Carts as they please.

4. The Woodmongers not having Carts to carry out Fuel, and Servants for whom on all occasions they must be answerable; will be a means to drive the Trade into the Out-parts, and the Citizens and Tradesmen will be incommoded either by hiring of Street Carts for Carrying their Fuel, or in going into the Out-parts for their Fuel; both which will not only be troublesom and dilatory but will advance the price of Fuel.

5. The Citizens will be lyable to the ill behavior and rude Language of the Town Carmen, whose abuses can no way be redrest without complaining to Christs Hospital, which it's possible may be thought both troublesom and tedious.

6. This is contrary to former Acts which have allowed a certain number of Carts to Woodmongers, which they desire may be still continued, they submitting to the Government of this Honorable City.

[handwritten manuscript text]

[636]

Entered in general catalogue 1889. p. 1015.
Removed from C.S.L. 1.120.

Broadsides
12.40.

---

25   THE WOODMONGERS' 'REMONSTRANCE'

The Company, despite its loss of Livery status, continued to defend its interests before the citizenry and the Common Council; here a Broadsheet (poster, early form of 'PR') argues the need to repeal the Act whereby the Woodmonger is excluded 'from the Carriage of his own goods in his own cart', also alluding to the 'ill behavior and rude Language of the Town Carmen'.

Evidence Old and New

This arrangement suited the Woodmongers but left the Carmen at their mercy. It started a protracted battle which was to last into the 19th century. In 1611, the Carmen and Woodmongers commenced suits against each other in Star Chamber. The Carmen accused the Woodmongers of various financial improprieties.

The Woodmongers' bill attacked the Carmen for attempting to overthrow the ordinances and charter of their Company. Star Chamber sought the advice of the Corporation of London who 'ruled in favour of the Woodmongers: both suits were dismissed.'

In 1617 the Common Council had to intervene once more, as it was now self-evident that the trade was virtually ungoverned, with the streets continually bottlenecked by unlicensed carts. The Council made detailed rulings about routage through London, keeping the cars to 400, including those of the Wharfingers: the orders introduced the one-way street to London, and also possibly the world's first 'traffic policemen' …

The following year the Lord Chief Justice, Sir Henry Mountagu [aka Montagu] affirmed the order, and the right of Wharfingers to hold carrooms before those of any other trade. The Wharfingers subsequently questioned the legality of the Woodmongers holding property rights over the carrooms … In order to affirm their right … in 1620 the Wharfingers appealed to the King and he referred the matter to the Bishop of London, John King … among others.

The commissioners sided with the Wharfingers … In 1621 the Wharfingers submitted to Parliament 'An Acte for the better orderinge and governing of Carmen and Care … The Wharfingers complained that the Woodmongers … often denied licenses to Wharfingers and continued to sell them to scriveners, ostlers and tapsters among othere … [also that] this had led to the overthrow of twenty wharves and a sharp rise in the price of fuel … [they] mounted a two-prong attack, and also printed a petition to the Commons grievances committee against the Woodmongers' monopoly …

In counter-attacking the Wharfingers, the Woodmongers also took practical action to ensure Parliament would be favourably disposed, and sent 'The Answer' to one of the Hampshire gentry, MP Sir Thomas Jervoise, to pack the Commons committee: 'a blatant attempt by the Woodmongers to influence the proceedings of the Commons', yet one not unusual for its time … 'whilst the Wharfingers' bill may have failed, the Company appears to have had greater success in the grievances committee … [which] agreed with the charges … Notes [taken by one of the committee, Edward Alford] reveal how the Woodmongers had used bribery and other dubious tactics to secure their position'.

During the mayoralty of Sir George Bolles (1617-18), after diverse complaints to the Common Council of London, the examination of abuses was referred to London's Recorder:

> The Woodmongers then presented the recorder's wife with a 'guilt [*sic*] Cup of a great value … [they] also managed to persuade the Attorney-General, Sir Henry Yelverton, to support them … He summoned the Wharfingers and Woodmongers but when they arrived at the hearing [he] summarily dismissed them … he then took up a position as legal counsel to the Woodmongers". The dispute dragged on through and beyond 1625 when Star Chamber again ruled in favour of the Wharfingers, a decision which seems to have been accepted by the Woodmongers.

Whatever the morality of the case, the Woodmongers exhibited here some very sophisticated 'management skills': 'petitioning and counterpetitioning, and the employment of legal counsel'. The rest of the saga is reported in the Carmen's history:

> Gradually the Carmen either began to believe that they must go out of business, or become uneasily dependent on the coal merchants'. As the situation on the streets became increasingly tense, a new trade, the watermen, entered the story, albeit at the margins of the Woodmongers' trade; [their impact will be set out in Chapter III]. The cause was the competition between the new sedan chairs and the customary use of the Thames as the sole City passenger transport: 'Against the ground we stand and knock our heels, Whilst all our profit runs away on wheels'.[49] Although two participants in the general mêlée of the fuel trade, the Carmen and the Porters, had been told by the Privy Council in 1628 to 'desist from their wonted disorderlie and violent courses', the standing of the Woodmongers was becoming no less unfavourable, perhaps unknown to their competitors.

New evidence from the proceedings of the Privy Council now shows how close to the winds of the Cities both of London and of Westminster they were sailing. By 1628, they had had to appoint Coal Meters to inspect for the 'false sacks and measures' – an ongoing abuse. On 26 May 1630, the prices of both the Woodmongers and, surprisingly, the venerable Butchers, were questioned by their Lordships in Star Chamber: 'informacion should be taken of the actors in these abuses … His Majestie should be moved to fines … and Mr Attorney should question the Charters of the Butchers and Woodmongers by a *quo warranto* or a *scire faciem*' (Edward I's legal devices for questioning assumed powers). By 1639, the Woodmongers had to 'certify names of offenders against the new coal trade regulations: J. How, N. Guy and "Galloping Jack" to appear'. Moreover 'the Lord Mayor [was] to examine into charges against the Woodmongers'.[50]

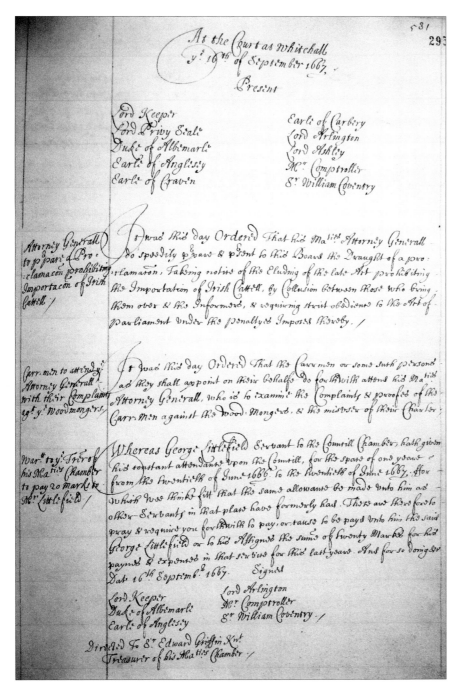

26   THE PRIVY COUNCIL ACTS AGAINST THE LIVERY

Minutes of the Privy Council for 1667, recording the reluctant movement of the Attorney General towards the final decision to require the Woodmongers to surrender their Charter (see Endnote 15, p.185).

Clearly, well before the final eruption of public disapproval emerged in the events of 1666/7, for the Woodmongers the writing was on the walls of both Cities. It would take a further two decades for the full effects to be seen, inevitably interrupted by an all-enveloping Civil War.

The market began to take on the semblance of a free-for-all: the epithets 'adventurers' and 'speculators' have been used to describe it. Wharfingers competed with carmen to carry wine and beer; woodmongers tried to hang on to their hold over all fuel. The Carmen's History sets out in detail the background to these trade wars, introducing a new element – competition between a newly burgeoning trade already referred to, growing from and closely allied to the Woodmongers, and that Company itself:

> In 1640, the Society of Coal Merchants told the King [that] the Woodmongers were interrupting tax-paid supplies; the Woodmongers replied [that] the coal was defective. The shippers were frustrated, and Scots skippers threatened to export coal direct to Holland ... In 1642 Parliament decreed that no 'Wharfinger, Woodmonger or other seller of Newcastle coals' should charge more than 23s the chaldron ... the reasonable price was 22s, and another twelve pence to encourage winter supplies.

On 26 April 1641, the House of Commons gave a second reading to a Bill which would have ensured 'the better government of the Corporacon of Woodmongers of London' and 'the relief of the Carmen of London' against the decrees of the Star Chamber. The Bill would have annulled the decree and restored the asset value of carrooms; the claim was that the decree was made without reference to the Carrmen, some of whom had lost their carrooms to Woodmongers 'to the greate wrong of the said Carre men'. Carmen also sought to end the Woodmongers' self-perpetuating oligarchy: 'no one should serve as Master or Warden for more than a year and a month, and Carmen should be eligible.'

Real political life now intervened: the outbreak of the civil war in 1642 stifled the Bill, but it did nothing to stifle the mutual public lobbying of Carmen and Woodmongers, who continued to accuse each other of all manner of wrongs.

By 1649, Christ's Hospital wanted redress for the failures of the two fratricidal trades under their charge to pay their dues. The Carmen, in a famous 'Remonstrance or a Reply to the false and scurrilous Papers of the Woodmongers', lobbied back, claiming 'embezzlement, fraud, false measures and price escalation', and asked Parliament to restore them to their separate Company status: all aborted. In 1653, 'the Woodmongers leant on the Carmen. Over forty acknowledged the Company's authority, and in 1654 an act of Common Council issued new rules against the disorders of the Carmen; it limited carrs to 420 – 140 for the wharves and 280 as street carrs, but there was an innovation: carrooms would be allocated by a joint committee of the Company and of Common Council.'

The Woodmongers had tried to palliate the Carmen, who then sought a better deal out of Cromwell – to no avail. Now, however, the Woodmongers were in trouble again: they had licensed 80 more carts than allowed: the Company's right to license carts was given to the Corporation of the Poor, whilst the Hospital still received its annual fee. The hard times of the first days of the Restoration in 1660 induced both parties to a truce: Carmen and Woodmongers joined forces and 45 carmen subscribed to Articles of Agreement: these included limiting carroom hire to Woodmongers' servants.[51]

iv: Restoration, Mystification, Deprivation

At this point in the 17th century, aside from political and international crises, the 'middling' way of life, which necessarily included domestic heating, was noticeably improving. However, economically, as the events of both the Protectorate under the Cromwells, and the 'Glorious Revolution' of 1688 would later underline, England and London were still unstable. Externally, the Dutch fleets in their 'capers' undermined eastern England's and London's water-borne life-line, the sea coal trade from Newcastle. Money for financing that ongoing international struggle posed a chronic stand-off between Westminster and the City of London. Revenue was always short; successive rulers had to resort to all conceivable sources for income, exacerbating endemic tension between Court and City.

There had emerged a strong element of Puritanism. Morality was infusing politics. In consequence, the Privy Council's 'publique advantage' was seen to be threatened by monopolistic practices: customs and traditions born of an earlier medieval world of protectionism had been called into question. Looking back to the 16th century, influential trades like the Woodmongers could be said, in Harold Macmillan's phrase, to have 'never had it so good'.

On 8 May 1660, Charles II was proclaimed King by the man to be the first and only Woodmonger Lord Mayor, Sir Richard Browne. It might have been surmised that life would now get sweeter for the Woodmongers, but by 1664 they had alienated public opinion too far with their practices – against the spirit of the new era:

> A committee appointed by the Aldermen found that the Woodmongers had been buying up wharves and wharfingers, stopping them handling coal, spreading rumours, using false measures and victimising protesters … They were accused of preventing ships from unloading at 'Smart's Key', forcing them to disgorge at their own wharves, fixing prices, cheating on weights, squeezing out other dealers and generally putting citizens 'under an intolerable grievance'. They absented themselves in summer to artificially delay shippers, reduce prices, and increase demand.

27 SMOKE VERSUS THE PLAGUE

It was believed that smoke, from coal or from tobacco, could kill the microbes of the Plague. Here a gravedigger is smoking a clay pipe to ward off the noxious vapours of the corpses being trundled into a cart. Coals supplied by the Woodmongers were burned at street corners for the same purpose.

If City Meters attempted to check measures, they 'fall upon them with evil and reviling language' … The basic scam was described: 'They labour to suppress all others' embargoeing stored fuel or buying it in at their own prices until they had 'engrossed the whole Store in their own hands'.

The list of wrongs was elaborated, but time was at last running out, not helped by various Woodmongers' actions at the expense of the City's widows and poor. The Aldermen finally proposed to amend the 1661 Act, to allow all carrs to carry fuel.

In June 1666, the Carmen had asked the King for separate incorporation; because the City for its own good reasons opposed the petition, it failed. There were further Woodmonger scandals; a Commons Committee adjudged that they had exploited the Dutch wars, to make profits of 200 per cent: their Clerk was arrested for refusing to produce the Company's books.

There is then cause for some surprise, and mystification: after much tit-for-tat and sailing close to the wind, totalling over 100 actions, it was resolved that the Company was illegal. Such a major step could not be effected over pricing, but it could be grounded in their monopoly over cars. Mysteriously, neither the State Papers nor the Journal of the City's Court of Common Council for 1667/8 show a record of any such final surrender. It is left to accept the Carmen historian's echo of Dale's comment: 'the Charter was surrendered on December 5, 1667, 'before Sir Walter Littleton, Master in Chancery, the record being drawn up in very dodgy Latin … to the *Magister, Gardiani et Societas Lignariorum … et Carricarii de Civitate de Londonii …*'. The Woodmongers did not just 'surrender' their lease on the car-rooms – it was forced out of their hands, and the government of cars was returned to Christ's Hospital.[52]

Those Stuart traders were made of stern stuff; in December 1668, the Carmen were complaining once more that they were 'soare oppressed by the Woodmongeres …', claiming that over 240 carrs were operating unlicensed.

Woodmonger William Fellowes told the Hospital that he had not claimed his carrooms because 'several members did perswade him not to come in'. The Woodmongers remained in being, their status damaged and their wings burned, but unknowingly they had begun to redeem themselves in the eyes of history, under the impact of two far greater burnings – that of coals for hygiene during the Plague of 1665, and the Great Fire itself of 1666.

With those disasters over, the Carmen would return to their particular hour of glory: the achievement through Christ's Hospital, on 28 April 1668, of their own 'Brotherhood or Fellowship as antiently they were'. For the Woodmongers, they had clearly become a powerful Company by this time, who thought that they 'knew the ropes'. In the broad context of the Fuellers' role in the history of London, the 17th century bears witness both to this lowest point in their journey, as well as to two of their own finest hours. The role of the Woodmonger-Fuellers' main product, coal, set against the sheer extent of the Plague, as well as against the scale of the fire and of the taxes that were needed to rebuild after it, give those 'finest hours' their rightful place in this narrative.

Woodmongers' Coals and the Plague

It was to be expected that the City was prone to disease. The Great Plague was the third in a sequence of such visitations. In a masterly piece of scientifically informed reconstruction, Defoe would later write of

> the trade of coals from Newcastle-upon-Tyne, without which the city would have been greatly distressed; for not in the streets only, but in private houses … great quantities of coal were then burnt, even all summer long which was done by the advice of physicians … Others said they granted that heat in the climate might propagate infection – as sultry hot weather fills the air with vermin and nourishes innumerable numbers and kinds of venemous creatures which breed in our food, in the plants and even in our bodies but that the heat of fire, and especially of coal fires kept in our houses, or near us, had a quite different operation; the heat being not of the same kind, but quick and fierce, tending not to nourish but consume and dissipate all those noxious fumes which the other kind of heat rather exhaled and stagnated than separated and burnt up. Besides it was alleged that the sulphurous and nitrous particles that are often to be found in coal, with that bituminous substance which burns, are all assisting to clear and purge the air.

Defoe then went on to comment on the effects of this emergency activity on the collier trade from the North-East, as well as on the woodmongers themselves, whom he saw, significantly, as identical and on a par with wharf-keepers and 'coal-sellers':

It was with no little difficulty that this trade was kept open, as we were in an open war ... the Dutch capers at first took a great many of our collier-ships, which made the rest cautious ... For the security of these northern traders, the coal-ships were ordered by my Lord Mayor not to come up into the Pool above a certain number at a time, and orderd [*sic*] lighters and other vessels such as the woodmongers (that is, the wharf-keepers or coal sellers [used here as a generic description, not as a title]) furnished, to go down and take out the coals as low as Deptford. Others delivered great quantities of coals in particular places where the ships could come to the shore ... as if to be kept for sale ... Yet all this caution could not effectually prevent the distemper geting [*sic*] among the colliery [the ships] ... especially at Newcastle and at Sunderland ...

The making so many fires, as above, did consume an unusual quantity of coals and ... the price of coals was exceeding dear, even as high as £4 a chalder [25 hundredweight] ... The public fires on these occasions ... must necessarily have cost the city about 20 chalders of coals a week ...

Defoe listed some 15 sites in the City where these putatively health-conducive fires were set up. Here at least, woodmongers had been busily engaged, clearly to the public benefit.[53]

28   THE GREAT FIRE, 1666
The Great Fire was the cause of the greatest blow ever to befall the Woodmongers, over a 12-month period that might well be called their annus horribilis*: 'a most horrid malicious bloody flame, not like the fine flame of an ordinary fire'.*

Annus Horribilis: 'The Malicious Bloody Flame'

The Great Fire of 1666 followed the Plague Year. One of the Fuellers' products – timber – was the unwitting cause for the greatest blow ever to befall the Woodmongers, over a 12-month period that might well be called their *annus horribilis*. The resolution of the damage to London's buildings could only be funded through the increases ordained by the Aldermen and Parliament in the coal dues already being levied through the Woodmongers and collected by the Meters. It will be the more important to investigate the value of those coal dues, given the misleading impression created in a recent account of the Liveries. The scene is set by Samuel Pepys, the sixth great English writer to become an unconscious contributor to 'The Fueller's Tale', His biographer, Claire Tomalin, rounds out the picture.

> As September 2nd dawned, Pepys was at first unconcerned by the news and the distant sight of the fire; he could see it to the west from his bedroom window at the Navy Office in Seething Lane, to the north-east of the Tower: 'Jane [his servant] called me up about 3 in the morning, to tell me of a great fire they saw in the City … I thought it far enough off'.

Pepys' initial judgment was mirrored on high. As the most recent writers about the Fire have put it: 'Fires were common enough in London, so perhaps it is unfair to record the first reaction of the Lord Mayor, Sir Thomas Bludworth: 'Pish, a woman might piss it out'.

A little later, like the Lord Mayor himself, Pepys became better informed and promptly did his duty as a public official:

> Jane tells me that she hears that some 300 houses have been burned down tonight … and that it is now burning down all Fish-street, by London Bridge … With my heart full of trouble, to the Lieutenant of the Tower, who tells me that it began this morning in the King's baker's (his name was Faryner) house in Pudding Lane, and that it hath burned St Magnus' Church … a lamentable fire, the wind mighty high and driving it into the City.

Later, Pepys describes the evacuation scenes, no doubt extending the workload of the City's Carmen, still formally Woodmonger-employed for fuel transport. His comments also confirm the predominance of coal in a domestic context by this time:

> River full of lighters and boats with goods … we to a little alehouse on the Bank-side … and there staid till was dark almost. I saw the fire grow … in a most horrid malicious bloody flame, not like the fine flame of an ordinary fire …[54]

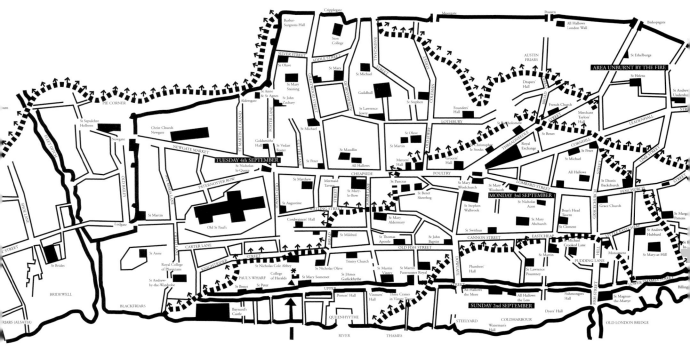

29 Burning of the Woodmongers' Hall

The Fire spread in three phases over five days – Sunday 2 September; Monday 3 September: (including [2nd] Woodmongers' Hall (*), above Poor Widdowes Alley, facing west to Paul's Wharf Hill, south of College of 'Heralds', now 'Arms'); extinguished between 4 and 6 September.

The Pepys biography fills out the domestic aspects (although 'household' should denote a reasonably middle-class dwelling – the poorer houses were still burning wood):

> Clothes, fine or plain, were hard to keep clean … Every household burnt coal brought from Newcastle by sea in its fireplaces and cooking ranges. So did the brewers and dyers, the brick-makers up the Tottenham Court Road; the ubiquitous soap and salt boilers smoke from their chimneys made the air dark, covering every surface with sooty grime.

In a description repeated once in 21st-century memory – the Buncefield Oil Depot fire of 2005 – Pepys' biographer observed that 'there were days when a cloud of smoke half a mile high and twenty miles wide could be seen over the City from the Epsom Downs. Londoners spat black'.

On 5 September, Pepys was again woken up in the small hours of the morning, this time by his wife Elizabeth, telling him that the fire was at the bottom of Seething Lane. With such treasures and valuables as they could muster they set off by boat, and no doubt by waterman, for a safe house in Woolwich. His return to the burning City is well described: 'He walked into the city, risking scorched feet from the hot coals underfoot everywhere, finding the main streets ... all destroyed'. Of the site of the Woodmongers' Hall, another observer noted: 'A great bunch of flame rose out of Baynard's Castle at the western extremity by the river, and burning in front of it were two churches, St Bennet's Paul's Wharf and St Peter's Paul's Wharf by Thames St ... Woodmongers' Hall was alight'.[55]

By 8 September, 80 per cent of the old City was razed to the ground. A report written at the height of the London Blitz in 1940 describes the damage:

> Debris which blotted out streets and sites alike masked the full loss. Later, statisticians were to compute the destruction at 13,200 houses, the Royal Exchange, the Custom House and the halls of 44 of the city Companies, the Guildhall and nearly all the City buildings, St Paul's itself and 87 of the parish churches, besides ... commodities valued at over three and a half million pounds ... In all they reckoned the bill at more than ten millions of currency of the time ... It was the greatest crisis in its history.[56]

'But by now the fire was miraculously under control ... minds were already turning to the tasks ahead, and thereby before very long to the future role of the dues to be levied through the Woodmongers' trade in coals: 'People speaking their thoughts variously about the beginnings of the fire, and the rebuilding of the City'.[57]

The overcrowding of the City at that time was plain to see – an urban timber-rich disaster waiting to happen; it was also easy to get a picture of the scope of the devastation wrought. For Pepys the effects were summed up in the words of a sermon he heard preached next day by Dean Harding: 'The City is reduced from a large folio to a decimo-tertio'.[58]

v: The Coal Dues: Rebuilding the City

The story of the coal dues has relevance for this History for three reasons. The choice for those taxes of an everyday object underlined the fact that coal was the most important item of merchandise upon the River Thames. Already in 1606, James I had granted the City of London the right to tax all the coals and other goods entering by the river; seven years later, all such coals would have to be landed on the legal quays. Government did not even try to raise tax through the importation of wood, that erstwhile mainstay of the Woodmonger's livelihood: 'The great advantage of coal from the City's point of view was that it was an essential to the life of the inhabitants.'[59]

Again, whatever charges of malfeasance could be levelled at the Livery, the trade manifestly complied with the Customs system operating from the London

30 WREN'S PLAN
– THE WOODWHARF

Sir Christopher Wren was asked to re-design a new post-Fire London, but much of his planning, including a new Wood Market on the east bank of the Fleet, above Bridewell Dock and below Ludgate, was not realised; likewise a grand octagonal 'Piazza' across the Strand area, and the triangular vista in front of the new St Paul's Cathedral.

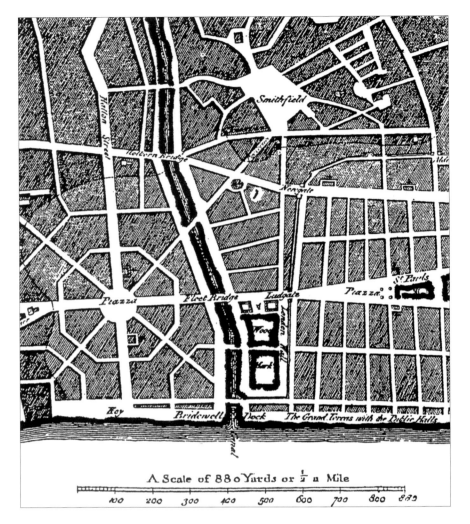

Customs Office; Woodmongers duly registered their incoming chaldrons of coal through the Wharfingers at the civic wharf at Billingsgate. The system is set out in the story of Robert Hooke's part in the rebuild:

> So that the Lord Mayor could perform and accomplish the work ordered by the act (the order of the Common Council], all coal brought into London sold by the chaldron or tun would be taxed at a rate of 12 pence (one shilling) for every tun, and the revenue paid to the Mayor. The money raised was to be used in the first place 'for the satisfaction of such persons whose grounds [are] to be taken for the enlarging of the streets and for the making of wharves and quays on the North side of the Thames …'.[60]

The effect of the coal dues can be seen in a true perspective, through Reddaway's pioneering research:

Three quarters of the extra duty was earmarked for the rebuilding or repairing of the great churches, with a proviso that a quarter of that sum must be spent on St Paul's, and the remaining quarter was assigned to the City … They only paid for the fabric of the churches. The altar, font, pews, lectern etc had to be provided by the parish … With seventeen years instead of seven, a duty increased by half, and the right to raise loans on its security, the City could afford to meet the clamour of applicants … By far the most expensive of the miscellaneous items were the convoys provided for the coal fleets during the Dutch wars – *The Loyal Catherine* and the *Experiment* … The coal dues not only saved the position of the City by paying for its new public buildings, but also made it possible for future citizens to live in a better and cleaner London … First and foremost came payments for widening streets and segregating markets. The Stocks market was purchased from the Bridge, its owner, while Leadenhall Market was enlarged. Next came the magnificent venture of the Fleet Canal … combined with it was the scheme for new laystalls … Expenditure on the general rebuilding programme [included] most aspects of the life and appearance of the rebuilt area … the coal dues paid for new landing places or 'stairs' along the riverside … to cleanse and repair old sewers … The list of items runs on and on like a roll call of the City's reviving activity.

Reddaway provided an estimate of the amounts paid out of the dues. 'Above all it can be said that thanks to the coal dues, the ultimate cost was not left as an intolerable mortgage on the future.'[62]

Token Characters

As a conclusion to this chapter it is timely to return from these major themes to the human level once more, for the period leading up to the surrender of the Woodmongers' charter in 1661 is replete with character as well as incident. One group of such characters, then considered to be at one end of the social scale, is still recognised as an aspect of a proud element within Britain's army – the Grenadier Guards. In between, two more Fuellers in the middle of society bear mention – Robert Bendish and Andrew Pope, who in 1666 sought licences 'to fetch coals from Newcastle in their ships'.

31   COAL AND WOOD: TRADE TOKENS
Two trade tokens from the period 1666-7 show: (i) the inscription 'Sea Coall Seller 1666'; (ii) the contemporary form of the Woodmongers' Livery Arms.

32   SIR RICHARD BROWNE, WOODMONGER LORD MAYOR, CITY OF LONDON

(Left) Royalist Sir Richard Browne was the Woodmongers' only Lord Mayor of London, instated after the Restoration of King Charles II; he was spared holding office during the period when the Great Fire burnt their Hall and their books, and the surrender of their 1605 Charter.

... SIR EDMUND BERRY GODFREY, FIRST CITIZEN, CITY OF WESTMINSTER

(Right) Sir Edmund's role was equivalent to today's Lord Mayor of Westminster. He was recently made famous once more through his tragic murder, portrayed at the heart of the best-selling The Plot Against Pepys.

At the opposite pinnacle of citizenry are two worthies who must rank among the best-known historical 'Fuellers', both enshrined in contemporary 21st-century images, and perhaps serving as token representatives of their age – Sir Robert Browne and Sir Edmundbury [Berry] Godfrey.

Prior to treating the stories of the first and last of these groups, 20 other Fuellers deserve inclusion, also placed in the centre of society. They emerge through the various Trade Tokens that had to come into use nationally in 1648-79, in a metal considered too base for the sovereign to sponsor – 'an 'illegal money of necessity'" – the Government having failed to issue sufficient farthings and halfpence. Their use as customers' small change signalled the credit-worthiness of the individual coining them, a further mark of the London Woodmongers' standing. The letter 'W' indicates the naming of a Woodmonger on the token:

> Robert Chapman at Bridewell Dock (his halfpenny; devices: The Woodmongers Arms, also Sword with a crown on the point from the Woodmongers Arms); Gilis Ray, 'W', at Bridewell Dock; Robert Austin, 'W', at Broken Wharf (on the obverse a bundle of wood between two stars. On the reverse a lion [or dog?] emerging from a wood: the Woodmongers' crest); Dan Burry, 'W', Cozen Lane, at Dowgat[e]. (A gate); Peter Tull, 'W', in Cozen Lane. (A plough); John Hudson at ye Brvrs [Brewers] [aka Brutts] Yard, King Street, Westminster. (The Woodmongers' Arms); Ralph Fancott, 'W', on Millbank. (Robin Hood and Little John); Richard Fisher, 'W', at ye Mill Bank. (A crooked billet); John Clarke, 'W', in Thames Street. (The Woodmongers' Arms); John Olay, 'W', in White Fryars, (1667, his halfepenny, A horse and cart); Govin Gouldegay, 'W', in White Friars, William Longe, 'W', Westminster, 1650, and Southwarke: (arms).

Museum of London tokens depict crooked billets, coalmen with sacks, coal carts, and various Woodmongers' Arms. There were also tokens purely for 'Seacoal Sellers' and 'Coalmen' (C):

> Nathaniel Robins, at the Haymarket, in Pickadilla, (his halfepenny, 1666); 'C', in Green Rentes, Bride Lane, (Three leopards' faces); John Burgesse, 'C', in Milford Lane, (1666, his halfpenny). A man carrying a sack of coals; Robert Farmer, 'C', in Milford Lane, Strand, (1668, his halfepenny. a horseshoe); At the Coale Yard in Nightinga[le] Lane. (A shield charged with three battle axes); Thomas Williams, 'C', (over against Strand Bridge, his halfpenny, A goat); Humphrey Vaughan, in White Hart Yard, 1666, his halfpeny. (A man carrying a sack on his shoulder: token); Mr Thos. Addisons, 'C', (men and horses unloading ships); At the Cole Yard in Barkin, (Arms, three battle axes).[63]

At the top rank of London's hierarchy must figure the eminent citizen already referred to, the only Woodmonger Lord Mayor of the City, and its first in London's 'Lord Mayor' tradition:

> The Woodmongers as a wealthy City Company with great constitutional powers were in a very strong position, and probably took every opportunity of turning their City connections to their own advantage. There is no doubt that one of them did. The Lord Mayor at the time of the Restoration, Sir Richard Browne, was a Woodmonger. At one time he was a strong Parliamentarian, and Major-General for Oxfordshire, Berkshire and

Buckinghamshire; but during his shrieval year he turned Royalist, and was removed from office, and imprisoned for five years. The City chose him as one of the deputation to Charles II at the Restoration; and as a Royalist at the time when the City needed to gain the King's favour he carried great weight with the Common Council and with the Aldermen. He was quick to use his influence; in October 1660 he was elected Lord Mayor, and on 23 July 1661 he obtained an [A]ct granting the Woodmongers a lease for (61) years for the disposal of car-rooms, the Company giving bond for £1,000 to pay £150 annually to Christ's Hospital.[64]

Then, as the narrative has examined earlier, the Woodmongers overreached themselves, with the well-known consequences.

A second prominent Woodmonger – first citizen of the City of Westminster, equivalent today to its Lord Mayor – was even more bound up in the commercial and political struggles of a time when the Civil and Dutch Wars had had the inflationary effect of pushing up prices. His story also illuminates trading practices, and re-affirms the evidence of a Company Hall:

> The coal-owner blamed the merchant, the merchant blamed the coal-owner, the consumer blamed them both. No doubt the Woodmongers in 1664 – or in any other year – looked after themselves; but during the years 1665-7 they had their own special difficulties. The case of Sir Edmund [Berrie] Godfrey is in point ... Upon leaving Oxford he set up in partnership with one Harrison at a wharf in Dowgate, where he succeeded so well that he was able to take a [wood]wharf of his own near Charing Cross. During the Plague Year Godfrey went about his duties as Justice of the Peace [for Westminster] with conspicuous energy and gallantry, and for his efforts was presented by the King with ... a knighthood in 1666'.[65]

A recent investigation, *The Plot against Pepys*, re-focused attention on this story; its political ramifications, and the Pepysian aspects lie beyond this History, although its undertones of terrorism echo today. Dale referred to Pepys' Diary, for January 1666-7, when Godfrey gave evidence before a Committee of the Commons: 'That he and others sold Coals to poor people at the price of Two shillings the Bushel, at his Wharf, which amounts to Twelve Shillings per Chaldron ... Which they repute a very great Extortion and oppression and worthy of the consideration of this House':

> Godfrey was in a difficult position. He was Master of the Woodmongers' Company; and while he himself had not suffered in the Fire, most of the Company had. He could either put up his price and be accused of extortion, or keep it down and ruin the market for his associates. Moreover the Company's Hall had been completely destroyed in the Fire; stocks of coal in wharves and in Companies' Halls and private houses had been burnt up ... the ingrain at which the House pointed so accusingly was an immemorial

custom of the trade; as far back as 1366 it was an established practice and in accordance with the custom of London.

Popular opinion denied such defences for this eminent citizen: 'the words coal-dealer and cheat were practically synonymous. Both as wholesaler and retailer the Woodmonger, like the coalseller after him, and in fact dealers in other commodities, was held up to public censure and reproof both in medieval times and later days for forestalling, regrating and engrossing.'

Godfrey is remembered, through a portrait, for taking an active part in the affairs of St Martin-in-the-Fields from his then home in Green's Lane, off the Strand. He had been:

> a wealthy London merchant selling coal and timber, and a Justice of the Peace, which combined the roles of magistrate, policeman and prosecutor ... On 5 September, Titus Oates ... had gone before Godfrey to swear his account of the Catholic Plot to kill the King ... On the morning of Saturday 12 October [1678], Godfrey left his house in Hartshorn Lane, by the Thames. He was seen walking in the fields to the north of Oxford Street and then failed to turn up for a lunch appointment ... At two o'clock on the following Thursday afternoon, two men ... walking along the edge of a field on Primrose Hill noticed gloves, a belt, and a cane on the ground ... When the rain stopped [they] went back to the spot. Nearby, lying face down in a ditch, was Godfrey's body ... His own sword had been driven right through him and the tip was sticking out of his back ... Godfrey's murder was instantly sensational and chilling. His name was on everyone's lips ... in a spreading wave of apprehension that this was the first of the onslaught of Catholic terrorist murders.

Dale recorded that 'medals were struck showing the murder ... The obverse of the medal shows the bust of Godfrey, surrounded by the legend [*trans*] "By dying E. Godfrey has put matters right again", and on the reverse [*trans*]: "A Church (it should be the Pope) turned upside down shows the face of the Devil".' Charles II had presented Godfrey with 'white plate' from which Godfrey had a silver tankard made. One of at least six copies is still displayed in Sudbury Heritage (*see* Fig. 18). Dale wrote: 'it is of the ordinary drum pattern with lip, handle and hinged lid. In front are the Royal arms of Charles II within the garter and crown, and below between palm branches are the arms of Sir Edmund ... It weighs 38½ ounces and bears the London hall mark for 1675/6 ... it of course cannot be the original.'[66]

The last colourful characters that fill out the picture of the Fueller over the centuries through to the 18th are surprising – the Grenadier Guards. Supported by contemporary evidence from the Guards' Archivist (and anticipating the reference to those trade forerunners, the Coal-Heavers, in Chapter III), the words 'Tow-rowrow' of the famous marching song are now clarified:

One of the privileges granted to the Grenadier Guards at the Restoration was the right to act as coal-heavers in their spare time, coal heaving being an arduous occupation requiring lusty men, a four-hour day being sufficient for most men ... The explanation is as follows:- A gang of coal heavers consisted of 16 men ... Each gang had their meeting-place at a particular ale-house, and the publican, to ensure the master of a ship asking for his particular gang, would promise him a gallon of rum if he did so. If the gang worked well, and cleared the ship rapidly, the master would pass the rum on to the gang. This was called the 'tow-row' for the British Grenadiers. The nickname of 'The Coal Heavers' still sticks ... a [treatise of] 1813 states that the coal heavers of the port of London may be estimated at about 1,000; but out of that number 300 were soldiers in the Guards, who had their pay still going on and some of them had pensions.[67]

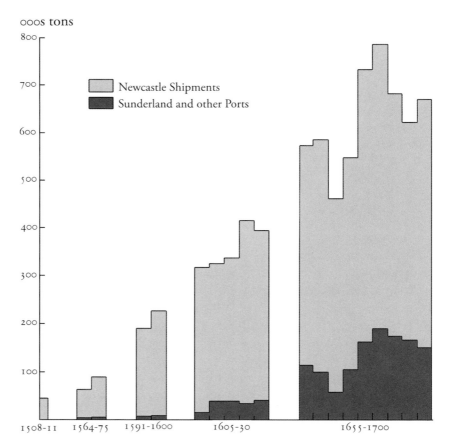

ooos tons

33   Growth in Coal Shipments from North-East England

This huge increase was principally for distribution by the increasingly wealthy Woodmongers' trade in London, from the 16th to the 18th centuries. Newcastle coal predominates (light shading) compared with coal from Sunderland and other sources (dark shading).

The Plague and the Great Fire were the two major events of national importance for the 17th century in which 'Fuellers' (in the widest sense of that title for the London wood and coal trade, embracing all aspects of distribution) played their different parts: Woodmongers, timber-merchants, Coal Merchants, Coal Meters, Wharfingers or Carmen. Lest any assumptions about their unfrocked hard core, the Woodmongers, or their trading colleagues, the Wharfingers, should imply a corresponding reduction in wealth, a sample of the poll tax returns at the end of that century suggest otherwise. Among the 26 merchants and tradesmen representing 201 occupations, even though only two Woodmongers and three Wharfingers were sampled, they were all paying at the full surtax level, alongside haberdashers, skinners, vintners and 88 general merchants. Yet of seemingly well-heeled trades such as the brewers and goldsmiths, only a majority paid surtax; others such as joiners, less than half, with the remaining 154 trades only taxed at 1s. There was still good money in fuel for London, whichever Livery underlay it. One charming instance of this continuing activity was the development of the Woodmongers' Barge-House, on the Thames frontage by Waterloo Road, known as Prince's Meadows. Use of this land as a wood and timber wharf continued under the Protectorate and into the Restoration; in the 18th century it was called 'Collyar's Yard'.[68]

Of other trades, Chapter III will trace the evolution of practices and disputes which both reached back into earlier centuries and forward into the new environments of the 18th and 19th. These next two centuries would show that, although the Fuellers' medieval Company, The Woodmongers, itself appeared to be on the wane, yet bursting forth from within it, Phoenix-like, their new wonder fuel – coal – was about to astonish the world.

34   NORTH-EASTERN COASTAL TRADE TO LONDON

*Two stages in the vital coal trade from the North-East to London: here a collier brig is first
being loaded at the Sunderland staithes. Colliers then had to brave the ocean: Joseph Heard's
painting shows a brig shortening sail in the North Sea. The perils were firstly man-made – the
threat of attack by the Dutch 'capers' during the war with Holland, but also inherent in the
route itself, if captains sailed too close to shore (as had once befallen Pepys on a celebrated
voyage off the Norfolk coast in his capacity as Secretary to the Navy).*

THE EIGHTEENTH TO NINETEENTH CENTURIES

The Fueller as Merchant Adventurer and Hostman; Fitter,
Factor, Crimp, Broker and Undertaker; Wharfinger,
Shipmaster, Coal Craft Owner and Lighterman; The
Emerging Coal Merchant – And the Last Woodmonger

from submergence … to supremacy

Fuel: The Socio-Economic Context – Coal and the Industrial Revolution – Wood v. Coal:
Tilting the Domestic Balance – Fueller Evolutions: Merchant Adventurers and Hostmen
– Fuellers All: Factors, Fitters, Crimps, Wharfingers – Trades at the Fueller Boundary – The
Final Turf War: Woodmongers v. Lightermen – Abuses, Grievances and Remedies – New
Concepts: Docks and Canals – Fueller Evolutions: Masters and Owners of Coal Craft
– Exeunt Woodmongers: 'King Coal' Supreme – Icon and Anathema

Two Liveries – the Carmen, and the Watermen – could be seen as a vestigial
'Fueller' continuity across this period. However, the natural driving impetus for
the future Livery were the non-liveried Society of Coal Merchants, the Society
of Coal Factors and the Coal Meters Committee; the 20th-century corporate
presence behind that force would be the National Coal Board.

A minor but far-sighted decision of the NCB's Chairman, Sir Derek Ezra,
was to sponsor a definitive history of the British Coal Industry; its contents have
already illuminated the opening chapters of the Fuellers' own History.

i: Fuel: The Socio-Economic Context

Much of that epic history's pages cover aspects of its once-great industry's story
beyond the orbit of the Fuellers' Ordinance as a Livery Company. It does, however,
offer insights into three areas of economic interest which are central to a Fuellers'
account. It sets coal, perhaps for the first time, in its correct relationship to the
Industrial Revolution with which it is associated; it also places the London fuel
market in its true national perspective. Third, it illustrates why the City's trade
achieved importance in Britain's economic history.

Coal production was of course already one of Britain's major industries; its era seems so near, yet also profoundly remote from today. It may be helpful to highlight some of the social factors that underlay London's changing fuel market.[1]

The increasingly populous London of Boswell's and Johnson's century has to be seen as a transition to the more familiar Dickensian nineteenth. Geographically, the Fuellers' city of the 18th century still echoes the dangerous, noisome and insalubrious stews, rookeries, courts, lanes and alleys of Stuart times as much as it anticipates the even more crowded hovels, nests and burrows of the capital of the Victorian era: 'from crazy piled-up tenements that had been villainous under Queen Anne to the squalid new warrens of the industrial age'.[2]

Under a stylish but thin upper crust – comfortably housed, servanted and fuelled – vast masses of the poor, above all indigent work-seeking Irish immigrants, eked out miserable existences, where even a chimney, let alone coal to burn in it, was luxury. Wealthier citizens, including no doubt the better-off wholesaling coal merchants, were beginning to move away from the City to more gracious suburbs, such as Hackney; thus trades like fuelling needed to reach out to an ever-wider catchment.[3] Wars occupied more than 50 per cent of the century, bringing with them not only periodic shortages, due to interruptions in the supply chain, but also the chronic insecurity and uncertainty of employment as a whole. The impression of good living, commented on by some foreign visitors, concealed a Hogarthian undertow of vice, disease, street violence, destitution. Thus while the need for fuel, and particularly coal, continued to grow in line with the needs of production, nationally even more than in the capital, London's population fell: the domestic market was far from homogeneous and regular – not a good recipe for continuous profitable trading.

Whilst the start of the 18th century was still an age of minute social distinctions – in trade and class – and the ancient liveries still had influence, by the turn of the 19th the restrictive era of the guilds was giving way to the expansive world of open commerce. London's trades evolved into three main categories: those dependant on the city's role as the country's main port; the highly skilled manufacturing trades, such as clocks; and those that catered for the growing taste for luxury. Fuel supply fitted roughly into the first of these groups: any ancient livery it might retain was not likely to keep the loyalty of an increasingly 'multi-fuel' merchant.

Coal and the Industrial Revolution

Coal output increased by 75 per cent during the first half of the 18th century, trebled during the second half, and doubled again in the first 30 years of the 19th century; over the whole period the expansion was ten-fold. It must surely have constituted a major element within the Industrial Revolution; yet it amounted to only some 2.2 per cent of the estimated gross national product.

Significance lies rather in coal's relationship within the industrial sector itself. By 1801, coal accounted for *c.*9.9 per cent of the total output of the mining, building and manufacturing sector taken together: 'For a single industry these are very substantial proportions and must place the coal industry in the ranks of the three or four principal industries in the country in the early nineteenth century'.[4]

Coal's importance lay in what it enabled to happen as well as in its sheer size. Driven by its own need to improve safety, drainage, ventilation, hauling, winding, lighting and transport, its technical advances kept coal at constant or even falling prices. Coal also had wider spin-off in the development of the steam-pump, canals, and most noticeably the railways. The *History of the British Coal Industry* illustrates the London coal trade's role within that wider picture of growth.

Output (*thousands of tons*)	1700	1750	1800	1830
Great Britain	2,985	5,230	15,045	30,375
North-East	1,210	2,070	4,005	6,915
North-East coastwise shipments	700	1,120	2,480	3,660
Imports (*thousands of tons*)				
London	445	677	1,234	2,079
London's imports as percentage of:				
Great Britain output	14.9	12.9	8.2	6.8
North-East output	36.8	32.7	30.8	30.1
North-East coastwise shipments	63.6	60.4	49.8	56.8

35 Shares of London Coal Market

Between 1700 and 1830, London's imports of coal rose from 445,000 tons to 2,079,000 tons. Whilst traditional coal shipments from the North-East actually rose from 700,000 to 3,660,000 tons, its imports declined proportionately to coastwise shipments from 63.6 per cent to 56.8 per cent, and London's share of the Great Britain output fell from 14.9 per cent to 6.8 per cent.

In fact, the London market only accounted for a minor share in the country's coal consumption. Although the largest single outlet, it was never preponderant in sales from the North-East. How, therefore, did that minor London trade gain its high national 'profile'? Here the Coal Industry *History* underlines a fact implicit in most of the earlier commentary in this Fuellers' history: the City of London had for centuries been at the centre of national power. For all its venality and vulnerability to 'creaking corruption', consonant with the political corruption on high under Walpole, the London market had become refined, imbued with vested interests, its political antennae at full quiver:

> the London market brought together perhaps the most articulate and influential set of customers in the country who invariably reacted vociferously to any sharp increases in coal prices, While the consumers of products of other industries might, in the general atmosphere of *laissez-faire* that prevailed during the eighteenth and early nineteenth centuries, have no alternative but to cut down their consumption in the face of raised prices, the consequence of a consumers' revolt in the London coal trade was an appeal to Parliament to restore fair and open trading …

A Report of the 1830s claimed that 'There are nearly 200 regulations and Acts of Parliament respecting the coal trade'. The outcome was a level of scrutiny and taxation making the coal trade a special case, meriting even by the mid-18th century the censure of Adam Smith in his *Wealth of Nations*:

> Coals carried either by land or by inland navigation pay no duty. Where they are naturally cheap they are consumed duty free: where they are naturally dear, they are loaded.[5]

In this next era, the industry basic to today's Fuellers' Company was steadily becoming crucial to the nation's economy, lending credence to the view that the Industrial Revolution was more a gradual, cumulative phenomenon, not a sudden eruption:

> At the beginning of the 18th century annual per capita consumption in Britain was probably slightly less than half a ton … by 1800 [it] had probably climbed to about 1.4 tons. By 1830 this had risen to just under 2 tons, not very far short of the level of the 1980s. The British economy that entered the Victorian era was indeed a coal-based one.[6]

Leading on to Britain's global dominance for a period of some 150 years, this was the era in which both the coal industry, and the nation which gave it birth, could still merit the epithet 'great'.

In its totality that one industry cannot be the sole theme for the Fuellers' story, yet economically, as successive histories of the British Coal Industry have made clear, it is certainly still the central, dominant theme of the London fuel trade for the period under review. A similar 'Fueller-based' distinction has to be drawn between this History and Raymond Smith's *Sea-Coal for London*: much of its invaluable detail, revealing its original objective as a history of just one link in the Fueller's long trading chain – the Factors and Fitters – has to be compressed for this present account. As that pioneering historian, steeped in the Guildhall Archives of which he was a leading member, so succinctly expressed it: 'It is the story of the transformation of the merchant in wood to the merchant in coal'.[7]

In this period, iron smelting was still dependant on the use of charcoal ('coal') as a fuel in the blast furnaces; the supply of charcoal depended on the supply of suitable timber, and suitable timber was becoming increasingly scarce. The charcoal most suitable for iron making was obtained from trees of about twenty years' growth. The thinnings of woodlands could be used in charcoal-burning, leaving the remaining trees to provide timber for constructional purposes for the future.

Difficulties arising from the high price of charcoal had been felt even as early as the 16th century. Many processes had begun to rely on either peat, or 'mineral coal' – pit coal, or 'sea-coal' from the Tyneside outcrops – instead of charcoal: coke, as evoked much later in the 'Coketown' of Charles Dickens' *Hard Times*, would now make its mark:[8]

> The main change making for progress in the primary iron industry during the earlier eighteenth century was the substitution of coke for charcoal in the smelting process ... The industrial developments of the eighteenth century called for a greatly increased output of coal, and therefore for a rapid expansion of the coal-mining industry. Even before the eighteenth century, coal was already taking the place of charcoal in a wide variety of industries, such as brewing, distilling, brick-making, pottery, sugar-refining, soap-boiling, cutlery, nail-making and the manufacture of glass.

These trends were mirrored on the domestic front and were exemplified in fundamental shifts within the trades that served the market in London, above all in the decline of the once-powerful legally corporate Woodmongers to an inevitably diminished status as individual, non-corporate 'woodmongers'. All the issues to be explored in this chapter are inevitably complicated by the fact that language and function are not fixed commodities: they evolve and change in response to need.

Wood v. Coal: Tilting the Domestic Balance

In domestic consumption, the over-reaction of the Elizabethans to an apparent scarcity in the supply of timber has already been noted as a factor in fuel supply.[9] Cheap, available coal had been used locally for heating on Tyneside from at least the early 14th century; as the price of wood for heating increased during the next two centuries, so poorer Tyneside people resorted to burning coal, to be emulated – interestingly – by wealthier households. Before the ancient Woodmongers' Company achieved its monopoly, individual merchants such as Richard Lovekyn, not a Woodmonger but a Stockfishmonger, had merited mention as the third Mayor of London (1358-9) and as a forerunner Fueller.

36   THE FLEET RIVER AND SEACOAL LANE, 1700
Right up to the 18th-century culverting of the Fleet River (Ditch) which descended from Hampstead Ponds, coal was carried in vessels of lower sail, enabling them to pass under London Bridge, up as far as the aptly- and still currently-named Seacoal Lane, to the north of Ludgate Hill; this brought merchandise into the heart of the City, for easier transportation along Fleet Street to the west or northwards up Farringdon Street (where basements still occasionally flood).

Operating out of Newcastle, it is recorded that he 'purposed by the grace of God to freight a ship called "la Weselere" of Dordright ... with seacoal and other merchandise ... to carry to the City of London'.[10]

During the 17th century, a myriad indications marked the final and irreversible shift from the domestic use of wood, in favour of coal. This trend acted as a seedbed for the eruption of the third and last 'turf war', between the Woodmongers and another former medieval guild – this time the Watermen and Lightermen – to be explored below.

The banning of timber for external and structural applications in favour of stone only began with the London Rebuilding Acts of 1667-70. However, woodmongers, and increasingly the specialised timbermongers, had an ongoing role, even if denuded of their one-time financial power as a City guild: timber was still required in quantity for reconstruction.

As to their now main fuel-product, the noxious effects of the use of carbon-rich sea-coal, causing adverse reactions in Elizabethan times, had become accepted, despite the stricture of the 17th-century diarist, John Evelyn.[11] Coal's salient role in commercial and industrial processes is already clear.

This next phase of the Fuellers' history nevertheless highlights a puzzle already alluded to. During the three centuries from 1700, the main fuel of the still extant noncorporate 18th-century woodmongers was achieving an even greater importance as the fuel that would drive Britain's Industrial Revolution. A recent story of coal industries round the world has underlined how vital that fuel would prove to be, through to the 21st century, globally if not yet again nationally.[12] Yet simultaneously the original purveyors of that fuel to its prime market, the City of London, were 'apparently' at their last gasp, as recorded by Dale:[13]

> Then occurred an event which sounded the death-knell of the Woodmongers' Company ... an Act was passed (29 September, 1700) which amalgamated the Watermen and Lightermen into a large Company. Woodmongers might keep lighters for their own use, provided their servants might be Watermen or Lightermen ... The Watermen's Company, however, promptly started to oppress the Woodmongers by refusing to register them as Lightermen.

In fact, as the story of the woodmongers' turf wars with the Lightermen will later reveal, despite this body-blow, they continued to operate under the title of their trade, albeit on an increasingly narrow front, until the mid-19th century. The key to the seeming paradox of their survival is reconciled in the word 'apparently'. As the embers of 'King Log' slowly cooled, a new king, 'King Coal' – through the medium of the 'Lords of Coal', the Hostmen – might be seen as ascending to the fuelling throne, thereby ushering in the woodmongers' successors, the sea-trading Society of Coal Merchants. The rise of that body, over the past five centuries, will be traced fully in Chapter IV.

ii: Fueller Evolutions: Merchant Adventurers and Hostmen

The breadth and depth of the Fuellers' history requires some chronological disciplining; inevitably, many themes and sub-themes in the story run across several centuries, constituting mini-histories on their own. It would be all too easy to allow a natural interest in one such major theme to become over-dominant – the British coal industry, which often appears to be synonymous with the lineage of the Fueller, as the concept can now be defined. Some of the sub-themes do, however, qualify for special treatment; the 'Hostmen' and the Guild of Merchant Adventurers from which they sprang, based on Tyneside (the 'Black Indies'), are one such theme.[14]

The definition will also later cover the 'Fitters' (evolving as the 18th-century Hostmen), the 'Factors', 'Crimps' and Brokers/'Undertakers', the Watermen and Lightermen, and the Shipmasters and the Owners of Coal Craft. These were the last in the long line of expositors of the Fueller's historic role which emerge from the records like the Russian Babouchka Dolls, each from within the other, all trades forming links in the chain bringing fuel to the capital, to a market that must now be seen as 'Greater London'.[15]

A line needs to be drawn beyond these trades. To the production end of the sequence, beyond the ambit of a 'Fueller', should be apportioned the Tyneside 'Keelmen' – the men who filled the 'keels' from the 'staithes'; as the Jackson *Diary* shows, these keels were rented by their skippers from the Hostmen.[16] Keelmen were renowned for their distinctive blue, white and yellow dress, their unique song, 'The Keel Row', and for their constant liability and aptitude for impressment into the Royal Navy; their role was included in Fig. 1.

It suited the Hostmen to purport that they had existed – in Brand's words – 'from time immemorial'.[17] They were certainly a feature of medieval trading throughout Britain and Northern Europe; (there were Hostmen in Yarmouth to deal with the Dutch herring trade). Their emergence in Newcastle from the 12th century had a direct bearing on the quality and pricing of solid fuel trading in London, since the rigid control over supply by their masters, the coalowners, together with the seasonality of the coastal shipping trade, meant that London was always at their mercy. Their background was set out in 1789 by John Brand, but has been updated recently in *Seacoal*:[18]

> The commanding position of the early boatmen may be gauged from the fact that William Jenison, the first Governor of the Hostmen's Company, was by that charter appointed mayor of the town, and the 42 hostmen named in the charter included also all the 10 aldermen, 5 of the councillors, and 4 of the other officers. Thirty-five of the original 42 Hostmen were also members of the … Company of Merchant Adventurers.

These Hostmen interfaced not merely in Newcastle, Stockton and Sunderland with Shipmasters and wholesaling merchants – Woodmongers as well as Coal Merchants: they also travelled to London for this purpose. Indeed, by the early 17th century, as evidenced in a protest from the mayor of Newcastle of 20 October 1634, many of them actually lived there. They also worked an 'unfree' coal trade in the City:[19]

> At the turn of the century, in 1703, Charles Atkinson and five other Hostmen were suspended for three months for assisting unfree gentlemen coalowners who confederated with the lightermen and buyers of coals in … London.

For these often overlooked reasons, the History does not limit their existence as merely the traditionally recognised Hostmen '*of Newcastle*'. Apart from the Hostmen's ownership of some 25 of the main collieries in the Tyne valley, there was London ownership, too, through the Knights of St John, Clerkenwell. This London linkage did not lessen two further interesting areas of conflict: first between the Tyneside providers and the coal shippers of East Anglia, for whom the Newcastle trade only ranked fourth in importance after Ipswich,

37   FIRST STAGE IN DISTRIBUTION: COAL WAGONS, COAL 'SHOOTS', NEWCASTLE, 1773

In Newcastle, keelmen formed a distinct community in the Sandgate area; they ferried coal in keelboats to collier ships on the river Tyne. By the late 18th century, coal staithes were able to load coal directly from rail wagons onto ships; here a boy is sitting on the back of the wagon, with his horse walking behind him down the slope.

King's Lynn and Yarmouth; nor did it, second, soften the pressures by the City against the monopolising 'combinations' of the Hostmen – some London pots were clearly calling other kettles black.

A complaint from the City of London of about 1595 indicates that the hostmen had already combined by that date to sell their coal at their own prices for their own advantage and to the public detriment, and in the words of the complaint 'diet and feed the Shipmasters and Merchants ...'.

> Other combinations of a similar nature but varying in detail were entered into in 1605, 1617, 1622, and 1627 ... In 1622 the Shipowners joined with the Woodmongers to declare that a great abuse existed at Newcastle 'in the mingling of good and badd coales together'. In 1623 the owners and masters of ships of London, Ipswich, Harwich and other coast towns complained to the Privy Council that the Hostmen of Newcastle combined to prevent free trade in coals.[20]

For semantic roots, Murray's *Dictionary* again supplies clues:

> The word 'host' is spelled in many ways ... including 'oat', 'oast', 'host' and 'hoast'. Of these 'oast' is the most frequent. and it would seem from its continued use up to the eighteenth century, that even when the 'h' was added ... that letter remained silent ... It is derived from the Latin 'hospes', through the old french 'oaste' and 'hoste', [and] the modern French 'hôte' ... and means a host, a guest, a stranger, a foreigner ... the Latin 'h', lost in Romanic, was generally readopted in old French and modern English spelling, as well as ... pronunciation.[21]

'Host' does not seem to have occurred before Norman times. Whilst Magna Carta's Clause 41 provided that all merchants should be safe and secure when trading in England, its Clause 13 reserved the ancient liberties and free customs of the City of London and all other cities and boroughs. For the origins, a recent publication of the Hostmen gives this summary:

> The initial role of the Hostman was to act as a host to visiting merchants and to be responsible for their social and commercial behaviour ... the Hostmen had formed themselves into a fraternity by the early 1500s. That fraternity was recognised and endorsed by the Royal Charter of 1600, in which Queen Elizabeth I granted them incorporated status and an exclusive right to trade in coal. By the mid-18th century the coal trade had experienced such growth that it was virtually the life blood of the town.[22]

Notwithstanding the claim of Liège to be Europe's first coalmining city, coal and grindstones had long been Newcastle's special products. They were not dealt with by any special guild, hence the opportunity for the Hostmen's monopoly. *Newcastle Hostmen* makes clear what is less well appreciated: that these Hostmen evolved from within a wider and older parent body, the Merchant Adventurers, incorporated in 1547, who in their turn should also properly be seen as early 'Fuellers':

> Every trade was privileged … The right of exporting coal would most naturally belong to the Merchants Company, and they undoubtedly dealt in coal in the early part of the sixteenth century. Indeed in 1516, they imposed a tax of eightpence per chaldron payable to their Company on all coal exported to Dieppe. Their books alone contain any reference to the hostmen before the incorporation of the latter. When that incorporation took place [as a legal entity] a large majority of the hostmen were Merchant Adventurers … [In the same books in their list of impositions for 1603 and 1618, no mention occurs of coals or grindstones, after the hostmen had been incorporated by royal charter].[23]

By now the Hostmen, whatever their business ethics, clearly justify in this History a capital initial 'H' for company status. An actual Company of Hostmen had first been referred to in the Books of the Merchant Adventurers guild in 1517.[24] Their trade included the form of sandstone mined on Gateshead Fell, specific to use as millstones for corn – 'grindstone'. Of the coal trade to London, another aspect of the hold which the Hostmen had built up over it is well described in *Seacoal*:

> There was also a custom, obtaining in towns throughout the kingdom, called 'foreign bought and sold' … any goods brought into the town by a 'foreigner', i.e. any Englishman or alien not a freeman of the town, could be bought only by a freeman; and any goods a foreigner bought had to be sold him by a freeman …[25]

These rights had been reiterated under successive monarchs – Edward III, Richard II and Henry IV. The concept of 'foreign bought and foreign sold' was seen, not as a narrow insular exception, but simply as asking for the same restrictions to be imposed on 'foreigners' as were imposed on Englishmen in other countries. They had been successfully asserted by the burgesses of Tyneside to force the coal-owning prior and bishop of Durham to stop selling products through Gateshead and Whickham.[26]

In Newcastle, the Hostmen's right to organise all parts of the growing trade in coal had declined under Henry VIII, but began to burgeon once more under Elizabeth I and later under the monopoly-hunger of the financially impoverished Stuarts. From a Newcastle perspective, an Elizabethan State Paper of 1575 elaborates the familiar commercial background:[27]

> the commodity of Newcastle and suchlike coals is of late years known to be of more value … for wood being grown to dearth and the severity of it felt more every day, causes many of the said coals to be used for fuel in London … by those who in times past used nothing but wood for fuel.

The complaints of the mayor and aldermen of the City of London underline how the freemen of Newcastle had started to exert the inflationary force of monopoly upon London's necessity. However, that same monopoly had attracted Charles I in 1638 to make an unpopular agreement with the Hostmen, giving the Crown the sole monopoly over the sale of coals – buying at a fixed price, but with discretion on the selling-on price. In 1644 the Commissioners of the Parliament attempted to institute a free and open trade in coal, but by 1645 the Hostmen's Company was back enjoying their old privileges. Throughout the Commonwealth the unfree among the coalowners had found a champion in Ralph Gardiner, not least through his pamphlet, *England's Grievance Discovered*.[28]

At the opening of the century, the *Impartial History* suggests that 400 ships were used in the Tyneside coal trade, half of which supplied London, the other feeding the rest of England. By 1649, Gray would record in *Chorographia* that 'There come sometimes into this river for coales three hundred sayles of ships. Many thousand people are imployed in this trade of coales: many live by working of them in the pits: many live by conveying them in waggons and waines to the river Tyne … one coal merchant imployeth five hundred or a thousand in his works of coals … This great trade hath made this towne to flourish in all trades.'[29] 'In the year 1655 … about [320] keels appear to have been employed each of which carries [800] chaldrons, Newcastle measure.'

A few years on, by 1662, the key statistics appeared to be 'twenty-eight acting "fitters", or hoastmen, who were to vend by the year 9,080 tons [*sic*] of coals, and find eighty-five keels for that purpose'.[30]

The Restoration of the monarchy two years earlier had allowed monopolies and vested interests to flourish once more. Three years further ahead, in 1675, this level of trade encouraged Charles II to try again for a lucrative monopoly where his father had failed, but nothing came of it.

38 COAL'S SEA-ROUTES TO LONDON, 1700

'Coalfields, principal towns, and navigable rivers, c.1700'.

During the evolution from the 18th to the 19th centuries, however, the power of the Hostmen to influence the London coal trade by right of 'immemorial custom' steadily receded. The so-called 'Richmond Shilling' – the duty of 12p per chaldron levied on coal from the Tyne by Charles II in favour of the then Duke of Richmond, Lennox and Aubigny – was bought out by the Lords Commissioners of the Treasury in 1799, and finally abolished by an Act of 1831. (The Richmond seat at Goodwood in Sussex endures as a permanent reminder of this distant event.)

Earlier, the parallel custom of 'foreign bought and sold' had disappeared from the books of both the Newcastle Adventurers and the Hostmen, in consequence of a failed law suit of 1726, although it still continued in other parts of the country. By 1835, the Municipal Reform Act would enable every person in every borough to deploy every lawful trade within the borough: the powers of the Newcastle Trading Companies were extinct, and London's Corporation no longer had to defend its interest. In the 21st century, the Hostmen, 'the premier Incorporated Company of Newcastle', retain a symbolic role: some 80 members meet each January in the Newcastle Guild Hall, and stage a banquet every Trafalgar Day. To commemorate their 'quarter-centenary 1600-2000', they published the booklet which has been quoted earlier – *Bound for the*

39 RALPH JACKSON, APPRENTICE HOSTMAN

Jackson's portrait was painted in 1763, when aged 27 years. His Diary provides a unique record of the initiating stage of the trade in coal, from the North-East collieries to the merchants in London. He was apprenticed to a Hostman, and progressed to some fortune, although he never formally became a member himself.

Tyne, Extracts from the Diary of Ralph Jackson, Apprentice Hostman of Newcastle upon Tyne 1749-1756. Although Jackson never in fact took up full membership of the Company, both he and his Hostman Master, William Jefferson, certainly count as early 'Fuellers'.[31]

iii: *Fuellers All: Factors, Fitters, Crimps, Wharfingers*

Meanwhile, three other Fueller antecedents in the coal trade, the intermediary 'Factors' and 'Fitters', and the 'Body of Wharfingers' had evolved (Fig. 52). Hostmen and 'fitters' were seen to be interchangeable by the beginning of the 18th century; their functions would also for a time merge into those of the 'Crimp' – to be examined below, p.83. Based on the records of 1716 onwards in the Guildhall Library, the historian of the resultant Society of Coal Factors provides an overview:

In the 17th century a group of middlemen arose in the London market who acted as brokers between the shippers who brought in the coal, and the buyers. In course of time these middlemen became known as factors, and in the early 18th century factors were given statutory recognition. For over a hundred years practically all London's coal passed through the hands of factors, and for a short time in the 19th century factors played a major role in the regulation and control of the London import. This control broke down before the mid-century and thereafter the factor ceased to act as agent working on a commission basis and became shipper and wholesaler or contractor in his own right.[32]

Woodmongers can also be placed in this wider context:

The factors of London originated … when the import trade was passing from the control of one ancient guild … the Woodmongers, to that of another, the Watermen and Lightermen … the Woodmongers were the fuel merchants of the middle ages and the coal merchants of the 17th century.[33]

Newcastle's historians record further background data:

The fitters … occupy a prominent place in the records of the Hostmen's Company … The Charter of 1600 mentions not only the governor, stewards and brethren of the fraternity but also their 'factors', servants and apprentices. By 1634 the term 'fitter' starts to be used … and after [1651] … 'factor' disappears from the books and the term 'fitter' alone is used. The verb 'to fit', however, is to be found at the commencement of the records. In January, 1601, the hostmen passed an ordinance that no brother by himself, his son, apprentice or servant should 'fit' the keel of any other brother without consent …

At the beginning of the 17th century, most of the hostmen were coal owners, and fitters were apparently their paid servants or agents, appointed by them severally, or by a group of them acting in a trade combination, to fix cargoes for coalowners with buyers from a distance, and to get the coals delivered by keels from the colliery staiths … At an early date, however … there came to be an increasing number of hostmen who were not coalowners, but who used the privileges of their position as hostmen to act as agents for unfree coalowners … and in course of time this completely changed the composition of the Company … to a fraternity of chartered fitters or privileged agents.[34]

Nevertheless, their position was becoming less dominant. As a speaker before a House of Commons Committee of 1800 put it:

The worker of the mine employs a description of men called fitters, to negotiate the sale of the coals with the shipowner. This fitter is in the nature of a *del credere* factor.

In the first half of the 19th century, the fitter was usually some leading member of a partnership of coalowners but, by the second half, most fitters reverted to their pre-1600 role – simply salaried servants to the coalowners, probably one of the chief clerks. By 1900, fitters were regaining something of their old importance, as salaried managers of the whole trading departments of the coalowners' concerns.

The dense syntax of the London coal trade of the 17th, 18th and 19th centuries is a minefield for the unwary. One more of its constituents needs to be described: the multi-faceted trade of the 'Crimp'. Defoe's simplified definition will need some elaboration: 'The Brokers of these Coals are called crimps'. Murray's *Dictionary* also oversimplifies as 'one that undertakes for or agrees to unlade a whole ship of coals'.[35]

Seacoal grapples with this elusive trade, but its role is complicated in at least five respects: (i) it changed several times over the centuries; (ii) it merged with the evolution of the Factor and the Broker; (iii) Lightermen also acted as Crimps; (iv) both also occasionally acted as buyers, not just intermediaries; (v) in different contexts, the buying role was carried out at a retail as well as at the wholesale level. As if this were not complicated enough, while the coal market developed, it created more specialisation, and the resultant fissures within the role of the Crimp led to polarisation – to the upper, financially controlling extreme, the Crimp as Broker, and at the other, artisan-employment extreme, to the Crimp as 'Undertaker' or Labour Agent.

40   DEVELOPMENT OF THE DOMESTIC GRATE, 18TH-19TH CENTURIES
The domestic grate became smaller and more 'integrated' with room design, and with the pattern of English comfort across the social scale; firebacks were replaced by basket grates, integral firedogs became separate.

To compound complexity even further, although both extremes could co-exist in a single market-entrepreneur, the role of this earlier sense of an 'Undertaker' would seem to lie at the very edge – if not just beyond – of what could be portrayed as an historical Fueller 'management' antecedent. The Crimp also played a significant and indeed primary role in the regularisation of the market, in co-operation with the Land Coal Meters – collection of the 'King's Duty' (*see* Fig. 48, p.101).

The Fuellers' History can here at least attempt to clarify one more obscure aspect, although the origins of the un-English, offputting word 'crimp' do not greatly illuminate matters; there is also need to observe differences in slang meanings between Smith's 1960s and today:

The word crimp was part of the vernacular of the dockside. Its etymology is obscure; it is considered to be of Dutch or Flemish origin, with the sense of screwing [*sic*] or scrimping, measuring under rather than over. And though in the course of its long history it was used to cover a number of different functions, it always carries something of its original association with the underworld between the river – or the sea – and the shore. From the time of its origin it is used in a pejorative sense, and in the 19th century it bears a like stigma. Even when it was applied to wholesale dealers and merchants in coal and became respectable, it still had around it some aura of its shady past.[36]

By Victorian times, a 'crimp' had degenerated further to become one more part of the dockland underworld, giving places like Rotherhythe and Stepney a 'bad reputation, with their contingents of whores, pandars, crimps, bullies ...'.[37] A noted historian of the 18th century has commented further: 'An education in brutality was given in the public spectacles at Tyburn and the pillory, by the constant floggings in the street, by the methods of press-gangs and crimps'.[38]

Trades at the Fueller Boundary

Just as at one end of the distribution lineage, the Newcastle keelmen 'on the shop floor' cannot be rolled in as direct predecessors to the merchanting Fuellers, so, too, do several other historic trades – all associated with the supply process (but not all included by Dale) require to be differentiated. Although vital links in the overall chain, neither the Fellowship of Billingsgate Porters, nor the then unorganised 'Coal-Heavers', 'Coal-Whippers' or several others can be viewed in the same line of descent as the 'Crimps' or Brokers. All these men were 'managed' by others, not acting in any vestigial management process, a noticeable characteristic of the Fueller over the centuries. There were still at least three lesser trades to be identified within the boundary of Fuellerdom: the Small-Coal Man, the Chandler's shop and the retailing Chapman.

Porters carried the coals ashore from lighters or barges on the Thames; they became freemen of the City of London, and indeed were so outside any conceptual 'Fueller' stream that in 1733 they not unreasonably had a controversy with the woodmongers as a body, in which they complained: 'In the time of King James the First ... the lighters and barges from which the Sea-coals were carried on Shore, were not above ten or fifteen Ton ... but by the increase of Trade, the Lighters are now from thirty to fifty Ton Burthen; and the Porters are obliged to carry ... thirty to ninety Foot and upwards'.[39]

Coal-Heavers (aka 'Colelabourers') unloaded the ships in the river, using 'vats': at first they were not organised as the Porters were. There was much activity between 1689 and 1706 for the creation of a fraternity, indicating that the organisation of riverside labour (a familiar problem of the post-Second World war London labour scene) had already even then become acute: 'The work itself was hard and dirty, casual and poorly paid ... The older hands sought to restrict intake

41   RISE OF THE COAL MERCHANT

By the 18th century, the coal merchant was becoming an established part of the domestic English scene, personally supervising the loading of his coal supply by coal porters onto his own carts, direct from the lightermen's boats at the Thames shore. Philip Fruchard's office was at the Golden Heart jetty, on All-hallows Lane, below Thames Street riverside.

into their gangs, by making things difficult for "colts" – newcomers – Labourers were engaged by shipmasters or their agents through heads of gangs … they were subject to extortion from the agents who employed them. Many of these were publicans … But not all those interested were labourers … There was obviously money in "undertaking" for others beside labourers … but a clearing "house for labour would have cut into the profits of crimps and dealers"'. (The Glossary and Appendix III(B) amplify.[40]) A bad harvest in 1767 led to the infamous Coal-Heavers' riots, starting at Wapping on 22 April, and raising a procession of 10,000 men and women with a call on the Coal Undertakers for higher wages. Men were killed, the Guards were brought out, arrests were made, the gaols were filled, and at least nine men were executed at Tyburn. Underlining the violence still lurking below the surface of 18th-century life, and foreshadowing the Gordon Riots of 1780, the *Gentlemen's Magazine* noted:

Hundreds of these coal heavers have again and again paraded the streets armed with bludgeons, cutlasses and other offensive weapons repeatedly crying out offers of £5 for a sailor's head, £20 for a [ship] master's; 'we'll cut the Lightermen's throats', they yelled, 'and murder all the masters, burn their houses and set fire to their shops [sic] without any men daring to molest us'.[41]

42 COAL WHIPPERS AND COAL PORTERS

These were two of the underpaid, unloved trades of London's riverside during the 18th and 19th centuries. The Whippers 'whipped' (hauled) the coals up from the holds of the colliers using large 'vats'; the porters ('labourers') then carried the coals ashore on their backs, in heavy sacks, to the wagons.

Two years later, a petition to the House of Commons of 9 March 1769, on behalf of 'The Poor Labouring Coal Heavers', stated: 'That they have for a series of years laboured under the greatest hardships through the cruel impositions of a set of men called Coal Undertakers to whom they have been obliged to give one quarter of what they earn or they could never expect to be employed by them, and also had to agree to pay for a pot of ale each ship provided, which ale was provided by the Coal Undertaker, and was worth nothing': Mayhew records the comment: 'We were compulsory drunkards.' As an evolution of the Crimp, a

Society of Coal Undertakers had been formed prior to 1758, creating their own labour Bureau; their role is embraced within the story of the Crimp.[42]

Coal-Heavers became a facet of London's street life: 'Easter Monday was their great festival day'. Hone, describing the traffic going to Greenwich Fair, says: 'then passes like some huge admiral, a full-sized coal waggon laden with coal-heavers and their wives, and shadowed by spreading boughs.'

By 1800, criminality in the London Docks was such that a police force was at last seen as necessary: 'defalcation' was estimated to run to at least £20,000 a year. Barges lying out in the river acted as 'Floating Warehouses', open to all kinds of 'nefarious practices': cut loose at night, towed to a quiet creek and systematically robbed of their contents. The 'thieving disposition … of the Coal-Heavers … being more powerful than the Ships' crews … removed such coals as remained on deck by force.' Sale of such contraband would later take place surreptitiously at Execution Dock – another, if illegal, link in the 19th-century distribution network.[43]

Yet later, in Mayhew's time, during the abortive Chartist demonstrations of 1848, the Coal-Heavers were proud to have turned out to a man for law and order as special constables. As added testimony to this hard, unremitting trade, there are at least two monuments still surviving for the eye of the 21st-century Fueller, over and above the eloquent displays in London's Museum in Docklands. In the Strand, just by the *Savoy*, that reminder of medieval John of Gaunt's palace and of the Woodmongers' early coal trade, the famous Bohemian soup-and-supper resort, *The Coal Hole*, bears a shining copper plaque recording the work of the Coal-Heavers who pursued their calling up to the late 19th century, by the riverbank, at the foot of Savoy Steps. As already outlined in Chapter II, this story also embraces the Grenadier Guards and the 'Tow-Row-Row'.[44]

Fifty miles away, in Lewes, Sussex, lies history's conclusion, a grimly evocative tombstone of William Huntingdon, a coal-heaver from Thames Ditton, who died there in 1815:[45] 'Here lies the Coal Heaver, Beloved of his God, but abhorred of men.'

Coal Whippers, introduced in 1786 to increase efficiency in these Coal-Heavers' gangs, were provided by Crimps acting as undertakers, licensed by the City authorities (later managed by the Factors): 'Cargoes were delivered by "whippers" … The coal was shovelled into baskets in the hold and the baskets jerked or "whipped" on deck by ropes passing through a pulley. There it was measured and unloaded into the barge which lay alongside. The undertaker received from the captain a penny for every chaldron. Publicans were prohibited from being undertakers, but the Act was evaded'.[46] There were pubs that were labour exchanges; most notoriously for the Thames coal-whippers, 'their gangmasters riverside publicans who required a goodly portion of their measly wages spilled in drink'. Other linked trades were the Trimmers, Trouncers and Waggoners.[47]

43 *THE COAL HOLE*, **STRAND**

This brass plaque, outside one of today's most famous London pubs, The Coal Hole, in the Strand, commemorates the use of Savoy Stairs, leading down to the river, as the access to the coal jetties, where lighters would bring coals ashore for the Coal Heavers – often soldiers from the Guards working for the 'Tow-Row' in their off-duty periods, supplementing the local Cockney workforce.

Small-Coal Men, Chandlers, Trolleymen and *Chapmen* had been features of London's street scene from at least the mid-17th century. The former might have been on the payroll of a Coal Merchant, or was self-employed. Half-pecks of coal were picked up from the latter three – all forming a last organised stage in the distribution process. Swift's *Morning in Town* of 1709 recalled that these were all aspects of the traditional 'cries of London': 'The Small Coal Man was heard, with cadence deep, Till drowned in shriller notes of "Chimney Sweep"'.⁴⁸ The drowning was not all vocal; other intermediaries were even less like Fueller precursors, albeit winning a kind of immortality – the scavengers at low tide, such as Mary Casey, one of the increasingly occurring illegal extensions of the distribution chain. In 1805, another impoverished lady, Peggy Jones, had been searching for loose coals with her toes, to carry off in a bag tied round her waist, to sell to coal merchants for 8d. a load. She disappeared, presumably lost in the Thames. Children had always collected coals and driftwood for family fires; through to the 20th century, 'Coal Boys' added to this chain.⁴⁹

iv: The Final Turf War: Woodmongers v. Lightermen

Whilst these direct or indirect forerunners of the Fuellers' coal trade were continuing at their different levels to gain supremacy for their fuel, the vestigial Woodmongers' interests had been touched in parallel by yet another of London's long drawn-out commercial boundary disputes. The Guild was the Watermen, then a separate Company whose Lightermen, as qualified 'Trinity men', rowed the lighters which transferred coals and other goods from the ships and colliers to the quays. They are in a different category compared with the Woodmongers' earlier competitors, the Carmen: 'Watermen and lightermen, by virtue of their fellowship and their apprenticeship and often the ownership of a boat, belonged to the class of skilled labour. Carmen (reputed an ill-mannered set) ranked rather with chairmen [carriers of chairs] and workers at livery stables'.⁵⁰ Although Smith, who 'blazed the trail for the whole history of the Port of London', speaks generically of 'the Lightermen' in relation to this episode, the title stands here best as Watermen and Lightermen. It is no accident that the first indication of their interest in coal, as a Company, had come a mere four years after the Woodmongers' loss of corporate status in 1667.⁵¹

44 SMALL COAL; THE MUSICAL SMALL-COAL MAN
Top: the 'Small Coale' deliveryman was almost the last link in the 18th-century fuel distribution chain. Bottom: a celebrated exponent of that trade was Thomas Britton, who contrived to combine his calling with the holding of musical soirées in the upstairs salon of his modest house in Spitalfields; his invitees included Handel.

Smith sums up: 'Whereas in the sixties and seventies of the 17th century the wholesale trade in London was in the hands of the Woodmongers, at the turn of the century it was dominated by the Lightermen who had been their servants.'[52]

This failure on the part of the Woodmongers to develop their niche in river transport is well portrayed by an anonymous, if grammatically quaint and partly untrue, satirist of *c*.1743-4:

> About half a century ago this Business was carried on in a manner very different from what it is at present: The Dealers in that Commodity had not then lost their antient name of Woodmongers; which it was obvious had been given them, when Wood was the principal Fuel of the City: The more pompous title of Coal-Merchant had not then been thought of [*sic*]; They lived on the Wharfs, kept Horses and Carts of their own, bought their coals at Billingsgate of the Masters of the Ships, and were there plyed by the Lightermen for their Business, that is to say, for the Carriage of their Coals from the Ship's Side to the Wharf, as Watermen now ply for Passengers at the several Landing-Places. In process of Time great ships being employed in the Coal-Trade, whose ladings were too large for any one or two Woodmongers either to purchase or dispose of, the Lightermen took the Hint to do what the Woodmongers could not; by which means from Carriers they, at once, became Traders of a superior Class.

> [They] found themselves in a Capacity to treat those who had been their Masters, as their Customer ... By these and such like Means, in less than thirty Years, those who had begged for a Lading of Coals, were enabled to keep their Coaches, and found themselves Masters of the whole Trade.[53]

The early history of this third, parallel 'turf war', needs ideally to be read in conjunction with the Woodmongers' simultaneous dispute with the Carmen; it is set out at length in the *Origin and Progress of the Watermen's Company*, which also contains historically important information on the development of London's coal trade.[54]

Its opening salvo might have been fired in a petition to Parliament of 15 October 1620 by the wharfingers, complaining of what the Watermen and Lightermen later termed 'the imposition of woodmongers and carmen'. This resulted in the by now standard exchange of published answers to the charges.

Consequently, on 5 March 1623, a Bill had been introduced into the House of Commons, but then not proceeded with, 'Concerning the taking and purveying of carts, carriages, etc by land and by water, for His Majesties service'; ever since the introduction of coaches in 1588, this loss of trade by the Lightermen had become an increasing problem for them. The Watermen's dispute lay also with the Crown, on the vexed question of the then unavoidable impressment of mariners for the Navy, as with the keelmen, in time of war. Charles II tried to further the river trade. Their Company 'consisted of watermen and wherrymen only, who were engaged in carrying both passengers and goods'. The lightermen were members of a separate Livery 'who most likely did not confine themselves to carrying goods on that part of the river within the city'.[55]

Abuses, Grievances and Remedies

The Thames was becoming inflammatory in other ways, too. At the start of the 17th century, 'in the eleventh and twelfth years of the reign of King William III' [1700], a Parliamentary approach was made to try to regulate the abuses which were now rife. A Bill recited the history of the problem:

> The lightermen rowing on the said river of Thames are grown very numerous and are at present, without rule and government amongst them, by whose rudeness and unskilfulness in working of lighters and other large craft, ships and vessels are hindered in the delivery of coals ... and notorious disorders are occasioned.

On 16 November 1703, the Lords appointed a Committee to examine the high price of coals; a call to the City's Aldermen led to a request to the Home Counties Justices to establish if there had been 'engrossment'. Smith describes the responsibility of the lightermen for turning Billingsgate from an open to a closed market, and also instances the Middlesex Justices' Report for its insight into the contemporary customers' right 'to satisfy themselves as to sorts, prices and goodness of their coals some of [the lightermen] aspiring to enrich themselves ... by many subtle methods to undermine and supplant the common customs of that market, and the right that every person has there ...'.

> These men, especially the richer sort ... even insult others as endeavour to buy fairly in the open market, by engrossing the whole ship and offering a price above the shipmaster's expectations ... the effect of their practices will be that in a few years time Billingsgate will be unknown to the coal trade, and every consumer and retailer will be at the mercy of the lightermen ... some of [them] are crimps as well, and not free of the City either ... the lightermen have also instigated many persons without any interest in the coal trade, who had money lying dormant, to put it with them 'for laying up private store' of coals against the winter, or the failure of the fleets to come in.[56]

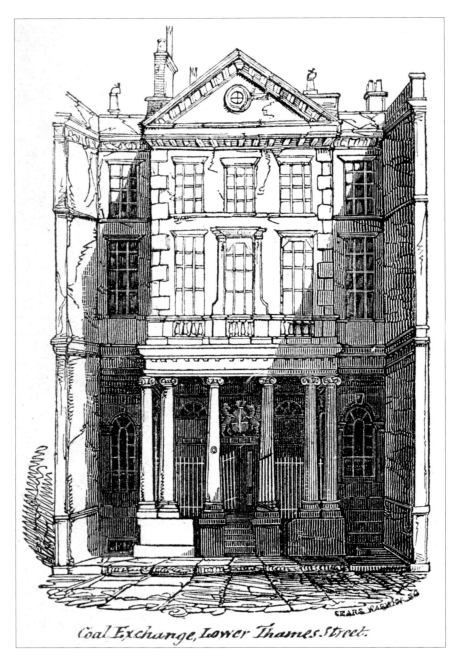

Coal Exchange, Lower Thames Street.

45 'OLD' COAL EXCHANGE, THAMES STREET, 1769

The three-storey 'Old' Exchange, a converted building on the site of the ancient 'Roomland' ('Romeland') space (possibly so-named after the former Roman marketplace?) was the trade's first organisational setting: it was an exclusive private market, closed to the less opulent. It nevertheless boasted the City of London's crest over its door. Here, merchants, factors and shipowners' representatives could at last do business more appropriately, compared with the taverns they had previously had to use.

By way of example, *Seacoal* records that the Surrey Justices submitted a list of persons with stores of coals on the south waterside – arguably yet another group of Fueller ancestors:

> In St Saviour's, Southwark, Mr Ashurst, sugar baker, had 30 chaldrons; Mr Richard Oldner and Mr William Smith, lightermen, 150 each; in St Olave's, Southwark, Mr Rowl. Gideon, a ... merchant, 300, and Mr Ryall (lighterman) 100; Peter Dawkins of Rotherhithe had 100 at Ipswich; Mr Newell, goldsmith, had 100 at St Olave's, Southwark and 300 in St Saviour's and 100 in Christchurch; three other brewers had 600 between them; while a few coal merchants were carrying from 20 to 25 chaldrons each.[57]

In 1728, a register was instituted at an office in London to ensure that ships should unload in turn, and on completion of unloading, each shipmaster was given a certificate without which, by arrangement with the northern fitters, no new cargoes could be supplied. Smith sums up the complexities:

> The Lightermen had a private war with the owners, and a public one with the woodmongers. The shipowners were trying to squeeze what they could out of the owners, but looked upon the Lightermen as the real peril. The coal-owners were in difficulties amongst themselves, but had a collective feud with the Lightermen ... The brewers and distillers of London and the Hostmen fitters of Newcastle were all embroiled in the affair, and in fact there was no one engaged in the coal trade whose interests were not implicated.[58]

Not surprisingly the Parliamentary Committee was overwhelmed:

> Witnesses for the shipmasters testified that coal-buyers and lightermen were few in number. One thought that about 10 of them bought two-thirds of the London imports; another that there were not more than 15 or 16 considerable dealers. Lightermen demanded premiums of 6d. or 1s. a chaldron from coal-owners ... if, however, the premiums were not forthcoming, the coals were 'blown upon' [an archaic term rendered in Murray's *Dictionary* as 'forced to pass by other means – in other words, to some third party']. One witness believed that the Lightermen received £12,000 per annum by way of premiums ... Ships whose masters did not accept prices were 'marked', i.e. the masters were boycotted [an anachronism, since the term only came in around 1880] until they climbed down or unloading was delayed.

A comment by George Oldner appears to be particularly apt: 'Masters and lightermen catch as catch can.'[59]

In 1700, the Lightermen, Wherrymen and Watermen had been made into one Company, and provision was at last attempted with regard to the interface with the Woodmongers' rights:

Owners of quays etc, betwixt the Hermitage bridge and London bridge, may use their own lighters etc, and employ persons qualified to row them. Woodmongers may keep lighters for carrying their own goods, provided their servants are watermen or lightermen [i.e. 'Trinity' men] … Any person who then was or should thereafter be a woodmonger, and keep a wharf or wharves for retailing [i.e. 'selling'] of fuel might keep, use and row by themselves or servants any lighters or large craft, for carrying their own goods so to be retailed and none others … All persons who … should be employed in … navigating any lighters or other great craft (Trinity men, fishermen, ballast men, western barges, and mill boats, chalk hoys, faggot and wood lighters, and other craft) … should be registered in the books of the Company.

Problems with the coal trade continued. In due course, the lightermen had adduced before the committee that 'About one half of the coals brought into the port of London were brought by about twelve lightermen, and the remaining half by about forty other lightermen … and that if coals were bought by persons not being lightermen, they were obliged to make use of a lighterman's barge to get them, as if the coal masters delivered coals to a non-freemen's barge, no lightermen would buy or take coals from such a ship'.

The Act which ensued in 1730 provided, among other ordinances, that dealers in coals could use their own lighters anywhere in the river, lighters to be entered with the Company of Watermen and Lightermen and 'marked' [registered]. No lighterman was to act as crimp, agent or factor; and no shipmaster was to employ a buyer as crimp.[60] An interesting distinction is made in the Watermen's history between the former Woodmongers' Livery, and those persons still pursuing that trade:

This Act has been commonly called the Woodmongers' Act, as extending the Act of eleven and twelve William III [1700] … by permitting coal merchants to carry coals in their own craft, on all parts of the river as lightermen had been accustomed, instead of confining them in carrying to and from their own wharves … This Act has no reference to the old Woodmonger Company of London, hereinbefore referred to, who were compelled by Parliament in 1667 to surrender their charter, in consequence of their malpractices.

A remedying Act of 7 May 1731 plugged gaps in the 1730 laws, such that 'cocquets' were to be delivered to Customs Officers within four days of arrival at Gravesend under penalty of £50. Raymond Smith's *Seacoal* highlights the importance of this fresh legislation in creating new conditions in the London market:

The powers of the lightermen were restricted both by the increased freedom given to other wharfingers and the scope given to independent factors … the lightermen lost the dominance of the market they had achieved in 1700 –

It was the factor who supplied the coal-buyer who succeeded the lighterman, and the coal merchants who succeeded the coal buyer. The ship masters of 1730, it is true, lost the battle for unloading in turn; but they won the fight to appoint their own agents. Twenty years later the Society of Coal Factors was in being, and there can be little doubt that the rise of factors to collective power dates from 1730, when they were given legal status, authority, and duties.[61]

In 1774, well after the Livery's supposed disappearance from influence, renewed complaints were made about the impact of the '*craft* [*sic*] of woodmongers'. On 31 August 'a standing committee was appointed to oppose and prosecute all woodmongers who should attempt to work in craft …'. The following year, the Watermen's history comments on the importance of the Coal Meters in the evolution of the 'market' (*see* Appendix III(B)):

> The importation of coals to London, which had risen in 1666 to [200,000] tons, gradually increased up to this year, when the import thereof amounted to [664,278] chaldrons, causing the employment of an additional number of ships, barges, lightermen, etc.

> The coal meter's office was on the north side of the church of St Dunstan in the East, and the market was held at this time on a piece of ground adjoining Billingsgate market, called the Room Land, nearly opposite St Mary-at-hill, described by Maitland as 'the place where the masters of coal ships, coal mongers [*sic*] and heavers, daily meet to transact their affairs'. The [second] coal market in Thames street was not erected until 1805.[62]

In 1794, a new Bill was ordered by the Corporation of London to regulate the Thames trade 'between Windsor and Gravesend', and the rulers of the watermen, wherrymen and lightermen raised questions about a new aspect of the woodmongers' practices: 'woodmongers and boat builders letting out boats without proper assistance.'[63]

A report arising from the subsequent committee of enquiry highlighted the predominance of coal and timber craft on the river, out of a total of 3,419 craft, of 110,156 tonnage, including sundry punts, sloops, cutters and hoys. There were, in addition, 3,000 wherries for passengers and parcels, and 155 bum boats licensed to hawk goods among the shipping:

Barges used principally for coal	2,196	85,103 (tons)
[Barges] employed in the deal trade	400	15,454 (tons)

The report also provides a fascinating insight into the employment that the river offered at this time, dividing the 120,000 individuals into two classes, employers and employed:

Many could be seen as acting as Fuellers of the 18th century, but now with less and less guild influence: the age belonged to entrepreneurs, guilds were increasingly seen as restrictive. Of 10,250 employers, some 4,100 were Merchants and Shipowners, a further 430 were Coal Merchants and dealers, 25 were Coal 'undertakers' for unloading ships, and 55 were Wharfingers, including the coasting trade. Among the second group, totalling 122,320, were included 1,400 Working Lumpers, 800 Coal Heavers, 450 Coal Porters, 450 Coal Carters, and the by now impressive total of some 200 Coal Meters and Meters' Men, to be compared with 155 Meters for corn, salt and fruit.

By the time of the French war, at London Bridge another major feature of the river trade was being recorded – its accidents: 'Loss of life was also frequently occurring through coal craft being taken through [between the piers forming cataract-like waterways under the bridge] two at a time by one lighterman, the coal merchants asserting a want of men, from the great numbers being impressed for the Navy.'[64]

v: New Concepts: Docks and Canals

In the days of Elizabeth I, 20 monopolistic 'legal quays' (of a mere 1,400 feet in length) had been designated on the north bank where all cargo was to be cleared by customs; their owners exploited their monopoly ruthlessly. In 1705, traders complained to the City Corporation and to Parliament, resulting later in the century in the introduction of 'sufferance wharves' on the south bank, which created a new monopoly; the vested interests so protected all throve on the chaotic conditions – lightermen, watermen, porters, and even the City Corporation itself. Although bulky coal might well not be its prime target, the overall situation encouraged crime – and a new vocabulary:

> 'River pirates', 'night plunderers', 'scuffle-hunters', 'light horsemen', 'heavy horsemen', and 'mudlarks'. The cant phrase for a crooked revenue officer was 'game'.

Secure docks were the answer. Three schemes presented in 1796 led to an Act in 1799, authorising the first commercial 'West India' docks, preceded in 1798 by the first river police organisation – 900 'lumpers' to work under some 200 constables. Later Dock Acts paid off the vested interests, but London and the nation missed the chance to make the new docks a public enterprise. Wharfingers and coal merchants were among those testifying to the growing menace of plundering. By 1800, the importation of coal to London had grown from 664,278 chaldrons in 1775 to just over the million mark – 1,005,352 chaldrons.

An 1800 treatise provides further background (*see also* Appendix III(B)). Some 800 coal-heavers worked on the River, of whom 600 might well be engaged in illegal practice, under the sway of some 24 publicans. Each collier needed 13 barges to serve it, adding up to some 1,170 barges 'above and below Bridge', bringing in a monthly supply of some 66,000 chaldrons of coal.

On 17 April that year, the Watermen's Company was required by the House of Commons to state the number of coal merchants and lighters in the port of London: of the 1,847 craft employed, 1,418 plied 'above bridge', 429 'below bridge'. The River, London Docks and the coal trade itself were all now assuming national importance. On 2 May, a committee was appointed under the coal lightermen's committee chairman James Wood to try to resolve the endemic problems of poor navigation on the nation's major river. On 23 June, a select committee of the Commons was set up to consider the state of the coal trade. By 1803, an Act was overdue to assist merchants, to form a free market, and prevent frauds: 'whereby the interests of the owners of the old buildings, for some time past used as a market, [were] purchased for [25,600] pounds. A new coal exchange was erected in Lower Thames street, opposite Billingsgate, which was opened in 1805, and remained until 1849, when a much larger building

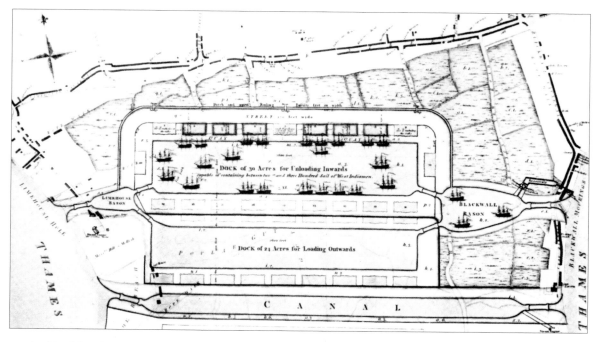

46 THE NEW DOCKS

'Plan of the West India Dock and City Canal … in the Isle of Dogs, Begun 1800.' Coal shipping would have a key role in the development of the dock system from the end of the 18th century onwards. This plan shows two docks – 'Unloading Inwards' (upper) and 'Loading Outwards' (lower), leading out both (west) to Limehouse Hole and the Thames (left), and again through Blackwall Basin ['Bason'] to the east.

was erected ... coals delivered at the wharf for the [Watermen's] company's hall being [54s.] per chaldron.'[65]

For the better service of the coal trade, that third coal-led development – the canals – was further involved, alongside the exciting new docklands. In this, London was at last catching up on the lead of the Duke of Bridgewater in the Midlands and in other coal-producing regions some 50 years earlier, following the much earlier precedent for private canal-building in Exeter.

Three years on, the City Canal was cut across the Isle of Dogs. Despite its eventual decline, its last years relieved the overall congestion. Some 7,000 colliers were using the port by 1825, when the Port Committee of the Corporation resolved that not more than 250 colliers should be permitted in the Pool at one time, and that harbourmasters should be directed 'to cause a signal flag (half red, half white) for stopping colliers, to be hoisted at the Blackwall end of the City Canal, whenever that number has been moored therein'.

Canals acted as links to the national river navigation network, still more important than the neglected roads for bulk distribution; nevertheless Midlands coal into London officially never exceeded the peak 1809 level of 17,300 tons per annum, as against the 1½ million ton North-East coastal trade. The small Regent's Canal Dock, on the north bank at Limehouse, had its fair share of this trade. A 1805 Act was introduced 'For allowing ... the bringing of a limited quantity of coals, culm or cinders to London and Westminster by inland navigation' ... no more than [50,000] tons might be brought into London by the Paddington Canal.[66]

Meanwhile the woodmongers were still clashing with their water carriers, but only the latters' records survive to tell the tale. On 10 March 1807, the watermen and lightermen were concerned about a new Bill, which 'would in a great measure infringe on the company's privileges' ... it was ordered that:

> the solicitors do endeavour to get a clause inserted limiting woodmongers and those doing business in coals, coke and fuel, from carrying goods as mentioned in the act of 3 George II [1730] ... The Act was passed 47 George III [1807]. By clause 61 it was enacted, that it should be lawful for any lighterman to enter into co-partnership with any woodmonger as a coal dealer, and to keep, use and employ their own barges for the carrying of coals to and from any wharf, dock, creek, etc, without being subject to any penalty ... provided that the same should not extend to authorize any lighterman to become jointly interested with a woodmonger in the trade or business of carrying in lighters, etc, for hire, any goods whatsoever, except only coals lightered in their trade of coal dealers.[67]

By 1808, the Lightermen and Watermen were noting that the price of coals had increased as a result of the Napoleonic war, the charge 'in the pool' being from 65s. to 70s. per chaldron. A breakdown of their 5,323 members showed 291 as Masters and owners of craft, including many Liverymen of the City of London, and 38 as Fellowship Porters, and Corn and Coal Meters (many of these are clearly seen in retrospect to be in the lineage of 'The Fuellers'). About 1811, a return of the number of lightermen for whom protection from impressment was required, highlighted the trades carrying in wood and coal:

Coal trade (2,000 craft, averaging 40 tons,
    requiring one man to every 8):   200 men

Deal [pine wood] trade, etc: 100 men

In his *London in the Nineteenth Century*, Jerry White has described the sprawling city as a sewage nightmare, with a 'shambling riverside of wharves, coalstacks and boatyards'. Despite such environmental problems, the development of the docks continued apace. In 1813, a Bill was brought in to compel coal vessels to discharge in a wet dock in the Isle of Dogs; the coal factors now come into prominence again with the coal merchants in opposing this, and succeeding. In 1814, nature intervened in London's trading, with the second great Thames Freeze: the coal barges were iced in, and coal merchants were compelled to draw their fuel from ships in the pool with carts and waggons, at an average price of 59s. per chaldron. There were also severe floods, with the river rising four inches higher than in the flood of 1774; intense fog and heavy snows were endemic hazards. There was a proposal to tax craft on the Thames, but the owners of coal craft, and also, apparently acting separately, the coal merchants, opposed it.

In 1828, a Bill for forming a collier dock and coal depot at Bermondsey was shortsightedly opposed, with regrettable success, by the rulers of the Lightermen; however a 107-clause Bill – '7 & 8 George IV *c.*75' [1827] – soon became law for constructing collier docks in the Isle of Dogs. It enacted:

That the power of the court of Lord Mayor, etc, to make rules and bye-laws should extend, and might be applied ... to lighters, boats, and vessels of woodmongers, and owners of laystalls, chalk hoys ... and all other lighters, boats and all other vessels on the river, although otherwise exempted.

The pettifogging rules governing Liveries were still a force to be reckoned with at this early stage of the new century, as illustrated by an incident which also exemplified the commercial interdependence of lightermen and fuel merchants:

In 1830 Mr Clement Peache, son of a timber merchant and barge owner of Lambeth, who had been bound apprentice to his father's lighterman, applied to the court for his freedom, which was opposed on the ground that he was not qualified, not having worked on the river, but in his father's counting house.[68]

By 1832, the importation of coals to London, amounting to 1,005,352 chaldrons in 1800, now rose to 2,139,078 tons – the first time that coals had to be measured by tonnage.

The Watermen's Books again balance statistics with humanity. On 15 June 1835, a coal porter, with a sack of coals, was drowned, the plank on which he was passing being forced from off a barge, due to the swell caused by passing steam boats.[69]

Delay was a growing problem. By 1835, there were 500 colliers in the Thames, some cargoes being detained for a month, waiting to be brought to market, and afterwards waiting for a weigher, the price being enhanced 3s. a month.

47 THAMES LIGHTERMEN
An earlier link in the fuel distribution chain was the Thames Lighterman, who rowed the loads ashore from the colliers or barges at anchor. Their realisation that this essential role could thereby give them competitive leverage in the contemporary fuel trade gave rise to the second of the Woodmongers' 'turf wars'.

A request was made to remedy this bottleneck. The height of tides and the effects of steam boats caused the interests concerned to petition the House of Commons, again through separate actions from 'merchants, importers and others in the coal, timber and stave trade of the Port of London' and 'from coal merchants and others'. A Bill was presented for building the London Collier Tidal Dock, at the Surrey canal at Deptford, but once more progress was halted, and the Bill not proceeded with.[70]

vi: Fueller Evolutions:
Masters and Owners of Coal Craft

Of the two other trades which bestrode the Fuellers' stage during the 18th century, in line with the Fueller concept, the Coal Merchants will be treated at length in the final chapter. The next trade that preceded them in the distribution chain, the Ship Masters, has already featured. They had published yet another of the typical lobbying 'broadsides' for that time, setting out their firm views and strong grievances, under the title: 'The Case of the Owners of Ships employed in the Coal Trade'. Its ninth clause appeared to attempt to rewrite history, re-asserting a 'canard' to support their continuity with the old 17th-century trading status:

> The Ship Owners never had any Charter of any sort, so could not lose same; and as for the Woodmongers, they did not forfeit their Charter

but voluntarily surrendered same freely to King Charles II above 60 years ago, which had it been otherwise, the actions of so long ago could not apply to any Woodmongers presently living.[71]

48 LAND COAL METER'S BADGE
The central role of the 19th-century Coal Meter (Official Weigher) was seen to be a mark of distinction within the coal trade – voluntary self-regulation in the originating ports of departure as well as in London, before legislation took over. It was exercised by senior figures of probity, meriting its own silver badge, worn round the arm (like the watermen) or possibly the neck. There were two divisions: on the dockside ('Land'); or, earlier in the distribution process, on the vessels themselves ('Sea'). This example is in the possession of a descendant of one of the best-known Coal Merchants and Factors, the family business of Benjamin Horne.

Dale nevertheless took the view that by 1763, when a new Act came into force regulating the price of coal at 25s. to 28s. per chaldron in the Pool of London, 'the Woodmongers Company seemed to have died of inanation. Many of its members being freemen of the Watermen's Company no longer saw any necessity for belonging to another Company. Yet the Watermen's Company embraced many others who were not interested at all in coal.'[72] He wrote that a Society of Owners of Coalcraft was created about this time, taking over as its inheritance the duties of the Woodmongers' Company: 'There is nothing known about the date when the last Freeman of this Company was admitted, but this title persisted, and as late as the inquiry of 1830, we find a witness declaring he was a Woodmonger but his son was a Lighterman and had served seven years to the oar'.

In the Lightermen's dispute, the 'Woodmongers and Sellers of Coal in London and Westminster' also published a broadside, which introduced an alternative trade title to the scene:

> The Lightermen published a counter broadside, entitled 'The Case of the Watermen and Lightermen' … 'The Woodmongers, who for reasons easy to be guessed at, have thought fit now to style themselves Persons keeping Wharfs, have lost many of their customers, and been in a state of declension'.[73]

Exeunt Woodmongers: 'King Coal' Supreme

In 1827, the Society of Coal Merchants wrote to Parliament; this led to a general enquiry in 1829-30 about the working of the trade. Among those giving evidence before the Commission were two names resonating into the 21st century – John Charrington, before the Lords, and William Horne, before the Commons. Dale's 1922 excerpts from the evidence offer illuminating insights into the trade in London at this time, including yet another name for a trade category – 'Brass-plate coal merchants':[74]

> The profit on sales was very moderate … The Coal Merchant made his real profits out of the discounts and ingrain and on working his barges, and cartage, and the charge for credit. Horne's expenses showed:[75]

	£	s.	d.
Rent of wharf and taxes	700	0	0
Hire of 9 wains at 25 guineas each	236	5	0
Interest and depreciation on horses at 15%	180	0	0
Horsekeep at 20s. per horse per week	1,248	0	0
Farrier at 5½ guineas per horse per annum	138	12	0
Sacks at 2d, per chaldron	157	10	0
Loading at 1s. per chaldron	675	0	0
Clerks	408	0	0
Total	3,743	7	0

There were 19 houses (27 individuals) of Coal Factors, or Colliery Agents, as we should call them now; 10 First Buyers who took the whole contents of a ship and sold to the Second Buyers who represented some 60 other firms, at 1s. per chaldron commission; and beyond these a vast number of brassplate coal merchants and dealers and retailers who sold by the bushel.[76]

The Coal Meters now re-surface after a meeting of some 70 parties on 22 December 1831, at the *London Tavern*, convened by the 'Woodmongers and Coal Wharfingers'. Out of this, a new Coal Meters' Society, to restore that valuable function to the trade, was set up by the Societies of Coal Factors and the Owners of Coal Craft; in 1836 this latter body changed its name to the Society of Coal Merchants.[77]

In 1836, when an inquiry was held into the City Companies, a summons was sent out to the Woodmongers; no one answered it or appeared to give evidence on their behalf. The year 1843 might be significant as the year when a Bill was brought before Parliament for a relief fund for one of the traditional participants already identified in the solid fuel world, the coal whippers. However, for the Fuellers, and their Coal Merchant forebears, its importance lies in this being the last year where any reference has been found to the survival of the first

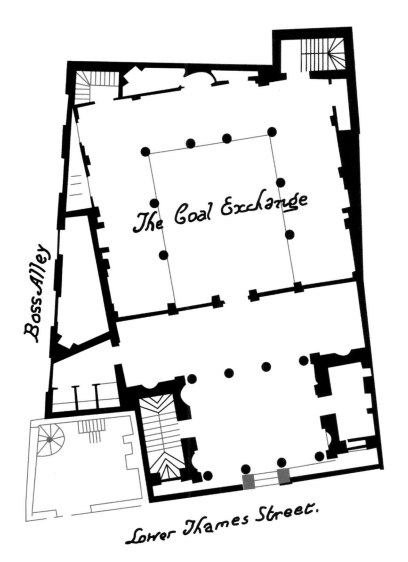

49   Plan of 'Old' Coal Exchange, 1804

The 1769 building, externally unchanged but internally improved, was about to undergo its second operational format. From 1805 its organisation would be radically different: taken over and now owned by the City Corporation, operating as an open market.

truly English exponent of their calling, the woodmonger, albeit in a case which appears to have had no resolution:

> In April, a dispute occurred with a Mr Temperley, as to granting him a woodmonger's number on an informal declaration, and he having written to and served notice on the clerk [of the Watermen], the solicitors were consulted, when it was determined to be guided by counsel's opinion, and a conference had with him thereon, which was submitted to the court of complaints.[78]

Later happenings in the Watermen's Books touch on the world of fuel, including the opening in 1844 of a coal whippers' office at King James' Stairs. The most important, however, arose in another significant year, 1849, when the third coal market was completed. The first Coal Exchange had been erected in 1768, by private subscription, in Lower Thames Street, the expense shared between the Coal Factors and the Coal Merchants.[79]

The historical background had been set out before the House of Commons Select Committee on the state of the coal trade, in 1830, by Mr Thomas Gillespy, an old Coal Factor – he was then 69, and had been on the market, from a boy of 14 onwards, for 55 years from 1775:

> When my father came on the market … in 1755, the practice was for the factors and buyers to associate together among the fish people, and endeavour to make an arrangement so as to make a purchase of coals; the Act of the 9th of Anne made it indispensable that the captains should be a party to such an agreement, and therefore whenever a factor could get one, two, three or four buyers, who engaged to take a cargo of coals, he got them to a public-house in the neighbourhood; the first thing was to order something to eat and drink, the factor to pay for the room, and they sometimes concluded a bargain … but the factor always paid the expenses, and they made a private bargain in the best way they could; it followed, of course, at that time, that no coals were sold unless the whole cargo could be disposed of; the practice at that period was, that there was generally something of a concealed price that was kept back, so that the price avowed to the public was more than the price really paid.[80]

The third market, with improvements to light and approaches, replaced the second Coal Exchange of 1805: it was to prove one of the fuel industry's greatest-ever state occasions, given front-page coverage in the *Illustrated London News*:[81]

> [On 30 October it was] publicly opened by H.R.H. Prince Albert, in the absence of Her Majesty the Queen from indisposition. The Lord Mayor … the Aldermen and Navigation Committee, in the city barge, took water at Southwark Bridge, and proceeded to Whitehall Stairs, where they found a large flotilla of boats, some belonging to men of war, and painted blue with gilt mouldings, belonging to the Royal Yacht, and close in shore was the royal barge, manned by the Queen's watermen, and the Queen's shallop and Admiralty yachts.

On the arrival of Prince Albert and the young princes and other distinguished visitors, a procession was formed arriving at London Bridge, the shipping in the river below were all dressed up, the crowds on board and in the rigging etc cheering lustily.

Icon and Anathema

It was the 19th century that began to make coal-mining and coal itself both notorious, even anathema, but also famous, even iconic, throughout the Western world. On the one hand, coal and mining became embodiments of folklore, settings for communal heroism, and emblems of man's struggle against nature. By the mid-20th century, children would read of *The Magic of Coal*.[82]

The notoriety derived from two sources – the increasing public challenge to the dangers of mining to miners and their communities, set against the backdrop of the other hazard – the effects on public health of unrestricted coal-burning in the technology of the day. This would later become known as 'smog', both domestically and industrially – a far cry from Wordsworth's idealised view of 1801 from Westminster Bridge:

All bright and glittering in the smokeless air.[83]

The socially-conscious literary evocations of European writers as diverse as Elizabeth Gaskell and Emile Zola bear witness to coal's dark side.[84]

50 THE COAL EXCHANGE IN ACTION, 1808
With the second phase in the evolution of the Exchange in full swing, still using the same site in Thames Street, the haggling and dealing market between sellers, middlemen and buyers could work more openly.

The beginning of records, through the Inspection of Coal Mines Act (1850), brought the facts home at last to the Victorian public, over disasters such as Lundhill, Yorkshire in 1857. As a commentator of 1920 would recall: 'The most painful feature of the coalmining industry is the heavy toll it takes on human life'.[85]

A century would have to pass before the very need for coal would be questioned, and its provision not simply accepted as part of life as an inevitable aspect of Mayhew's *London Labour and London's Poor*.[86] Thinking with his customary irony, George Orwell would later write:

> People have a way of taking it for granted that all work is done for a sound purpose. Coal-mining, for example, is hard work, but it is necessary, we must have coal.[87]

King Coal's renown was of a different order, the reverse side of that dark coin: its power to feed Industry, to create wealth, and so to carry forward the momentous processes of industrialisation.

Coal's fame was married to its sheer familiarity and ubiquity. Is it more than just a happy accident that one of the greatest popular heroines of the Victorian era, acclaimed and taken into the hearts of the British public on her triumphal

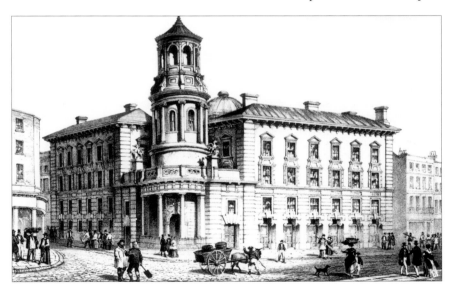

51 'New' Coal Exchange, 1849, exterior

The four-storey, L-shaped 'New' Exchange, to the design of the Corporation's Architect, J.B. Bunning, bursting with early Victorian confidence, and occupying more ground, would far outshine the more modest 1769 Georgian edifice, with a grander, semicircular entrance portico, triumphantly graced by the City's heraldic beasts, above a balustrade. The high-dome of the iron-framed inner space, the new dealing-room, can be seen behind the bell-tower, enclosed by offices for merchants, Coal Meters, the dozen wholesaling Factors' firms still trading – and even the new Coal Trade Benevolent Fund.

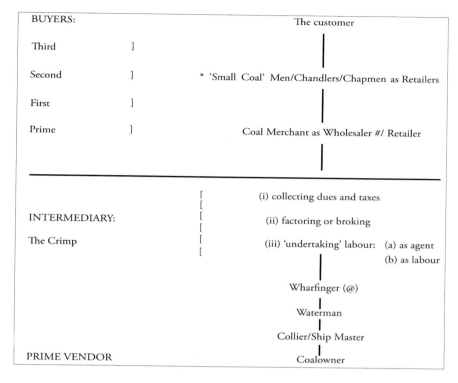

```
BUYERS:                                    The customer

Third            ]
                                 * 'Small Coal' Men/Chandlers/Chapmen as Retailers
Second           ]

First            ]

Prime            ]               Coal Merchant as Wholesaler #/ Retailer



                               [
                               [     (i) collecting dues and taxes
INTERMEDIARY:                  [
                               [     (ii) factoring or broking
The Crimp                      [
                               [     (iii) 'undertaking' labour:  (a) as agent
                                                                  (b) as labour

                                          Wharfinger (@)

                                          Waterman

                                      Collier/Ship Master

PRIME VENDOR                              Coalowner
```

52 LONDON COAL TRADE: EVOLUTION OF THE 'MIDDLE-MAN'

First buyers: negotiated sale from factors, whole cargoes.
   Second buyers: merchants, bought from first buyers, smaller quantities, retailing outside London.

* *Third buyers: small London retailers, sold to customers from small sheds; (categories evolved by the late 18th century).*

By 1770 a Society of Coal Buyers had emerged (Lightermen owning their own lighters) 56/57 strong, acting as wholesalers, buying and selling at the Coal Exchange. They must be seen as indirect Fueller forerunners of the land-based Coal Merchant.

@ *By 1800 a formal 'Body' of Wharfingers had come into being, replete with a Chairman, to represent the interests of yet another unit in the distribution chain. (For wider aspects of the London fuel trade at the turn of the 18th century, see Appendix III(B)).*

return from her humanitarian, but also very down-to-earth, work in the Crimea, rejoiced in the name of Mary Seacoal?[88]

Coal's sustained rise and its century of popularity, against the competition of alternative fuels; its subsequent decline, in the face of those new fuels, yet ultimately the distant prospect of the rediscovery, through 21st-century technology, of the ongoing qualities of that great fuel-source; the merchants who brought fuel to the market; their adaptation to the new anti-carbon environment, and the 'Firebird'-like rebirth of their ancient Livery: these will be the background themes of the History's final chapter.

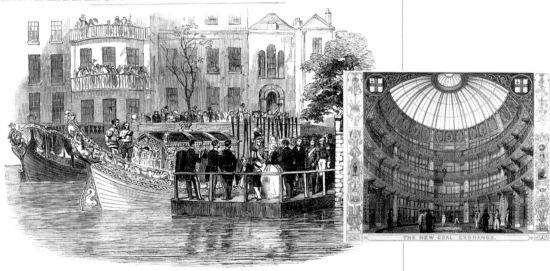

53 'Blessings': Royalty Honours the Coal Trade, 1849

The royal opening of the 'New' and most magnificent (but also the last) Coal Exchange, in the mid-19th century: it seemed to be ushering in a limitless future for coal, the fuel of the Industrial Revolution – indeed, for the ascendancy of fossil fuel as a whole. The front-page feature in the nation's foremost news medium, Illustrated London News, *under the heading, 'The Blessings of Coal', appeared unquestionable. Yet a century on, UK coal resources would be diminishing and their social costs challenged, with alternative power and heat sources coming increasingly into competition. This 'New' Coal Exchange could even be regarded as both its third and fourth 'setting', if the temporary transitional structure of 1847 is counted. It was finally – and symbolically – demolished in 1963; London thereby lost its glorious 'Raffaelesque' interior – with wall panels depicting collieries, the main coal-bearing rivers, and replicas of carboniferous fossils, as well its 4,000-piece wooden block floor, in effect a reminder of the trade's woodmongering origins. Its site was covered over, like that of the ancient Woodmongers' Hall, for a new priority, the needs of modern traffic. See also* Fig. 50, 51, pp.105-6 *and Chapter III, p.69.*

IV

THE NINETEENTH TO TWENTIETH CENTURIES

The Fueller as the Livery for Energy

from Provider ... to Authority
The Worshipful Company: Redefinition and reorientation

A Mixed Economy: Coal, Gas, Electricity, Oil – Signs of Competition – Evolution of the Coal Trade – Coal as Icon – Re-forming a Company – A Livery Reborn: The Background – The Course of Events – Heraldry, Ceremony and Authority – The Active Fueller: 1979-2009 – Charitable Objectives – Energy and Industry – Fact, Fiction and Faction – Double Claim to Uniqueness – Future Role: A Resource for Energy Policy

The Phoenix-like re-emergence – from the ashes of the medieval Woodmongers – of the modern Fuellers' Livery was a long drawn-out but creative process.

This Phoenix benefited, however, from one major difference: it was able to evolve from an existing and flourishing entity, the Coal Merchants' association (initially styled The Society of Coal Merchants of London Limited) from which it could draw its initial sustenance – human, financial, and also in a broad sense, spiritual. Of these re-birthing factors, perhaps the spiritual was the most unusual and the most significant: the coal industry and its trade had long been 'fired' by a fierce belief in their value to society – coal as icon – and in a history as proud and ancient as that of the Woodmonger-Fuellers themselves.

None of the pre-Fueller entities fully spans these next two centuries. Thus it is appropriate for this final chapter to move from the narrative to the thematic: to focus initially on two topics – the long story of the trade of the coal merchants; and the short span of years in the late 20th century in which their Society was able to bring into being the City Company which then in its turn engendered The Fuellers.

The previous chapter has anticipated the 19th- and 20th-century ascendancy of that major energy industry – coal – and of the two alternative energy sources

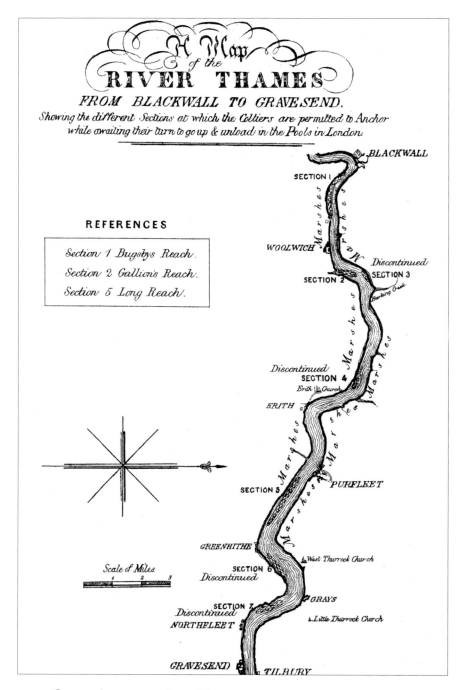

54   COLLIER ANCHORAGES, RIVER THAMES

The early 19th-century map illustrates the partly discontinued 'sections' – from Tilbury (see Fig. 67) to Blackwall – 'at which the Colliers are permitted to Anchor while awaiting their turn to go up and unload in the Pools [sic] of London'. Three of the seven sections are identified: 1: Bugsbys Reach; 2: Gallion's Reach, and 5: Long Reach (see also Appendix III(B)).

that grew directly out of it, town gas and electricity, as well as their collective new competitor, oil. It has also identified the course of the trade organisations that provided a transitional stage in the triumphant Victorian dominance of their fuel.

Although this chapter cannot seek to cover that vast canvas in detail, it must nevertheless first outline the main factors in the world of energy supply which precipitated that development, and show how, following the resurgence of the London Livery concept in the late 19th century, these many economic strands came together by the end of the succeeding century in the reincarnation of a new London Livery Company.

i: A Mixed Economy: Coal, Gas, Electricity, Oil

As a setting for the blossoming of The Fuellers' Livery, a brief multi-fuel overview of the background is now timely. Taking first the period which the coal industry's *History* dubs that of its 'Victorian Pre-Eminence' – 1830 to 1913, domestic UK coal consumption in 1830 was already 12 million tons, 38 per cent of the total output. By 1913, some 35 million tons – only 12 per cent of the total – were being burnt, mainly in British homes. The UK was then the world's largest exporter of coal fuel, a record it only conceded to Australia by 1991.[1]

Throughout this period, London's consumers took some seven per cent of total production, but the sources altered considerably. From an almost exclusive reliance on the North-East coalfields in 1830, the opening-up of the railways to coal from the pivotal year, 1845, radically changed things. By 1860, the London and North Western, the Great Western and the Midland Railways were all competing in the London market, eventually benefiting the coalfields nearest to London: Derbyshire, Leicestershire and Warwickshire.[2]

55   Coal Unloading at Paul's Wharf

An artist's view from 1881 of the ancient timber-built wharf still being used in the late 19th century to unload coal from the barges moored by St Paul Wharf, Thames Street. The dome of St Paul's Cathedral can be seen in the background.

To match this expansion in the fuel trade, the London market concept and its Coal Exchange had developed in parallel, rebuilding amidst much royal pomp, circumstance and press coverage in 1849.[3]

By the 1890s, the screw-steam coastal trade had retaliated, the coastwise market to London being proportionately the largest, at between 75 and 80 per cent of the total before 1870; after 1900, coastwise shipments to London industrial users continued to exceed the inland supplies, mainly for domestic customers. Colliers were larger, unloading facilities improved, and Port of London bunkering for bulk industrial users, including another child of the Industrial Revolution, the rising gas industry, all contributed.

If eventual size were the criterion, gas would merit a chapter on its own, transforming itself 'from a failing also-ran of the fuel industries to a major supplier of heat services'. In principle, with today's Fuellers focused on a total energy concept, the gas industry is a vital part of their hinterland. However, in the 19th century, the impact on domestic coal consumption (as oppposed to its dependence on coal for the production of town gas) of what was in fact initially a two-fuel industry – *vide* the Gas, Light & Coke Company – was small.

Following William Murdock's lighting of his Redruth cottage by gas in 1792, the new era was signalled from 1805/6 by the first gas lighting in the northern textile factories, and from 1812 by the first large-scale public supply. The lighting of streets and public buildings created most of the demand before 1850. Later (before the arrival of Swan and Edison's electric light bulb in the late 1870s), gas-lighting, through revolutionary gas mantles, replaced oil lamps and candles in better-off private homes and, from the 1880s, for heating and cooking, too: all indirectly increased the industrial demand for coal.[4]

Although domestic demand for gas was accelerated by the subsequent emergence of a force new in the fuel market – an innovative appliance industry – fortunately for the coalmen, Victorian gasmen found themselves on the horns of a dilemma: 'service' or 'sales'? As engineers they were firmly placed on the 'commodity and safety' side of that dilemma, not on the more profitable side – selling better utilisation of their fuel. The new industry's appliance developments had to come from outside it, and then not much before the 1890s, with burner improvements, the oven thermostat, and the German Ascot instantaneous water heater. By the 1870s, gas, too, in its turn was being threatened by another new fuel, oil, after 'Colonel' Drake had struck oil in Pennsylvania in 1859. American kerosene was dumped onto European markets; paraffin lamps and heaters were born. Their sequel 100 years on was the heavily advertised 'Mrs 1970' central heating revolution, solid fuel and gas having led the way.

Despite the advent of electricity, coal persisted as a fuel for heating, domestically as well as industrially. Even for cooking, solid fuel could look forward to a long life. The history of the British gas appliance industry (taking its

56 COAL-GAS LIGHTING

Coal-gas lighting was first successfully developed in this country by William Murdock, for the firm of Boulton & Watt, who used it in 1802 to light their Soho factory. During the early 19th century its use spread rapidly for lighting streets as well as buildings. Here early-style gas lamps illuminate the Westminster gasworks.

image *Burning to Serve* from one of the fuel industries' best-known 20th-century brands, 'Mr Therm'), identified, from a gas perspective, one of the key elements in this long-drawn out survival of coal in the hearths of Britain:

> Somehow the innate conservatism of the British would have to be overcome. There was the prevalent notion that the only way for meat to be roasted was in front of an open fire. Even as late as 1910 the *Encyclopedia Britannica* was able to claim that 'No kitchen can be complete without an open range' ... The British love affair with the open fire was incomprehensible to others: on the continent of Europe the closed stove for cooking and heating was preferred for its efficiency. In America closed stoves had replaced the open fire ... in the majority of homes by the end of the Civil War; only traditionalists of British origin disliked them ... Edwin Chadwick ... visited the Paris exhibition of 1867, and saw the efficient coal appliances then available. Afterwards he remarked that it would take at least a generation before the British could be persuaded to give up their open fires; he would have been nearer the mark if he had said at least a century.[5]

Signs of Competition

Behind the appliance revolution, trade liberalisation and diversification were developing apace. The elegant and informative Trade Cards of the merchants offer abundant visual evidence. In the 18th century, Messrs Love & Lawrence of Clerkenwell had combined the basic craft of woodturning – turners – with the trade of woodmongering ('All sorts of wood bought and sold').

The firm of Rainals & Jones provided an example, at the opening of the 19th century, for the combined trade of 'Timber and Coal Merchants'. By 1827, T. Downing of Wapping (Fig. 57) was acting as both 'Coal Merchants' and 'Corn Dealers'.[6]

The predecessor firm to the 20th century's Rickett & Cockerell was limiting itself by 1858 to the more normal specialisation of 'Coal & Coke Merchants'.[7]

Underneath these outward signs, the whole national fuel industry, and in consequence the trades that served it, would now undergo a revolutionary process of technologically-driven change. Through the course of the 19th century, the very idea of a physically-located, predominant solid fuel 'market' would give way to multilateral commercial dealings between coalowners and larger-scale industrial users; the coastal trade would become a mainly industrially-bound supply, not least to the fuel-burning industries proliferating along the Thames; the factors would become increasingly similar to merchants in their role, and by 1900 to all intents and purposes synonymous.

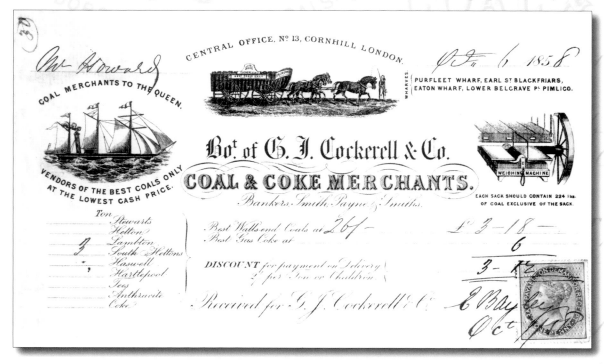

6. Clay Cross Company Price List, 1910

57 COAL 'MARKETING': MERCHANTS AND PRODUCERS

Trade cards were used to assist the sale of fuel by merchants such as T. Downing (of Fenchurch Street and Hope Wharf, Wapping) in 1827 (below), and G.J. Cockerell (of Earl Street, Blackfriars and Eaton Wharf, Pimlico) in 1858 (opposite). Downing still dealt in the traditional mix of coal and corn, charging also for 'shooting' and 'metage'; Cockerells, 'Coal Merchants to the Queen', combined coke with 'best coals only', at a guaranteed weight. Literature from the Clay Cross Company, Chesterfield (left), 'Contractors to H.M. Government', of 1910, indicates how, by the start of the 20th century, the marketing process had extended back to the colliery itself. Branding was also evident among this colliery's fuel products for 16 different 'markets'.

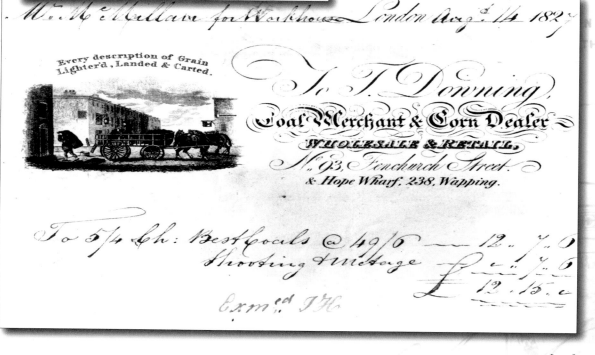

Railway coal would become a domestically determined supply, with merchants setting up yards near the new railway stations, from which to sell both wholesale and retail to the domestic market; centralised subsidiary functions like that of weighing, traditionally carried out by Coal Meters, would be bypassed by the weighing plants of the wholesalers and retailers. At the receiving end, the systems for notifying the arrival of colliers would move upstream from Gravesend to Tilbury, and the mechanisms for passing this information back to the 'market' would evolve in line with developments in communications through sail, steam, and human intervention, to the telegraph and then finally to the telephone. As the size of operations increased, so did the need for larger units of operation become apparent, and mergers of various interlocking functions – wholesaling, retailing, factoring and metering – grew apace.

This text cannot do justice to these manifold developments. The background picture is only relevant insofar as it will illustrate the evolution of the 'Fueller' concept. (Some attempt to amplify this account is however made in Appendix III(B): Meters, Factors and the Market, supported for additional detail by the Glossary.)

ii Evolution of the Coal Trade

The catalyst for coal's domestic survival into the 20th century was Britain's rapidly expanding fuel merchant trade. The history of The Fuellers' Livery is indissolubly linked with the trade's collective body, the Society of Coal Merchants, and, by later extension, with the relationship between the coal trade and the National Coal Board – 'NCB' – (and subsequently the privatised British Coal). It is perhaps not surprising that nothing was attempted in the period between the wars to reinstate the ancient fuel trade Livery; the harsh but telling descriptions that have been officially applied to the industry during this time have been 'stagnation' and 'inflexibility'. Nevertheless, between the two wars, the trade engaged in many entrepreneurial activities, some of which have been highlighted in the recently-unearthed Minute Books of the period.[8]

Exigencies in both wars enforced realignments and new thinking across Europe, although Britain did not have to retreat as far into history as the French, who under occupation turned back to wood-and-coke burning *gazogène* vehicles to replace petrol. From midway during the 20th century, the position of the UK trade in its turn can only be understood in terms of the increasing politicisation of the coal industry from what has been called its 'apotheosis' at the outbreak of the First World War.[9] With nationalisation in 1947, while the production side moved into monolithic public ownership, domestic marketing remained in a myriad private hands. Whilst each side needed the other commercially, tensions in that split were inevitable.

The Fuellers' History has no call to detail this vast topic, but significant echoes in the evolution of the merchanting interests need to be identified.

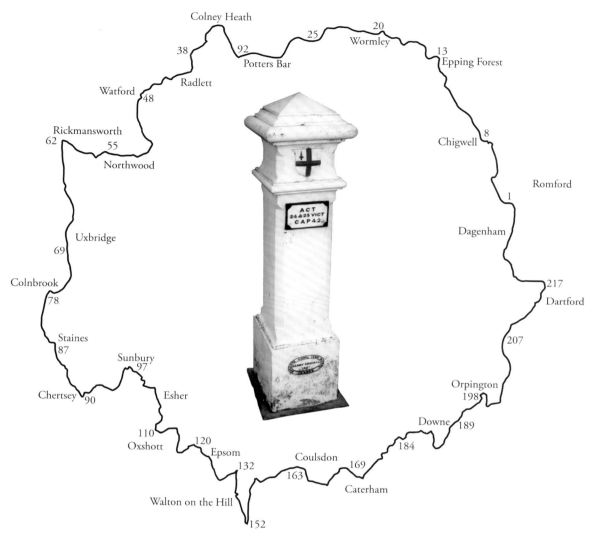

Colney Heath

38   92

25   20   Wormley

Potters Bar   13
Epping Forest

Watford   Radlett
48

Rickmansworth   8
62   Chigwell
55
Northwood   Romford

1
Dagenham

Uxbridge
69

Colnbrook   217
78   Dartford

Staines   207
87
Sunbury
97   Orpington
Chertsey   Esher   198
90
Downe   189
110   120   184
Oxshott   Epsom
132   Coulsdon   169
163   Caterham

Walton on the Hill
152

58   TAXING COAL IMPORTS TO LONDON: THE COAL POSTS
Typical coal post at Oxhey Lane, Pinner, on the boundary between Hertfordshire and London; it was stolen but recovered. It carries the City Corporation's arms, and the legislative legend, 'Act 24 & 25 Vict, Cap 42'. This sketch shows post locations around London: there were originally 270/280 boundary marks: 210 now survive, from the 219 recorded in 1972.

In parallel with an ongoing spirit of co-operation was an element of suspicion on the part of the smaller private sector towards the massive public sector. Huge organisational changes were needed by the fuel trade to cope in these post-war years.[10]

Given its role as the cradle for The Fuellers' Livery, this is the natural moment to bring up to date the four centuries of collective activity embodied in that system, the coal and solid fuel trade's central body, the Coal Merchants.

THE "FULHAM"

59 REVOLUTION IN COAL TRANSPORT: FROM WIND TO STEAM

By the mid-19th century, steam was replacing the wind-power of the collier brig, encapsulated here in the 'brig in a bottle' presented to PM Richard Horne c.1975, on the occasion of his appointment to the Coal Factors Society and Coal Meters' Committee (below). The growing ascendancy of steam is represented by the 'flat-iron' collier, the Fulham (above).

The evolution of that trade to its 21st-century format has been shown to be tortuous, with terms bearing different meanings over time, or even simultaneously. Two Tables offer partial explanations, Fig. 1 and Fig. 52. One aspect of this problem was that 'Coal Merchants' in the 17th century could be (i) both wholesalers and retailers, and indeed, later during the 18th and 19th centuries (ii) highly capitalised wholesalers, owning colliers (for example the firm of Stephenson Clarke); in this sense they also evolved as 'Coal Factors'.[11] A brief retrospect is now necessary.

A Society of Coal Merchants ('The Governor and Corporation of Coal Merchants') first saw the light of day, primarily as a political stratagem, for two short years, through an Order of the Privy Council of 2 May 1638. Its monopolistic existence was the price the Council had to pay a group of London coal dealers and East Anglian shipowners headed by Thomas Horth, a wealthy Yarmouth merchant, in order to squeeze out another existing monopoly, the Newcastle 'combination' of Hostmen. The contract with Charles I of 1637 had to be cancelled only one year later. Earlier, in 1622, the Woodmongers had already joined with ship-owners, declaring that a great abuse existed at Newcastle 'in the mingling of good and badd coales together'.[12]

A sense of common cause also arises in the records on 2 July 1638; through his brother, Pepys confirms that 'Woodmongers, Carmen and others' joined in tripartite deliberations, as equally-interested parties, over the period 1638 to 1640.[13]

This short-lived Company also clearly protected the interests uniquely vulnerable to war and weather risk of the emerging coastal trade in coal; the implication must be that the historic Woodmongers' Livery, who as wholesalers dealt daily with these shipowning business partners, did not sufficiently focus on this aspect of their overall fuel trade.

The end was quick. In January 1640, a House of Lords enquiry into one major effect of this new cartel – the 'excessive price of coal' – led the Lord Mayor and his City officers to recommend that 'a freedom of trade may be established which hath of late been interrupted by the new Corporation of Coal Merchants': the Coal Merchants appear to have died out in this corporate manifestation a few months later, nor did they seem to feel any need to form their own separate Livery either before or after the 'Surrender of Letters Patent' in 1667; many of their members must also have been Woodmongers, *faute de mieux*.[14]

From the 17th century onwards, contemporary commentaries refer increasingly to the need for competitive multiplicity in all forms of trade; umbrella terms like 'Dealers in Fuel' are used, implying many forms of participation.[15] By 1756 Maitland writes of 'Coalmen' and 'Woodmongers' meeting together at Billingsgate, to do business with

60 PEACEFUL CO-EXISTENCE
(Top) the coal-heaver and the carman (carter) portrayed at last as working co-operatively: print from 1850. (Right) coal porters at work.

the collier-owners' representatives.[16] By the early 19th century, 1831, this broad-based merchanting trade split further into what seemed to be its constituent parts – a wholesaling 'Society of Coal Factors' (subsuming the earlier 'Fitters'), and a 'Society of Owners of Coal Craft'.[17] They had come together to reform and revitalise the Coal Meters' function. By 1836, the Society of Coal Craft Owners was changing its name to 'The Society of Coal Merchants', to concentrate on the real purpose of their trade.[18]

The story of the ensuing two centuries bears witness to coal's initial supremacy as the country's economic backbone. As a result of both environmental trends and earlier union policies, the circle would be rounded in 2008: UK coal production at 15 million tonnes, from a mere five deep pits, would finally fall below the pre-industrial level of 200 years before, with two-thirds of UK consumption now coming from overseas.[19]

Coal as Icon

Inevitably, with the shifting of The Fuellers' focus to embrace all forms of energy, its nature starts to broaden out from the former sense of coal as a very domestic, human subject, to fuel utilisation in general: from the heart to the mind.

Before following that shift in focus, it is relevant to touch on the influence of coal and its industry on British culture, in its widest sense: 'Coal as Icon'. Coal became part of national life: merchants' names like Charringtons, and Rickett Cockerell, became household words, and the coalman, and his coal-holes in the pavement ('opercula') a feature of every street-scene.[20] Equally symbolic of the ubiquity of coal for the City were the Coal Posts (p.117) located around London's periphery.[21]

The miner himself must be at the centre of the picture, as hero of fiction and film, from Zola's *Germinal*, and D.H. Lawrence's *Coal Dust*, to such epics of the screen as *How Green Was My Valley*. Mining has also generated its own culture, through autobiographies such as *When the Dust has Settled*.[22] That elemental confrontation with raw nature also inspired many artists such as Henry Moore, Ron Gribbons, or Josef Herman in his NCB-commissioned drawings of the 1960s.[23] The pithead and slagheap scene had also long been an iconic feature of the British countryside, offering, through disasters such as Aberfan, a ready, sometimes deserved, target for the attention of environmentalists. Whatever the future of coal and

61   The Iconic Miner
An award-winning tribute to an icon: photograph of an 18-inch seam by PM 'Mac' McCombe.

62 Technology replaces Muscle
Cory's 'Atlas' rig for the hydraulic offloading of coal midstream from collier to moored barge, Thames, 1862.

its trade and industry, with the new Kingsnorth power station ratified in 2008 as a portent of a new governmental approach to fuel consumption, all these symbols will become yet another set of markers in The Fuellers' long history.

Re-forming a Company

Moving ahead to the late 20th century, information that only came to light in 2008 through the diaries of Thérèse Clarke suggests that at least two senior figures in the coal trade – her husband Charles, and Jack Charrington, 'the boys', as she called them – began talking about the possibility of recovering the 1667 Charter as early as 1970. It still remains of interest why the coal trade took 400 years to re-address its energies, and its wealth, to this public task. Informal interactions with Sir Derek and Lady Ezra in 1973 and August 1975 could well have provided further opportunities for what may be distinguished as 'the gang of six' to discuss the topic, with the added weight of the NCB behind it. Other industry figures, such as Past Master Bill Pybus, may well also have been involved in the 'loop' early on. Significantly, later that same year, at the Society of Coal Merchants' meeting, on 7 October, the topic was raised informally: the seeds were being sown.[24]

The next point of importance was at the 23rd meeting, on 8 July 1976, when the Secretary, Arthur Puttock, reported that on 21 May the Companies Registration Officer had refused to accept the proposed name for the Society, on the grounds that it implied that its Coal Merchant members served the whole country; perhaps some alternative such as 'South of England Coal Merchants Ltd' might be considered?

Not so! – at a Committee Meeting that autumn, on 11 November, it was recorded that on 29 October Windsor Herald of the College of Arms had advised that a new formula, 'Society of Coal Merchants of London Ltd' would be the answer: it was historically accurate, and they could still be known colloquially as 'The Society of Coal Merchants' (SCM). By 16 September 1977, the first of two professional advisors, Jordan & Sons, Bristol, were brought in to draft new Articles. A milestone was reached on 8 May 1978 when the new Company, 'The Society of Coal Merchants of London Ltd' celebrated its formation (373 years after the Grant of a Charter to the Woodmongers' under James I, in 1605). On 10 May, it was agreed that a 'Memorial' should be presented to the next in the required sequence of historic dignitaries, the Earl Marshal, for approval of the Grant, and of the proposed Arms and Crest designed by Windsor Herald. Some discussion would later take place as to the appropriateness of the joint depiction of a dragon ('representing all that is evil', according to one commentator) and its sworn enemy, a panther, but these concerns would be negated by the prevailing heraldic view that the dragon was traditionally seen by 'the upper classes' as a sign of pride! These heraldic matters will be pursued below.

From a Fuellers' vantage point, it was the Society's meeting of 8 December 1978 which marked the shift in focus from the SCM itself to the future Fuellers, for it was now, arising from a letter of congratulations on the new status received from the already interested NCB Chairman, that one of the earliest references appeared in the Minutes as to the possibility of the evolution of a Livery Company for the coal trade: a baton passed.

iii: A Livery Reborn: The Background

It is opportune to explain the steps preceding the birth of any City Livery Company, let alone the rebirth of one long defunct. The sequence of events behind the second, re-petitioned 20th-century 'origins' of the Fuellers' Company, although covering 23 years in all, 1970-93, must accordingly demand pride of place in this concluding chapter. This account is an amalgam of the Minutes of the four bodies concerned, under the lead of the Society of Coal Merchants (SCM); the Coal Meters' Office (CMO); the Coal Factors Society (CFS); and the newly constituted Fuellers themselves. Detailed recall of those early days has proved hard to come by. SCM members have emphasised the early and continuous part played by Arthur Puttock, the first Clerk, and his colleagues; ex-NCB sources point out the energising role played by Sir Derek, later Lord, Ezra.

63   The Coal Exchange in its Prime: at Work – but in a Panic

Merchants, factors and coal-owners' agents gather to do normal business in 1892, in the Coal Exchange's final format as a single market location. Suddenly, panic set in, disturbing the accustomed calm, on the news that 400,000 'colliers' (miners) were taking a 'fortnight's holiday' in order to keep up the price of coal. In the 'general rush to [buy from] the coal merchants, coal went up 38s. per ton', causing press criticism of the 'middleman's bloated profits'.

The story has benefited from discussions with a few participants of the early days: Lord Ezra, Thérèse Clarke, Colin Brinkman, Roger Cloke and Mary Chandler.

As far back as 1921, Hylton Dale had bewailed the fact that there was no City Company to represent fuel interests: 'It seems a pity the London Coal Trade does not think sufficient of itself to petition the Lord Mayor and Court of Aldermen to revive the Old Company, whose direct successors they are.'[25] Whether the basic idea of a City Company automatically also implied to his readers the ultimate ambition of status as a Company with Livery can only be conjectural; historically, as the previous chapters have shown, it did not always follow. Thoughts about a possible Livery Company for the London solid fuel community had been around in some form before the Society set up its Committee. A Minute of the Fuellers' first meeting in the *Goring Hotel* Drawing

Room, to celebrate the formation of the new Company, of 17 February 1981, referred to the birth of the project in that same room 'eight years ago', i.e. 1973!

The concept of the former vehicle, a 'Company', certainly resurfaced through the voice of Arthur Puttock, SCM Secretary and later the Fuellers' first Clerk. His successor in the SCM, Peter Stafford, noted: 'it was the Society who, in 1974, took the first positive steps by agreeing to initiate proceedings to reinstate the regrant of the Charter surrendered in 1667 ... in order to do this the Society became a Company, The Society of Coal Merchants (London) Ltd' (here embraced as the 'SCM'). The Livery concept first appeared in the SCM Minutes in 1976.[26]

Motivation must here be distinguished from effect. One of the Company's progenitors, Lord Ezra, explained to the author and to former Fueller, John Josling, at a meeting on 3 November 2006, that the broad idea in the minds of coal trade leaders had been to develop the community of the UK solid fuel trade at a time when it was still riding as high, in commercial terms, as in morale. It is possible that Sir Derek Ezra periodically re-convened Charles Clarke, Jack Charrington, and their wives to exchange notes on progress. When Sir Derek wrote to George McGechan on 25 April 1979, after having presented the SCM Chairman's first chain of office, he added: 'I hope we may have a chat before long about the Livery Company aspect.'[27] The idea was boosted when the NCB Chairman invited Lord Mayor Sir Peter Gadsden, with NCB Finance Director and future Fueller Master, Brian Harrison, to the customary lunch at Hobart House, in his year of office 1979/80. Pursuing one of his traditional mayoral duties – promotion of the City livery idea – the Lord Mayor asked why there was no Livery Company for the UK 'coal industry'? Its eventual effect, at a subsequent time when the industry's fortunes had started to wane, was as a mechanism for binding the threatened national solid fuel community together in a way that existing structures were not positioned to do.

Like any other group of citizens seeking to be a Livery Company of the City of London, all concerned needed to become aware of the delicate conventions implicit in the process. They would require advice from experts in the formalities involved, and in the tax and financial intricacies, and the intermediation of a Sponsoring Alderman who could vouch for their credentials.

They would also need solicitors familiar with the legal niceties – and with the likely time factor. These inputs would come through Sir Colin Cole KCVO, Garter Principal King of Arms at the College of Arms; the Assistant Clerk to the Chartered Accountants; the Beadle to the Bakers; Christopher Mowll, Clerk to the Clothworkers, and John Finchett; former Lord Mayor and Clothworker, now Senior Alderman, with past links with coalmining, Sir Bernard Waley-Cohen; and through the law firm of Linklaters (& Paines);

64 BOYS AND GIRLS TO THE FORE

(Below) Evolution of a further link in the distribution chain – 'coal boys' of the 1890s taking coals direct from the King's Cross railhead to local domestic customers. The formation of smaller coal markets at the main London train termini steadily eroded the central role of the Coal Exchange, effectively a fifth step in the evolution of the London 'market'. The first women 'Fuellers', 1916 (left). To free men for the front, women took over many erstwhile male preserves, including London's coal deliveries, 1916.

also the Comptroller and City Solicitor, Stanley Heather. Moreover, many of the potential Members for the proposed Company would bring experience as Liverymen of other Companies, mostly the outcome of long-standing connections – for example the Horne family through the Clothworkers, or Lord Ezra's educational involvement with the Haberdashers.

A picture of a 10-stage qualification process gradually emerged. Basic was the obligation to convince the Lord Mayor's Office and the Court of Aldermen that the Society not only sincerely wished to deepen its existing presence within the City's life and traditions, but that its current members did indeed carry on the trade to be described in its proposed title. It was also vital to establish that it

65   NCB ERA DAWNS – AND THE THREAT OF COAL SCARCITY, 1947

This Illingworth cartoon highlights the austerity regime of Chancellor of the Exchequer, Stafford Cripps (a relative of three eminent Fuellers) and coal-merchanting Minister of Fuel & Power, Emanuel Shinwell; brick-laying Minister of Housing, Aneurin Bevan, looks on. Pithead poster announces confident new public ownership under the National Coal Board (above).

could raise the appropriate head of steam, in terms of membership, and not least of all financially: a target of some 150-200 was deemed desirable, to a maximum of some 300, and a perceived ability to pay an annual 'Fine' (*see* Glossary) in the region of £400-450.

For the SCM, the first step in pursuit of these fundamental criteria was to ensure the united involvement, from the outset, of anyone who for whatever reason might be thought of as a constituent faction within the solid fuel industry – the CMO and the CFS, as well as the NCB, the Coal Trade Benevolent Association (CTBA), and the Coal Industry Society (CIS). This would eventually be arrived at through the Society's setting up of a Joint (advisory) Committee composed in equal numbers of themselves, the CMO, and the CFS.

The evident interest of the NCB, manifested through Sir Derek Ezra as its Chairman, would soon unintentionally highlight the first two of three hurdles across the Committee's path. The suspicion surfaced that Aldermen – traditionally 'apolitical' – might have reservations about this form of involvement with a nationalised industry, at a time when nationalisation was still an economic *bête noire*, quite apart from the question as to whether such a corporation might be precluded anyway by its statutes from such activity. This would in no way reflect on Sir Derek himself, who, as Sir Bernard Waley Cohen would later confirm, 'was held in the highest regard by the City'. Secondly, if the Committee hoped to apply for a possible two-year 'fast-track' for its application to the Court of Aldermen as a 'special case', through its original supposed incarnation as 'Woodmongers and Coal Sellers', the narrower concept of 'selling' fuel would be paramount (the medieval connotation) as opposed to the broader theme which has set the boundaries for this History – its marketing and distribution.

The NCB had had a long-standing interest in the marketing of its products, and Sir Derek Ezra was particularly involved in this aspect. Nevertheless, an early casualty would prove to be the impossibility of realising his dream of a Livery explicitly open to the entire coal industry; these aspects of future membership would have to stand over for subsequent resolution.

The remaining nine stages necessitated, firstly, the creation of a basic Company, paving the way for a Petition granting it the status of a 'City' Company – at that stage 'without Livery'. There would also be the prerequisite of building up an initial list of potential members, together with the composition of the group of officials appropriate to a City Company, and of its Court of Assistants. These Members would automatically become Freemen of the Company itself. A Trust Fund would have to be formed, to cover the Company's anticipated charitable status. With the ultimate attainment of full Livery status and Letters Patent, seen as the desired goal from the word go, would come finally an application to the City Chamberlain for these Liverymen to become Freemen of the City of London.

There were also several informal factors at work that would not be immediately clear. A Company's candidature would only work if its creation did not impinge on the ground of any existing Livery Company. There was also another perception affecting the issue: a feeling among Aldermen that there might currently be too many Companies applying for Livery status. Further it was believed that someone 'on the inside' had advised that there was only one current 'vacancy': (this story was later doubted by a former Clerk of the Chamberlain's Court). The road ahead might well be fraught, if anything went wrong, leading either to a stultifying delay of several years, or – the worst-case scenario – eventual rejection by the Court of Aldermen. A subtle weighing-up by the worldly-wise Charles Stephenson Clarke of the various options that would present themselves would prove to be one of the factors that now ensured success for the Fuellers.

The Course of Events

The sequence of events had opened in 1974/5 when the SCM, in pursuit of enhanced status within the community, started on the path of securing the regranting of the Charter. At no stage did the circumstances of 1667 affect matters. At an historic moment in time, through the Companies Acts, 'The Society of Coal Merchants of London Ltd' became a Company limited by guarantee.

An SCM Committee meeting of 8 December 1978 debated how the new Coat of Arms could be used, if necessary in conjunction with the old Arms, and how Livery status might later eventuate. Arms and Crest were duly granted by the College of Arms on 29 December. At the new Company's first Committee Meeting on 31 January 1979, the possible problems of the new format were explored in relation to the Armorial bearings; if the Society were to become a Livery Company, the formulation 'Society of Coal Merchants of London Ltd' would surely become unnecessary?

It was the essence of the project that the Company's identity had to be the qualifying vehicle for any new Livery. Some realistic if short-term concerns surfaced as to the chances of the Society losing its 'identity and prestige' if a Livery Company came into being. This cautious train of thought emerged again at the Company's Committee Meeting on 21 March 1979: would the Society of Coal Merchants (London) be 'overpowered' in this event by the NCB?

On 24 April 1979, Garter Principal King of Arms presented Letters Patent of the new Arms and Crest, and Sir Derek Ezra made a personal presentation of a new Chairman's Badge and Chain. On 22 May 1979, the Company convened a vital meeting with the CMO at the *Bonnington Hotel*, to confer as to how best to achieve the next stage of evolution – Livery Status; its deliberations form the opening to the future Livery Company's Minute Book. Presiding over this historic meeting was the SCM's Chairman, Joseph C. Brannigan, supported by nine other leading members: John Pugh, Colin Brinkman, Frederick E. Carr, William V.T. Ferraro, George McGechan, Stewart J.G. Hutchinson, C. James Sears, Leslie A.H. Tasker and Martyn Wakefield. The putative Chairman of the Joint Committee to be set up, Charles Stephenson Clarke, could not attend. The CMO was represented by Douglas Cory-Wright, Peter Brewis, Lester Horne, George B. Pugh, Hugh Lloyd Davies and Errington Brewis. In attendance were Mrs Mary Chandler, then Chief Clerk to the CMO; the driving force for the project, Arthur Puttock, Secretary to the SCM; and again Colin Cole, to advise the new Company on procedure.

He stressed that Livery Companies were 'of great religious significance', with a relationship to 'the church of their own particular parish'. Although, as the History has shown, the 1605 Charter referred only to 'Woodmongers', the proposed title was 'The Company of Woodmongers and Coal Sellers': the Company would need to establish its claim to such an ambitious title.

At the Joint Committee's meeting on 25 June, the CFS was drawn into the frame. Meanwhile with the SCM, on 20 August, Sir Derek Ezra's alternative – and as it transpired, prophetic – suggestion for a title was tabled: 'The Company of Coal Fuellers'. For the SCM, pragmatism was still the watchword: given that the prerogative for the title lay with them, it was believed that the trade favoured what it thought to be the 'old connection' – 'The Company of Woodmongers and Coal Sellers'.

Furthermore, would the CIS and the CTBA be part of any new Livery? If an application for a Livery were to be turned down, would there be any second chance, since it might well then be difficult to find an existing Livery Company to support their application? If Letters Patent were granted, could they carry the cost of the formal Banquet on the occasion of the Lord Mayor's presentation? As a next stage in their discussions, the Committee meeting of 19 September noted that the CTBA could not act as a basis for the Livery's necessary charitable status.

At meetings in November and December, the parties learned from Linklaters' Alan Ground, Comptroller and City Solicitor Stanley Heather, and Chief Commoner G.M. Stitcher, that there was much enthusiasm in City circles for their aspirations, and that Mr Stanley Cohen, who had previously been involved with the Society in the Campaign for Clean Air, would offer his support. The question now arose as to whether any other Livery might conceivably claim any ancient right to the title 'Woodmongers'.

Much activity in the new year 1980 preceded and followed a meeting on 3 June, at which Linklaters tabled a letter from the Comptroller and City Solicitor signalling the green light for the formal presentation of a Petition for the Society's recognition in its new *persona* as a 'City Company without Livery'. In the same vein, on what would prove to be the tricky subject of the title, the Committee's Secretary noted, a little optimistically, that 'he did not anticipate any objection by the Carmen as he had already been in touch with them verbally'. He would also consult with the Joiners & Ceilers, the Carpenters, the Furniture Makers, the Plaisterers, and the Watermen & Lightermen, who raised no objections.

By the start of the next new year, 1981, with 62 letters of intent and 40 replies awaited, all seemed set fair. On 5 January, four representatives were mandated 'to proceed with the formation of a City Company, and the setting up of a Trust Fund'. Ratifying meetings of the CMO and the CFS were held.

Accordingly, it was announced that the 'Company of Woodmongers and Coal Sellers' was now formed, the title felt by the CMO, and a number of individuals, to be a basic essential. By 10 April, the first phase for the City Company would appear over: with 75 names already behind any Petition, its elected officers were named. The first and founder Master – Charles Stephenson Clarke; first Senior Warden – Martyn Wakefield; first Junior Warden – Peter Errington Brewis; first Clerk – Arthur Puttock, and Assistant Clerk – Mary Chandler.

As to advocacy to the City, the original meeting on 22 May 1979 had taken the view that this might be well secured by contacts with the Clothworkers. Despite those valuable links, the Committee decided to ask again for the help of Sir Derek Ezra, as the person best placed to approach his friend the Lord Mayor, Sir Peter Gadsden. The purpose had been to sound out his informal reaction to the idea of such a new City Company, incorporating the name 'Woodmongers'. The Lord Mayor's office, with its necessarily special overview of wider Livery interests and backgrounds, had in fact predicted that there might be one Livery, the Company of Carmen, who would object. Their reasoning was surmised to lie in the events of four centuries earlier (as already recounted in Chapters II and III) when the Company of Woodmongers had had to yield its Grant of Arms and Charter back to the Crown. Sir Derek Ezra now advised the coal trade leaders to think again, with as much dexterity as they could muster. Although, as this History has established, the re-born Woodmongers' tradition preceded any formal assumption of trade rights by the Carmen, nevertheless in the eyes of City pundits it could be argued that an existing Company's 'ground' might be 'infringed': precedent, however interpreted, was all.

Charles Stephenson Clarke had reported that at a meeting on 16 December the Carmen's Master was after all objecting to the Company's proposed use of the title 'Woodmongers': the third 'hurdle' had appeared. Sir Bernard Waley-Cohen advised the new Company to 'stand firm', as Garter Principal King of Arms had intimated 'full recognition' in April 1979. Although they could see the dangers of questions being raised in the City, the Secretary duly wrote to the Master of the Carmen. However, a subsequent meeting between Charles Stephenson Clarke and the Carmen's Master, Lt Col Geoffrey Clarkson, on 16 May 1981 made it clear that the Carmen would indeed cross-petition to challenge use of the title 'Woodmongers' ('part of their history') unless Sir Derek Ezra's idea for a 'Company of Fuellers' was substituted.

The third (and last) meeting of 'The Woodmongers and Coalsellers' on 11 June ratified the decision. This solution asserted their right to that alternative title, equally valid historically – as the History has already shown – but happily more wide-ranging. The Carmen's History records the satisfactory compromise:

Then in 1980 came the ghosts of conflicts past. The Woodmongers returned. The Society of Coal Merchants had decided to ask the Aldermen for a Livery as the Worshipful Company of Woodmongers and Coal Sellers. The Court erupted. To put it mildly, Assistants were not amused. The Company regarded itself as rightful successors and, given the conflicts of the past, was 'not happy with the title of Woodmonger', let alone its use by anyone else … Master Geoffrey Clarkson told the Coal Merchants the Court thought it 'most unfortunate and undesirable for two Livery Companies to lay claim in succession of the old Woodmongers Company and we reserve our rights'.

What started ominously quickly ended. 'The Company extended the hand of friendship to the coalmen [sic], and helped them progress – as the Worshipful Company of Fuellers. The last spark from the embers of the past flickered, and died.'[28] All unknowingly, The Carmen had in fact done The Fuellers a great service: the new title would soon position them to take a more holistic, comprehensive view of what would turn out to be a unique role within the whole field of global energy. The prospect of this wider vista did not, however, stop two members of the Livery resigning in protest.

66 FROM COMPETITORS TO FELLOW-FUELLERS: GAS
Coke, as a gas by-product, is promoted in the post-war period for domestic heating under the popular branded 'Mr Therm', leading later to the coal industry's solid fuel central heating campaigns. Today, from being seen as a commercial rival, the gas industry is now an equal partner in The Fuellers' 'total energy' Livery.

A great Grate for saving fuel

See this cheerful, glowing fuel-and-labour-saving open fire at your gas showroom. Gas ignited—it needs no laying. You can *control* the heat; with 'all-night' attachment the fire keeps in till morning; you come down to a warm room! Burns any solid fuel and is excellent on coke, which is smokeless. Several handsome models to choose from. Prices from £4 . 1s . 6d. Your gas showroom offers expert advice on installation.

GAS IGNITED

All Fuel ECONOMY GRATE

Burns coke or any other solid fuel

SOUTH EASTERN GAS

Arrangements could now be put in hand for the usual Celebratory Luncheon in the Egyptian Hall at the Mansion House, on 29 March 1982. This would symbolise a nice rounding-off of the renewed interaction with the Carmen, for Sir Christopher Leaver, the new Lord Mayor, was also a Carman, and had indicated that he would be glad to propose a toast to the new Company.

Over a protracted period, starting with a meeting of the Court of Assistants of The Fuellers on 17 May 1982, matters ceremonial were resolved. In a letter of 18 February, Colin Cole had presented the College of Arms' designs for the Armorial Bearings and Supporters for The Fuellers' coat of arms. These were approved save only that 'the finials of the crown from which a dragon emerges should be red (Gules) instead of black (Sable), and that the Coal Factors' ship held by the dragon should be a two-master'. There was discussion about the Company's motto to be placed under the crest. In addition to the SCM's *vis unita fortior* and the CFS' *per mare per industrium*, some other suggestions were: (i) United Strength by Sea and by Industry; (ii) Coal, the Fuel of the Future; (iii) United we Stand; and (iv) Our Strength is in Coal (or Fuel). At a later meeting the College's translation of *in carbone robur nostrum* (Our Strength is in Coal) was agreed; the appropriately symbolic dual meaning of *robur* as 'the oak, appeared not to have been mentioned. A nicely witty proposal from Colin Cole – *firmiter coalescimus* (We Grow Firmly Together) was also tabled.

On 28 October 1983, a first Master's Badge was presented by Mr C.E. Needham, the Chairman of Coalite Ltd. At meetings in July that year and finally on 26 January 1984 the College's designs for formal gowns for the Master, Wardens and the Clerk would also be agreed, and placed with Thresher & Glenny for execution.

On 29 June 1982, the new Master, Wardens and Court of Assistants petitioned the Lord Mayor and the Court of Aldermen for recognition as a City Company without Livery. On 13 October, the City and Aldermen agreed that the Company Ordinances should be enrolled in the City of London records. A letter from the City offices of 21 October recognised 'The Company of Fuellers' as a 'City Company'. By the meeting of 26 November 1982, membership had reached 100 – with the election of Lord Ezra. By 20 October 1983, the formal Ordinances and Objects had been documented.

By May 1984, the new Company had been granted Livery status. At The Fuellers' Court meeting on 28 June, it was promulgated that on 17 October the new Livery Company's Letters Patent would be presented at a luncheon at the Mansion House by the Lord Mayor and the Court of Aldermen: in the customary language they would be 'well liked', as 'part of the life and history of the City'. In parallel, the Fuellers' Charitable Trust would be registered with the Charity Commissioners on 8 November.

Following the 19 November Court Meeting, a celebratory luncheon was held at Fishmongers' Hall. Attending this event was the Company's new Chaplain, the Rev. Basil Watson. Presentations were then made: by Charles Needham – the Master's Badge; by the Founder Master, Charles Stephenson Clarke –

the Senior Warden's and Junior Warden's Badges; by Mrs Thérèse Stephenson Clarke – the Master's Lady's Badge; and by Peter Brewis – a Mace and Staff.

Thanks to good steerage, and powerful advocacy within the City, the formal steps had only taken an impressive four years. As the concluding reference in the Minutes of the extant Society of Coal Merchants would rightly record, given that such a process might well last the emerging norm of 'four years plus four', or even the earlier traditional apprenticeship of 'seven plus seven' years, 'The Company of Fuellers was now well under way – a major achievement in such a short space of time'.

The final post-hoc rationalisation of the Livery was for it to petition that it should widen its Ordinances beyond 'coal', and indeed the implicit distribution of all fuels, and thus appeal to those associated with every aspect of the energy market. There were precedents for such extensions and it was later agreed by the City authorities on 16 March 1993, twenty years after the first 'gleam' in anyone's eye. As NCB Director of Staff and Fueller Master, Dr Paul Glover expressed it, no doubt with unconscious irony, in *The Fueller*, in the opening Autumn issue of that same year: 'What foresight our forebears had in their selection of the title 'The Fuellers' instead of the more restrictive, if earlier, "Woodmongers and Coal Sellers". The Worshipful Company of Fuellers now has entrée to all the energy industries of the nation …'. At the third in an unprecedented series of joint Livery occasions – the Carmen's and Fuellers' 'Woodmongers' Suppers', on 11 November 2008 – a witty version of an 'Oklahoma' song would be sung, summing up today's relationship between the two Companies who had once been bitter rivals: 'The Fueller and the Carman should stay friends!'[29]

iv: Heraldry, Ceremony and Authority

That luncheon on 19 November 1984, celebrating The Fuellers' recognition as the 95th Livery Company, was held with fitting symbolism in the Hall of the Company whose dock the Woodmongers had anciently shared – the Fishmongers. Its menu recorded an even nicer symbolism – a critique of the blazon of the Livery's Armorial Bearings, embodying all the vital corporate elements:

The Shield: The shield of arms resembles that of the Coal Merchants' Society but has added to it the Sable Lozenges, or black diamonds, which are a feature of the Armorial Bearings of the Society of Coal Factors.

The Crest: The Society of Coal Factors is also commemorated heraldically in the Crest, where the wings of the Dragon have been charged with the Arms of the Coal Factors. The Dragon has been chosen as the Crest Creature that is suitable because the Society of Coal Merchants in its crest was granted a Dragon, so that the said Dragon holding up the Collier Brig, also deriving from the Armorial Bearings of the Coal Factors, can be said to stand for the way in which the two Societies have united to form the Company of Fuellers.

The Dragon emerges from a 'Crown rayonny', that is to say, a Crown or Coronet the finials of which are in the form of rays, this type of Crown thereby suggesting heat and energy. The Crown is tinctured Gules, red, as it is in the Arms of the Society of Coal Merchants and it can also be interpreted as standing for the Coal Meters' Committee which has joined with the other Societies in the founding of the Fuellers and which, not having any arms of its own, would not be otherwise represented heraldically.

The Supporters: The Supporters are heraldic Monsters, and certainly can be said to have a carboniferous quality in that they are depicted Sable, black, the colour of coal, and are in other respects suitable emblematically to represent Fuellers.

The Dexter Supporter is a 'Caretyne', an heraldic Monster, the very name of which, 'Care Tyne', pronounced in this way suggests that the Tyne or the area of the Tyne where coal is produced should be safeguarded, which in a notional sense can be said to be one of the objectives of [a] Company such as the Fuellers, concerned as it is about one of the substances which is used as fuel. The Caretyne is always depicted in heraldry with flames coming from its ears and jaws, like the Panther in the Arms of the Fuellers, and thus like the latter by reason of this characteristic, can be regarded as typifying suitably the interest that the Fuellers have in the production of heat, energy and light.

The Sinister Supporter, a 'Cockatrice', has the wings of a Dragon and a Dragon's head at its tail end, and in heraldic mythology is linked with such a creature of the earth as the Dragon. Its name of 'Cockatrice' by its first syllable provides a play upon [the name of] another kind of fuel, Coke, so for this reason also it can be regarded as allusive [to] the Fuellers' objects, and as both Supporters are shown with their heads 'reguardant', that is to say, looking watchfully over their shoulders; they can be said to symbolise the care which it is the purpose of the Company of Fuellers to provide in the case of necessitous persons engaged in the Coal Trade. [The 'Sinister' Supporter (in fact shown 'right') was a risky choice: the evil Cockatrice was deemed heraldically to have been 'hatched on a dunghill from a cock's egg by a serpent'!].

Each Supporter is shown collared, and pendant from each collar there is a chain of three links. This has significance also, symbolising the union of the three groups who have come together in the formation of the Company of Fuellers, namely the Society of Coal Merchants, the Society of Coal Factors and the Coal Meters' Committee. This meticulous description of the new Company's Arms is eloquent of the care with which the Company's scope and objectives have been designed and defined. Subsequent events in 1993 and 1996 further refined those aims, providing the firm basis with which the Company exercises its contemporary authoritative role.

67 Heraldic Symbolism: Arms for the SCM – and The Fuellers

Royal grant of armorial bearings, 1979, to the 'Society of Coal Merchants of London Ltd', lineal successor to the Fellowship of Woodmongers (left). Full achievement of the coat (shield) of arms of The Fuellers (below), embracing the details of the Society's bearings – the panther and the inverted fasces – but blazoning the coal-diamonds, a collier-brig and the two supporters: in carbone robur nostrum (see text).

Ceremony

Furthering these heraldic symbols would come many silverware items representing the Livery's various functions. These are detailed in Appendix II(C), gifts by individual Masters or Liverymen, or subscribed by the Livery as a whole. They include candlesticks, a Master's goblet, and a new chain of office, with badges and brooches.[30]

From time to time, ostensibly social occasions performed important historical and symbolic functions. The Fuellers count among the 31 'Modern Companies' within the City, hence their attendance at the regular dinners for this class of Liveries; (see Appendix II(E)).[31] Similarly, a dinner inaugurated in September 2004 and officially designated as a Joint Fuellers' & Carmen's Ladies Court Supper was in fact also entitled 'The Woodmongers' Supper', intended to put to rest any lingering echo of the past dissension recorded in this History.[32]

IN CARBONE ROBUR NOSTRUM

68 VESTIGES OF THE OLD DAYS: TILBURY SIGNAL STATION

Through to the mid-20th century, signals were still being hoisted mechanically at the Collier Signal Station, at Tilbury, to alert the officials upstream as to incoming colliers (see Appendix III(B)).

Authority:

Energy policy Livery status may bring authority with it; The Fuellers have earned such authority in two fields. The first has lain, and continues to lie, in the field of energy policy. In an increasingly energy-conscious age, during the latter decades of the 20th century and into the first decade of the 21st, the Company has become, through the accumulated expertise of its members and its own gravitas, a source for advice with regard to the evolution of new strategies for the better use of fuels. The conclusion to this History, complemented by Appendix I(A), will record that the invitation to the Company to contribute to the Government's 2006 Energy Policy Review has been one of its most outstanding inputs to date.

Law Commission The second avenue for the Company's authority in the public domain is as a resource on solid fuel matters with regard to the repealing remit of the Law Commission. In this, the Company is consulted with another interested Company detailed in this History, the Watermen and Lightermen, as well as with HM Treasury and HM Revenue & Customs, the DTI, the City of London Corporation and Westminster City Council. At the time of going to press, this concerns the repeal of six Victorian Acts of Parliament, long in disuse. These are: the London Coal Trade Act, 1805; the City of London Coal Trade Act, 1824; the Port of London Coal and Wines Import Duties Act, 1840; the Port of London Coalwhippers Act, 1843; the Coal Duties (London and Westminster and adjacent Counties) Act, 1851 and the Coal Duties (London etc) Drawback Act, 1857. All this legislation was designed for an age when minute changes of public or commercial policy required formal Acts of Parliament, and a considerable passage of time, for their resolution; it sought to remedy a range of problems.[33]

The first Act provided indemnities to people working in the then new coal market who incurred penalties during the month of January 1805, the re-opening month of the Coal Exchange, as a result of a previous Act of 1803. This Act had imposed new obligations to record full details of contracts for the sale of coal; any sale agent failing to comply was liable to a fine of £100, and thus could face ruin if the law had been strictly enforced against them.

The Act of 1824 authorised the City of London to borrow money, on the security of the revenue from the coal duties received by the City pursuant to the same Act of 1803, all dating back to the coal dues levied to pay for the costs of the Great Fire.

Obscurely, the 1840 Act was to continue, from 5 July 1858, some duties on coal and wine: the duty on both had originally been imposed by an Act of 1694 – '(Orphans, London)' – but that on coal (at 6d. per chaldron) would have expired due to a later Act of 1829 ['10 Geo.4 c.cxxxv] ('London Bridge Approaches'). Regulation of a trade inoperative for more than a century was the subject of the 1843 Act – the Coalwhippers; it was only meant to run anyway until 1 January 1846.

The last two of these old Acts throw up the greatest interest for The Fuellers' History. The first amended earlier legislation about the sale and delivery of coal in the Cities of London and Westminster and surrounding areas, ensuring the quality of coal and the payment of duties thereon, whether brought into London by sea, canal, road or railway, within a radius of 20 miles from the GPO in St Martin's-le-Grand. The Law Commission's own wording bears recording:

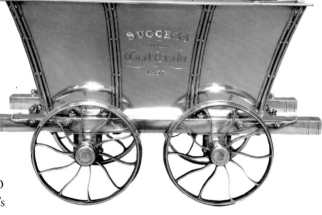

69 AN ASPECT OF STATUS: THE LIVERY'S SILVERWARE

Traditionally, a Company's silverware symbolised both its wealth, and its power over its Members. The 1813 coal chauldron cart, proclaiming 'Success to the Coal Trade', is one item from The Fuellers' collection, which is housed at the Tower of London, under the care of the Company's Beadle, Colin Smith MBE, BEM, who also has charge of its maintenance and presentability (see Appendix II).

The 1851 Act provided for this 20 mile distance to be marked by boundary stones or other permanent markings. (Approximately 200 remain situated around London. The posts are no longer in a neat ring, after the London Coal and Wine Duties Continuance Act 1861 reduced the size of the area within the boundaries). Any coal ... as it came into London attracted the duties although there was provision for remission of duty (known as 'drawback') in cases where the coal merely passed through London without being unladen. The enforcement ... was in the hands of the Clerk and Registrar of the City of London Coal Market. The purpose of the 1857 Act was 'to allow a Drawback on the Duties payable on Coals, Culm, Coke and Cinders'. Given the closure of the Coal Market and the abolition of the tax on coal brought in ... (by the London Coal Duties Aboliton Act 1889) both [were] redundant.'

v: The Active Fueller: 1979-2009

Beyond these public remits, the Fuellers' Court has addressed its energies to many good private causes during its first 25 years' existence. These have included benefactions through The Fuellers Charitable Trust Fund, and inputs to its affiliated Military Service links: these are illustrated in the Pictorial Review and identified in Appendix II(D).

So too have its 26 Masters, each directing attention to an especial cause or target. Particularly interesting among such causes was the possibility that arose during the Mastership of Michael Bryer Ash in 1994-5. As a past President of the CMF and National Chairman of the CTBA, his contacts were many and varied. Whilst he was Chairman of the CTBA he had as his President The Duke of Westminster, who was landlord of Hobart House. Michael realised that, with the ending of the lease, there might be a possibility of funding a new Hall for the Fuellers; intricate negotiations were taking place, the lease had a lengthy term to run, and he established that The Grosvenor Estate had to pay £20 million to recover their building.

Michael arranged a meeting with Neil Clarke, the then NCB Chairman, and with the founder Master, Charles Stephenson Clarke, to seek the Chairman's support for the idea of Michael now approaching the Duke, asking if £2 million could be paid to The Fuellers, and £18 million to the Department of Trade & Industry (DTI). Neil Clarke gave his support, and Michael achieved the Duke's consent, but when Michael reported back to Neil Clarke that he had agreement to his proposal, Neil said that the Department were insisting that all the £20 million went to them.

Michael's letter to Gerald Grosvenor of 20 December 1995 adds an extra dimension: 'It is tremendously important to preserve some of the history … of this once great Industry … There is an answer, covering the general situation at Hobart House, and the valuable lease …'. On 20 January 1995, Michael had to write again to the Duke: 'Neil Clarke … explained that his power is much reduced, with the smaller size of the Industry, and the Privatisation moves – these facts together with the heavy involvement of the DTI in the negotiations with Grosvenor Estates have resulted in no flexibility. It is very sad …'. In the event, the opportunity passed by; the one chance for the creation of a new Hall was lost. It would have been a wonderful way of making good the ravages of the Great Fire of three and a half centuries earlier.[34]

Charitable Objectives

Charitable objectives have been at the heart of each of the 26 Masters' years to date. These have tended to fall into five broad categories: (i) The Fuellers' own special causes, principally their four affiliated military service links, including such extensions as the 'Flying Angel' launch. During Vaughan Williams' Mastership, these links extended to embrace the RAF: a possible link with the Grenadier Guards was mooted, celebrating the 'Tow-Row-Row' story, but it did not materialise; (ii) general contributions subsumed under Lord Mayors' Appeals, such as the Lord Mayor's Treloar School and College, and SSAFA; (iii) ventures in association with other Liveries such as the annual 'City Dips'; the regular bailed 'imprisonments' in the Tower for causes such as the Red Cross; more recently for the 'Swimathons', and the traditional, historic sheep-driving event in the company of 450 other Freemen across London Bridge in 2001 and 2008; (iv) a general heading as beneficiaries of The Fuellers Charitable Trust Fund; (v) Masters' one-off personal events such as Past Master Vaughan Williams' inclusion in the Lord Mayor's London Marathon unit in 2000, and Brian Harrison's abseiling, tandem skydive and cabaret act in 2001. Over the first 25 years of their existence, The Fuellers have contributed their full share of the £140 million given by Livery Companies to such good causes. They have been both for individuals and for corporate bodies, well-known as well as relatively unknown.[35]

Most notable among such activity has been the award of The Fuellers' Prizes to service men and women in their fuel-linked military units. Recipients have covered members of the RN engineering training establishment HMS *Daedalus*, now HMS *Sultan*, at Gosport; 216 Squadron ('The Re-Fuellers' – InFlight Refuelling) at RAF Brize Norton; the Defence Fuels Group at Wimborne, Dorset, and the RFA fast fleet tankers *Wave Knight* and *Wave Ruler*.[36]

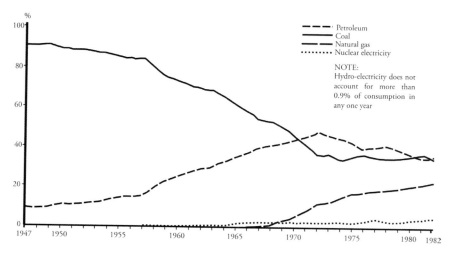

70 ENERGY: THE FUELLERS' OVERVIEW

The chart underlines the dramatic relative changes in British energy consumption over the post-war period, 1947 to 1982. The Fuellers now pursue an overview of all fuels, in their membership as in their public stance.

Two additions to this range of benefactions were the introduction in 2002 of the Fuellers Freemen Apprentice scheme and its first award to Apprentice Miss Ronnie Carey. This was followed in 2005 with the institution of the Charles Stephenson Clarke Memorial Prize for students at The City University.[37]

Among the targets for the general Trust Fund have been the Chicken Shed Theatre Company; the New Horizon Youth Trust; the City of London Sea Cadets; the London Taxidrivers' Fund for Underprivileged Children; the now adopted City Church, St Michael Cornhill; and the 2004 Paralympic Team. Individuals who have been assisted in their studies have included Hannah Thomas and Elinor Moran. An important departure into education has been the adoption of Stockwell Park High School and the signing of an 'MOU' (Memorandum of Understanding).[38]

Energy and Industry

This Livery's History can at least record that one of its prime policies has been to run a continuous programme of educational events to a wide variety of locations bearing on the debate about energy. These have included Nuclear Electric's A & B plants at Sizewell, the *Electricité de France* site at Gravelines, and the underground pumped station at Dinorwig in Snowdonia, organised by Fueller Paul Mott.

Also embraced have been exhibitions with strong Fueller associations such as those at London Docklands; Duxford, Cambridge; the Black Country Museum; 'HMS *Warrior*' at Portsmouth; the 'Bevin Boy' exhibits at the Imperial War Museum; and the 'Milestone' exhibition at Basingstoke. Industrial sites visited ranged from 'Europe's Detroit'; Ford's Dagenham complex; the Transco Terminal at Bacton; Past Master David Port's ATH Resources open-cast mine at Garleffan, Ayrshire; to Texaco's oil refinery at Milford Haven; and Thames Steel at Sheerness.

There were also visits to places of general Livery interest: Past Master Edward Wilkinson's Army Benevolent Fund event at the Royal Military Tattoo on Horse Guards Parade; trips on the Thames on the only operational coal-fired paddle steamer, the 'Kingswear Castle', and on the Severn; and excursions to sites as diverse as London's Globe Theatre, the London Eye and Smithfield Market; and Master 'Mac' McCombe's visit to various historic mills in future Master David Bell's 'territory' in the Midlands.

The Fueller has also recorded tributes to the services of many Fuellers and Livery officials, not least to its 'pen' of Clerks – Arthur Puttock, Wg Cdr Henry Squire, Simon Lee, Ralph Riley and Sir Antony Reardon Smith; and Assistant Clerk Fran Algar. Honours have included the names of Colin Brinkman and Roger Cloke as Honorary Court Assistants, and David Bell and Chris Lefevre as Almoners. The pageant of the years demonstrates a Livery Company appreciative, active, informed and outwardly turned.

vi: Fact, Fiction and Faction

It is worth recording in conclusion that one remit for this History was to establish the truth about The Fuellers' story.

What has emerged from the research process has proved to be a compound of confirmed truths, some myths, and a few fictions that charitably ought to have been true – 'factions' – despite lack of evidence to support them.

The two accounts rendered by Dale from his background as a Charrington 'insider' have proved to be broadly right, even if necessarily short on data that he could not have known about. Earlier evidence about the trade has now placed the record some three centuries earlier, just as new sources position the last woodmonger a century later than originally thought. On the down side, notwithstanding the admiration that is due for Dale's extensive readings, some of his reports could not be validated. It is a fortunate irony that his work was made possible through an enforced sabbatical caused by the national strike of 1921, on behalf of the very industry that had lain at the heart of his own and the former Woodmongers' trade – coal.

The most salient positive fact established has been that the Woodmongers were indeed not merely a guild or a Company, but a recognised Livery Company of the City.

Second – a negative finding but an excusable 'faction' – it has not been possible to substantiate the title 'Coal-Sellers'. Nowhere in the archives, at the Bodleian nor at the British or Guildhall Libraries, is the term 'Coal-Sellers' used as a Company title in its own right. Its value in the evolution of 'The Fuellers' is now to be seen as a linguistic convenience to highlight their undoubted role as pioneers of coal-selling under the name of the ancient Woodmongers.[39]

The third major point has been to document the fact that the Woodmongers were indeed the first Company to carry on that trade. The Carmen, as their medieval transport suppliers, followed them into Livery, and were first their unwilling subordinates and later equal partners, later still their competitors. This esteemed fellow-Livery can certainly claim, as it did, a long association with the term: in the event, the competition for any primacy in that association has happily proved a beneficial 'non'-event for today's Fuellers.

Fourth comes a question as to how the Livery might in future be classified, as a 'lapsed' Company. City literature only shows the foundation year as 1984, yet another lapsed Company, The Tobacco Pipe Makers (revived 1960), is credited with 1619 as an original date.[40] The official criterion is: 'the earliest clear evidence of a Company's formation, ordinance or charter.' At the very least, should this suggest the year 1605?

A confirmed truth comes fifth: the definite existence and probable site of the second Woodmongers' Hall, south of St Paul's Cathedral and south-west of the College of Arms, by the land leading down to the new Millennium Bridge over the Thames.

The pages of *The Fueller* have also carried myths as well as truths over the years. One such myth concerns the number of Woodmonger Mayors of London, and the nature of the trade and Livery of the most famous of them all, Dick Whittington. *The Fueller* of December 1998 reported the new Master's assertion that the Woodmongers had provided a number of Lord [*sic*] mayors of London, the most famous being 'Dick' Whittington, more properly Richard Withingsdone, 'coal merchant'. Sadly, the History has unearthed only one Woodmonger Lord Mayor of the City. A learned article had already made clear some 30 years earlier that Dick 'was three times a master of the Mercers' Company, in 1395-6, 1401-2 and 1408-9'; that although 'his interests were deflected from mercery "proper" … he never belonged to any other company', and that 'he was elected mayor of London for the third time in 1409'.

Whether his name was ever rendered 'Withingsdone', or whether his 'deflections' from mercery proper might have included some interests in coal importation can only be conjectured: the nearest he is known to have got to 'coal' was an address in Coleman Street. Although his death is only known as 'before 8 March 1423', 'one of the Brut chroniclers wrote: Also Richard Whyttyngton, mercer, died ye xiiii day of Marche'. Given that by 1395, Fig. 12 (Chapter I) has shown that the Woodmongers were only just emerging as a relatively modest 'craft' sending members to the common council, it seems highly unlikely that a prestigious and wealthy Mayor, all-unknown to the scribes, would have also bestowed his patronage upon them: alas![41]

Double Claim to Uniqueness

A claim to uniqueness in any field has to be treated with care: in one basic sense everything is unique. A brief assertion was made in the Introduction to this History as to a kind of dual uniqueness for The Fuellers. The conclusion on the previous pages about the Company's contemporary stance as an expert witness on the topic of global energy explains one half of this claim.

The ancient half lies in the apparent fact that, unlike many of the British Liveries, for example the Weavers, the Woodmongers have no counterpart anywhere else in the world. The reasons for this historical uniqueness can only be speculative, since on the face of it, other major cities in Europe would have had the same fuelling trades, with a progression through wood, to coal and solid fuel, and into the modern world of multisourced energy. Why did London alone develop such a specialty? The reason must lie in the very nature of early English society: strongly hierarchical, insular and therefore conservative of all tradition, but lacking in ample supplies of lignite – brown coal – such that wood came to have high scarcity value, and therefore to engender the need for some form of protection for its trade. No other explanation seems to be appropriate.

Future Role: A Resource for Energy Policy

From 2005 onwards, the annual Energy Lectures, initially sponsored by founder-Fueller Lord Ezra, have become the mainspring for the Livery's commanding position in the public eye: an expertly informed resource, truly unique among the Livery Companies, for energy policy and its effect on the environment. That stance has been maintained and strengthened through the series of reports in *The Fueller* under the heading 'Fuel for Thought', carrying news of developments across the spectrum of UK fuel consumption and policy. It has been further enhanced by virtue of the breadth of experience embodied in the backgrounds of individual Fuellers, today fully representative of the field of European and international energy. Such experience includes nuclear power generation, the oil, gas and electricity industries, the wide field of renewables, as well as the 21st-century manifestations of the solid fuel world, from research and production to marketing.

The Livery also plays its part in the debates that are aired at the annual Energy Industry lunches, and periodically stands ready to offer informed and above all impartial witness for governmental policy consultations. In a 56-page paper sponsored by the Company, but edited by Liveryman Paul Mott, and produced by Roger Cloke, for the 2006 Energy Review, The Fuellers were able to argue several key issues: the UK needed nuclear replacement, clean coal, coal gasification, carbon sequestration, renewables, and solutions to curb the growth in emissions from road and air transport. The Renewables Obligation and Climate Change Levy should be replaced with a life-cycle carbon valuation that would allow sequestration, as well as nuclear and renewables options to compete equally alongside clean coal and Combined Cycle Gas Turbines. The paper also urged incentives for smart metering so that business and householders could see the realtime costs of their energy consumption; it is now published on the Fuellers' website, *www. fuellers.co.uk*.[42]

Perhaps the first, if unacknowledged, fruits of this lobbying process could be seen in the March 2008 speech to the Adam Smith Institute by the Secretary of State for Business, in which John Hutton said: 'As a country we have to accept the reality that, even in meeting our EU 2020 renewables target, fossil fuels will still play a major part for the next couple of decades for the very least.' This development was further enhanced by a paper in *The Times* of 9 September 2008, entitled, 'How a new power station could make coal the fuel of the future'; it reported a new commercial pilot coal-mine embodying 'carbon capture and storage' (CCS) at Spremberg, the '*Stink Stadt*' of the former East Germany.[43]

These outputs are summarised in Appendix I. They add up to a picture of a contemporary Livery whose Members continuously think beyond and outside any intellectual 'box' that a City of London ambience might, however erroneously, imply: that important role will undoubtedly increase in the uncertain environmental future that the UK and its planet now faces. The motto of the Company could well merit a wider translation and acquire an added significance: a strength in the public arena, firmly grounded in an understanding and deep experience of the earth's capacities – *in carbone robur nostrum*.

71 START OF A NEW CITY TRADITION

Charles Stephenson Clarke, Founder Master and first Master, The Worshipful Company of Fuellers, 1985, here wearing the Livery's livery design of gold and red flames. With Sir Derek Ezra, and then through George McGechan and Arthur Puttock, 'Charlie' Clarke was the main architect of the reincarnation of the Woodmongers' Livery as today's Fuellers.

V

Corporate Life: A Pictorial Review

The Fuellers' History concludes with an overview of the corporate life of the Fuellers and the entity that preceded them, the Society of Coal Merchants, from 1979 onwards – from the early days when the SCM was making its first moves towards incorporation, creating the vehicle for The Fuellers' Company, to the time of the 25th anniversary year of The Fuellers' Livery, in 2009/10.

The Review also provides the opportunity to record some of the more informal, community aspects of the Company's affairs since its inception. Year by year, the Fuellers' Company has undertaken increasingly ambitious tasks, the most work-intensive and entrepreneurial of which has undoubtedly been the educational association formed with one of the new Science and Technology Academies, Stockwell Park High School, in 2007. The aim of the Academies is to give children who have a gift for, or a particular interest in, a subject to pursue their interest to levels that are not offered within the national curriculum – in this case a business and enterprise specialism. In the first year, this led to various initiatives: support for the Army Cadet Force Detachment, badged to The Rifles; the formation of a Girl Guides troop (unusual in a school, already regarded by the Department for Children, Schools and Families (DCSF) as a role model, and so befitting its status as a specialist training school); and an impressive variety of other projects, including monthly scientific or technological challenges.

All these developments have been faithfully and fulsomely reported every six months or so in the now four-colour pages of *The Fueller*, which has been edited and largely written by PM 'Mac' McCombe MBE. From modest black-and-white beginnings in 1981, each issue now runs to some six to eight pages of information and topical interest, making it surely one of the best publications of its kind in the Livery world. 'Mac's retirement in 2008 after 10 years in the editorial chair was marked by a presentation, evidence of the Company's appreciation of his devotion to the cause; he has also acted as Chairman of the Book Committee which has helped the author to produce this History. From now on, Editorship will pass annually to the newly incumbent Junior Warden, that job being first assumed in 2009, by Michael Byrne.

One important editorial feature created and contributed by 'Mac' was the compilation of vital statistics about the energy market – 'Fuel for Thought'. Pressure of work and on space has meant that this valuable series has had to be discontinued, but it must be hoped that other means will be found for keeping Liverymen up-to-date with the key facts and figures – and the ever-burgeoning terminology – of the rapidly evolving world of energy conservation and fuel production (*see* Glossary).

Publicly, that role is performed annually by the Fuellers' Energy Lecture, founded and initially funded by the former NCB Chairman, Lord Ezra. Space limits to these pages have precluded anything more than a brief reference to the subjects and names of the various distinguished speakers (*see* Introduction) that have so far graced this now prestigious, indeed nationally anticipated occasion. Perhaps an exception should be made here with regard to that given on Tuesday 2 June 2009 by a Fueller who might be described as an indirect coal industry successor to Lord Ezra, as CEO of Powerfuel plc, PM Richard Budge, on the theme: 'Carbon Capture and Storage from Coal. A Cleaner Environment from a Secure Supply'. His outstanding presentation, the first to be in electronic form, was delivered to a large audience at Fishmongers' Hall. Richard touched on a number of key issues in today's environmental debate, notably that 'Coal will play an important part in the UK's and the world's energy mix for a long time'. All new coal-fired power plants 'must be ready to be 100 per cent switched to CCS by 2020 if a technology assessment organisation, expected to be the EA, deems the technology is ready': a 'CCS demo must form part of all new projects with at least 300MW net production or 400MW gross capacity of the total capacity of the facility'. Richard exemplified his argument through the optimum solution design for the Hatfield Power Station, based around his own colliery at Hatfield, Doncaster.

Richard and 'Mac' are but two of the 26 Liverymen and Court Members who have been elected to the Master's chair during the past 25 years; their names and backgrounds are detailed in Appendix II. Each Master has to commit him- (or her-) self to an enormously heavy workload – as well as to a gastronomic and, dare it be mentioned, financial marathon – the extent of which may not always be understood by the wider Livery.

The year's events need to be planned some two years in advance, if they are to interlock with other City and national venues and calendar fixtures, not least of all those of the Lord Mayor of the year. Only a few of such events can be highlighted visually in this Review, but a summary of the programme of John Bainbridge, the current Master at the time of publication, may serve by way of illustration of all the Masters' yearly ambitions. Some events may well become recurring features: the Epsom day out in June; a Cocktail Party in July; the activities surrounding the Lord Mayor's show in November – which in 2009 would see the Fuellers aboard their own float for only the second time, a coal-fired steam lorry, the 'Sentinel' from HMS *Sultan* supported by contingents from HMS *Sultan*; 216 Squadron RAF and the Cadet Force from Stockwell Park School; and a continuing interest in the Royal Fleet Auxiliary fast fleet tankers, RFA *Wave Knight* and RFA *Wave Ruler*, and the Defence Fuels Group.

Organisation of the recurrent events is no less time-consuming than those which the Master himself has to devise. By the time of this History's publication many had already happened, including a visit to EFDA-JET, Culham Science Centre, the flagship of the EC fusion programme, but later in May would come the Fuellers' Weekend in Worcestershire. A two-day London-based event is intended, a tour of the Sir John Soane Museum, an evening visit to the Bridewell Theatre off Fleet Street; and the next day a visit to a London landmark with strong Fueller overtones: the Charterhouse, refounded in 1611 as a hospital by a man who had made money in coal – Thomas Sutton.

The traditional link with the Clothworkers (alluded to visually below), was enhanced by holding the 2009 Installation Court and Dinner at their Hall, the scene of the meeting at which the Company's ordinance had been extended in the 1990s from solely the Coal Trade to embrace the entire Energy industry (a vital topic covered in Chapter IV). Another historic event would be a Founders' Lunch in July 2010. Much else besides, by no means all of which can be depicted here: an extraordinary schedule.

The following pages encapsulate the broad spread of these events over the Company's first 25 years.

I   24 April 1979

The reception line at Plaisterers' Hall, when the Society of Coal Merchants of London received its Armorial Bearings and Letters Patent from Colin Cole, Garter Principal King of Arms: [left to right] – Mrs Joy Puttock and Arthur Puttock (subsequently Founder Clerk of the Worshipful Company of Fuellers), Mrs Brannigan and Joe C. Brannigan (subsequently Assistant on the first Court of the Company), Mrs Doreen McGechan and George McGechan (subsequently Master of the Company 1989-90).

II   1979

New Badge and Chain – Sir Derek Ezra, at Plaisterers' Hall, presents the new insignia to George McGechan. The Badge and Chain had been specially commissioned by the NCB, and were designed and manufactured by Brian Fuller, a designer-silversmith from Amersham, Buckinghamshire.

III   17 October 1984

Presentation of the Letters Patent at The Mansion House: Senior Warden Martyn Wakefield; The Lord Mayor Dame Mary Donaldson GBE; Master Charles Stephenson Clarke; Junior Warden Peter Brewis CBE; The Clerk Arthur Puttock.

IV 21 MAY 1987

Formal signing of the Letters of Affiliation between HMS Daedalus and the Fuellers' Company, at HMS Daedalus, Lee-on-Solent (forerunner to HMS Sultan): [left to right] seated: Capt Max Kohler RN (Commanding Officer, HMS Daedalus) and Master Martyn Wakefield; standing: [left], Past Master Peter Brewis CBE; Senior Warden Richard Horne; The Clerk, Wg Cdr Henry Squire OBE. Also in attendance, Cdr R.F. Edmunds (Executive Officer, HMS Daedalus) and Cdr A.J. Bruce (Director of Air Engineering, HMS Daedalus).

V 13 APRIL 1988

The Fuellers' Livery Luncheon, Clothworkers' Hall: [left to right] Charles Stephenson Clarke (Master of the Worshipful Company of Clothworkers, and Founder Master of The Fuellers) and Mrs Thérèse Stephenson Clarke, greeting Master Fueller, Richard Horne JP, and Mrs Cherry Horne.

VI 10 OCTOBER 1991

The Installation Luncheon was held at Cutlers' Hall following the installation of Master Geoffrey Stokes. The new Master is supported on his right by Senior Warden John Boddy DL and on his left Junior Warden Dr Paul Glover MA.

VII **SEPTEMBER 1993**

Annual awards to members of the affiliations of the Company: these are an important aspect of the military service links. Here, Master John Boddy DL presents The Fuellers' Prize, the Daedalus Trophy, to Chief Petty Officer Kevin Sargent (at HMS Daedalus*).*

VIII **8 NOVEMBER 1995**

Ross House, Captain's Residence at HMS Daedalus *on the occasion of the final dinner to commemorate the Battle of Taranto. From left, Senior Warden Brig. Edward Wilkinson CBE TD DL. Captain David Newberry, Master Michael Bryer Ash, Rear Admiral Terry Loughran, Flag Officer Naval Aviation, and Clerk Simon Lee.*

IX *Menu from the Taranto Dinner, showing the Fairey Swordfish biplane torpedo bomber aircraft that flew from HMS* Illustrious *to attack the Italian fleet in a highly successful operation in November 1940. In their wake, the 21 Swordfish left the battleship* Conte di Cavour *sunk and the battleships* Littorio *and* Caio Duilio *heavily damaged. Of the six battleships, seven heavy cruisers, two light cruisers and eight destroyers, all were either sunk or damaged. In one night, the Royal Navy had succeeded in halving the Italian battleship fleet and had gained a tremendous advantage in the Mediterranean.*

X   30 MARCH 1999

In discussion with the Rev. Basil Watson OBE, The Fuellers' first Chaplain, at the annual Livery Luncheon, Painter Stainers' Hall, is Liveryman Frances Algar, former Assistant Clerk to The Fuellers, who played a major part in the foundation of the Company.

XI   12 APRIL 2000

'Clothing' in Company gown by Master Vaughan Williams, in presence of The Fuellers' Clerk Ralph Riley. New Liverymen are: [centre] Neil Lamberton (already 'clothed'); [to his right], Gas Engineer and Systems Manager, John Sharp; [back] temporary Beadle Tony Parker.

XII 2001

Visit to the 'Milestones' Living History Museum, Basingstoke, including a reconstructed coal merchants' siding for 'Wood & Co., Coal and Coke Merchants'. Admiring the exhibit: Mrs Marjorie McCombe. (The Fuellers had earlier also contributed to the refurbishment of a Coal Yard in the Black Country Museum, at Dudley.)

XIII APRIL 2002

Master Richard Budge presents The Fuellers' Prize to Initial Training Instructor POAEM Andrew Claxton, HMS Sultan *(the successor unit to HMS* Daedalus*).*

XIV   SUMMER 2002

Visit to the then HMS Sultan, *Gosport, together with members of the Blacksmiths, Plumbers, Turners and Engineers [seated, left to right]: Mrs Jessica Bell, Mrs Marianne Bainbridge, long-serving Court Assistant Mrs Jane Ayre, and Mrs Shelagh Mott; [standing, left to right]: Liveryman David Bell, Senior Warden Andrew Bainbridge, Liveryman Nigel Draffin, Liveryman Paul Mott, accompanied by Lt Craig Simm representing the hosts.*

XV   6 OCTOBER 2004

Installation Dinner at Skinners' Hall: Guest of Honour Lord (David) Owen of the City of Plymouth responds on behalf of the guests; [to his left] Master David Port; [to his right] Mrs Lynn Port.

XVI   17 JUNE 2004

The first 'Woodmongers' Supper', on board HQS Wellington, the Hall of the Master Mariners. The performers in A Brief Interlude, are [left to right] Clerk to the Fuellers, Sir Antony Reardon Smith Bt; Master Carman Jack Henley; Past Master Carman Clive Birch; Master Fueller Doug Barrow; Clerk to the Carmen, Walter Gill. (The first supper was organised by Master Doug Barrow.)

XVII   17 JUNE 2004

On the same occasion, Clerk Sir Antony Reardon Smith Bt stands alongside a portrait of the founder Master Mariners. In the portrait, his grandfather Sir William Reardon Smith Bt, JP is seated on the right of the group of three founder Master Mariners immediately behind him.

XVIII   OCTOBER 2004, SKINNERS' HALL

Past Master David Waring JP [left] receives from outgoing Master Doug Barrow [right] his newly designed Past Master's jewel (on red ribbons), an element within the Ceremonial of the Installation Dinner for the new Master, David Port.

XIX   APRIL 2005

Mrs Jane Ayre, and (right) Liveryman Dennis Woods, being instructed about ATH Resources' open-cast coal mine during visit to Garleffan, Ayrshire, South Scotland, operated by Master David Port: this site produces over 20,000 tonnes of nationally-valuable coal per week. Fuellers also rode the RH120 excavator.

XX   20 MAY 2005

Liveryman Lord Ezra MBE, former Chairman, NCB, early protagonist for the Company's formation, was presented with a plaque of the Company's Arms, and a silver bowl, on the occasion of his giving the inaugural Fuellers' Energy Lecture, at the Hall of The Haberdashers' Company, a Livery with whom Lord Ezra had long connections.

XXI   8 JUNE 2005, COURT DINNER AT TALLOW CHANDLERS' HALL

Honorary Court Assistant Roger Cloke [left] and Court Assistant Michael Byrne [right] toasting Freeman [then] Group Captain Paul Atherton, following his return from duty in Basra, Iraq; Paul was awarded the OBE in September that year.

XXII   17 MARCH 2006

Visit to Thames Steel. This photograph includes two Masters of City Liveries: third from left, John Lockyer, Master Plumber, and third from right, William King, Master World Trader.

The Fuellers in full voice, at their dedicated church, St Michael, Cornhill, prior to the Election Court lunch.

XXIV 19 APRIL 2006

Master's traditional procession to St Michael, Cornhill: Master 'Mac' McCombe MBE, with temporary Beadle, Tony Parker. Senior and Junior Wardens Nigel Draffin and David Bell are in support.

xxv *Brian Harrison CBE, Master 2000/1, raised significant sums for the Fuellers Charitable Trust and other charities through Gala Charity Dinners at Guildhall in 2001 and Plaisterers' Hall in 2007 and sponsored activities. From left, Brian commencing his abseil at The Design Centre, Chelsea Harbour, on 3 June 2001; at the Election Luncheon, held at Merchant Taylors' Hall on Thursday 5 April 2001, wearing the Master's Chain of Office which he generously presented to the Company; and skydiving at RAF Weston on the Green, Oxfordshire, on 10 June 2001.*

xxvi May 2006

The Fuellers' weekend in Worcestershire includes inspection of ancient Charlcott charcoal-burning blast furnace, part of a 'Windmills and Watermills' visit, to explore how The Fuellers' forebears harnessed wind and water.

XXVII   14 FEBRUARY 2007

On the occasion of the annual Court & Ladies' Dinner, this year at Innholders' Hall, the ladies are, by tradition, guests of the Master [left to right]: Past Master Brig Edward Wilkinson CBE TD DL, Court Assistant Air Vice Marshal John Price CBE DL and Mrs Joy Wilkinson.

XXVIII   2007-8

The exchange of Affiliation documents with the Royal Fleet Auxiliary vessel, Wave Knight, at Harwich; [right to left] Master Nigel Draffin, Capt Ian Pilling (CO, RFA Vessel Wave Knight), and Commodore Robert Thornton (CO, RFA). In December 2008, the Master, Mike Husband, helped hoist the Fuellers' RAS (Replenishment At Sea) flag on her sister-ship RFA Wave Ruler, in Portland.

XXIX   27 FEBRUARY 2008

The Fuellers' visit to Sutton Bridge Combined Cycle Gas Turbine (CCGT) and Gedney Drove End Wind Farm, Lincolnshire. Here, in the Sutton Bridge control room, Liveryman Paul Mott, who organised the event with Station Manager, Trevor Thorpe, explains to Senior Warden Mike Husband and the group, how the national electricity market works.

XXX   Three Masters of the Company in formal and relaxed style. From left, John Pugh, Master 1988/9, in a formal portrait *for the Company; Bill Pybus, Master 1994/5 fishing on the Spey; and Colin MacLeod, Master 1997/8, and Kay MacLeod at a Pattenmakers' Banquet at Mansion House in 1998.*

XXXI   14 JUNE 2008

A group of Fuellers was invited by Wing Commander Steve Chadwick to join the Company's affiliated 216 Squadron RAF in a Lockheed Tri-Star, as part of the Fly Past over Buckingham Palace, to celebrate the Queen's official Birthday. On their return to Brize Norton base on time at 13.30 hrs, the Fuellers expressed their thanks to the Squadron and Fl Lt Tucker, Flt Lt Margetts and the aircrew for another memorable day in their seven-year association with 216.

XXXII   18 JUNE 2008

The June Court at Watermen's Hall; [left to right] Senior Warden Michael Husband, Master David Bell, Junior Warden John Bainbridge.

XXXIII   8 DECEMBER 2008

Master Michael Husband and Trust Chairman Past Master Nigel Draffin officiate at the award by the Charitable Trust of the Charles Stephenson Clarke Prize to City University's David Mead, for his project on 'Practical Options for Sustainable Energy Sources for Dairy Farming'.

XXXIV 11 NOVEMBER 2008

The Third Woodmongers Supper at Armourers' Hall. The highlight was the singing of an 'Oklahoma' parody: Past Master 'Mac' McCombe, erstwhile editor of The Fueller, *and Chairman of the Book Committee, with Master Michael Husband.*

XXXV 2 JUNE 2009

Past Master Richard Budge, CEO, Powerfuel plc, presents the 5th Annual Fuellers' Energy Lecture at Fishmongers' Hall on the theme: 'Carbon Capture and Storage from Coal. A Cleaner Environment from a Secure Supply'.

XXXVI 15 OCTOBER 2009

Installation Court and Dinner, Clothworkers' Hall. The date for this occasion was the nearest it was possible to the anniversary of the Grant of Letters Patent – 17 October 1984. Master John Bainbridge responds to the toast to the Fuellers. To his right, Lt Gen Sir Freddie Viggers KCB CMG MBE. In the background, Beadle Colin Smith MBE BEM.

XXXVII   14 NOVEMBER 2009

Celebrating the 25th Anniversary, the Fuellers had their own float in the Lord Mayor's Show. The steam lorry Super Sentinel, from HMS Sultan, 216 Squadron and the Army Cadet Force from Stockwell Park High School. The main picture shows Senior Warden Michael Byrne, Master John Bainbridge and Junior Warden Stuart Goldsmith greeting the crowds in the grandstand by St Paul's. Disappearing left of the picture is David Marsh with Liveryman Carrie Marsh, stalwart supporters of the Fuellers' banner in atrocious weather.

XXXVIII   20 NOVEMBER 2009

The annual Coal Meters' lunch, held at the Goring Hotel. The Fuellers owe a tremendous debt of gratitude to the Meters Committee for their continued support over the years and for their help in preparing this book. The picture includes seven Fuellers. From left, Coal Meters Clerk Ralph Riley, John Watkiss, Edmund Stephenson Clarke (son of Founder Master Charles Stephenson Clarke), Liveryman Liz Lockley, Liveryman Gordon Banham, Debbie Phipps (daughter of Past Master Richard Horne), Hon. Court Assistant Colin Brinkman, Liveryman Frances Alger, Past Master David Port and Past Master John Boddy DL. The host at the lunch, but not pictured, was Past Master Michael Bryer Ash (Chairman). The guests included Liveryman Lord Ezra MBE and Master John Bainbridge.

THE WORSHIPFUL COMPANY OF FUELLERS
THE HISTORY

The Worshipful Company of Fuellers is 95th in the Order Precedence of Livery Companies of the City of London. Whilst its history is steeped in coal, its membership actively extends into the energy market generally and already includes representation from gas, electricity, oil and nuclear industries in addition to its traditional connections within the coal industry.

The original Livery of Woodmongers and Coal Sellers first appears in the City records in 1376. The Royal Charter was granted by King James I in 1605. Responsible for the collection of coal dues and taxes, the Company handled most of the moneys required for the rebuilding of the City after the Great Fire of 1666, including the present St. Paul's Cathedral and St. Mary at Hill (the Coal Church).

The Charter was surrendered on 5th December in 1667 following a variety of disputes with the Authorities mainly regarding prices and the collection of taxes but also because of a Charter with The Carmen which was considered illegal. However references to the 'Fuellers' continue in the records until the mid-19th century, and a number of other institutions arose which separately represented the differing interests of their members.

In 1981....

xxxix   Two pages from the beautifully presented Masters' Book, *which was presented to the Company by nine Past Masters (see App. II (C)). The Masters' Book is updated annually and contains details of presentations made to the Company, historical information, and names of the Masters and Clerks who have served the Company.*

THE WORSHIPFUL COMPANY OF FUELLERS
THE MASTERS OF THE COMPANY

1984/85	Charles St. George Stephenson Clarke, Esquire
1985/86	Peter Errington Brewis, Esquire, CBE
1986/87	Martyn Richard Wakefield, Esquire,
1987/88	Richard Neale Horne, Esquire, JP
1988/89	John Beresford Pugh, Esquire
1989/90	George Arthur McGechan, Esquire
1990/91	Matthew Anthony Leonard Cripps, Esquire, CBE DSO TD QC
1991/92	Geoffrey Stuart Stokes, Esquire
1992/93	John Anthony Boddy, Esquire, DL
1993/94	Dr. Paul William Glover,
1994/95	William Michael Pybus, Esquire
1995/96	Michael Richard Toraville Bryer Ash, Esquire,
1996/97	Charles Edward Wilkinson, Esquire, CBE TD DL
1997/98	Colin John MacLeod, Esquire
1998/99	David Rupert Tremayne Waring, Esquire, JP
1999/00	Vaughan Martyn Floyer Williams, Esquire
2000/01	Fred Brian Harrison, Esquire, CBE
2001/02	Richard John Budge, Esquire
2002/03	Andrew Bainbridge, Esquire
2003/04	Douglas Gordon Fleming Barrow, Esquire
2004/05	David Charles Port, Esquire
2005/06	Cyril 'Mac' McCombe, Esquire, MBE

Appendix I

The Energy Debate and the Fuellers' Inputs

(A) Paper for the Energy Review 2006: (ed.) Fueller and Liveryman, Paul Mott.

(B) The Fuellers' Annual Energy Lectures:

   (i)   May 2005: Founding Lecture: Lord Ezra, former Chairman, National Coal Board: 'A Personal Review of Energy and Related Issues over the Past Century'

   (ii)   May 2006: John Harris, Chairman of the Coal Authority: 'Whither Energy Policy?'

   (iii) May 2007: Sir Bernard Ingham, Secretary, Supporters of Nuclear Energy: 'Energy Policy – The Struggle between Myth and Fact'

   (iv) May 2008: Lord Browne of Madingley, former Chairman, BP: 'A New Energy Mission for Europe?'

   (v)   June 2009: PM Richard J. Budge, CEO, Powerfuel plc: 'Carbon Capture and Storage from Coal. A Cleaner Environment from a Secure Supply'

Appendix II

CONSTITUTIONAL AND CEREMONIAL

Abbreviations:

ACMS	Approved Coal Merchants Scheme
BC	British Coal
CBI	Confederation of British Industries
CCT	Chamber of Coal Traders
CIS	Coal Industry Society
CMF	Coal Merchants' Federation
CTBA	Coal Trade Benevolent Society
NCB	National Coal Board
NFC	National Fireplace Council
SCF	Society of Coal Factors
SCM	Society of Coal Merchants

(A)(i) CURRENT PERSONALIA

MASTER: John Bainbridge
SENIOR WARDEN: Michael Byrne
JUNIOR WARDEN: Stuart Goldsmith
IMMEDIATE PAST MASTER: Michael Husband

COURT OF ASSISTANTS: (* = Past Master)

Mrs Jane Ayre; David Bell; James Bellew; John Byrne; Michael Byrne; Neville Chamberlain CBE; Paul Cutill OBE; Nigel Draffin*; Stuart Goldsmith; Janet Harrison; James Hill; Christopher Le Fevre; Cyril McCombe MBE*; William Pretswell; Rex Rose; Patrick Helly; John Sharp; Gerard Strahan; Russel Warburton; Dennis E. Woods

HONORARY COURT:

Andrew Bainbridge*; Doug Barrow; John Boddy DL*; Colin Brinkman; Michael Bryer Ash*; Richard Budge*; Roger Cloke; Dr Paul Glover*; Brian Harrison CBE*; Richard Horne*; Michael Husband*; Colin MacLeod*; David Port; Air Vice-Marshall John Price CBE DL; Anthony Shillingford; Edward Wilkinson CBE TD DL*; Vaughan Williams*

HONORARY FREEMEN

Sir John Guinness CB; Sir Paul Newall TD DL MA DLitt; Sir John Parker FREng

HONORARY LIVERYMEN

Air Commodore Sue Armitage Maddox MBE RAF; Wing Commander Steve Chadwick RAF; Commodore Alan Rymer RN; Commodore William Walworth OBE RFA.

CLERK: Sir Antony Reardon Smith Bt GCLT
HONORARY CHAPLAIN: The Rev. Dr Peter Mullen
ALMONER: Janet Harrison
ARCHIVIST: Rex Rose
BEADLE: Colin Smith MBE, BEM

(A) (ii): MASTERS 1984-2009

1984/5 Charles St George Stephenson Clarke, Esq AMIF, MCIT, FID: b.19.iv.1924; educated Eton College; m.1959, two sons. Joined Stephenson Clarke 1942; War service RAFVR (T), Flt Lt Managing Director, Powell Duffryn Group 1966; non-executive director, P.D. Oil & Storage, 1981; Chairman, Edric Property & Investment Co., Shires Investment Co. Ltd, Winston Investment Co. Ltd, Ramteazle Ltd, SCF; Governor, Clothworkers Foundation, member, Court of Assistants, Clothworkers Company; Master, 1987-8. Fuellers, 1981-2002, Founder Master 1983-4, first Master 1984-5; d.2002.

1985/6 Peter Errington Brewis Esq CBE: b.5.iii.1924; educated, Rugby School and RAF; three sons, two stepsons. Past President, CMF, past Chairman, CCT; Chairman, Brewis Bros. Fuellers: 1981-1993; d.1993.

1986/7 Martyn Richard Wakefield Esq: b.3.vi.1920; educated, Maidstone Grammar School; three daughters. Chairman & Managing Director, Kenstone Properties PLC 1982; past Chairman, SCM, member, trade committees; past President, Rotary Club, Maidstone; member local review committee, HM Prison, Maidstone. Fuellers: 1982-2000; d.2000.

1987/8 Richard Neale Horne Esq JP: b.18.xi.1926; educated, Eastbourne College and Oxford University; three daughters. Former Fellow, Institute of Quarrying, Institute of Energy, Institute of Petroleum; former Chairman, Sheffield Division, Boddy Industries Ltd, English China Clays Ltd; Chairman, TBL Fibres Optics Group; High Sheriff, Sth Yorkshire 1984-5; member, Lansdowne Club; former Master 1991/2 & member, Court of Assistants, Clothworkers' Company; former National Chairman, CIS & CTBA, Fuellers: 1982-present.

1988/9 John Beresford Pugh Esq: b.21.ix.1926; educated Sutton Vallance; two sons. Chartered Accountant; Honorary Steward, Wimbledon Tennis Championships. Fuellers: 1981-2004; d.2004.

1989/90 George Arthur McGechan Esq: b.14.iii.1924; educated Harrow Weald County Grammar School; one son, one daughter. Managing Director, A. Wooster & Sons Ltd; President, National Chamber of Trade, & CMF of Great Britain, Rotary Club of Harrow & Greater Harrow Chamber of Commerce; member, City of London Guides Association; Honorary Steward, FA Wembley; member, Wimbledon Association of Honorary Stewards of All England Tennis & Crocquet Club. Founder member, Fuellers: 1982-1996; d.1996.

1990/1 Matthew Anthony Leonard Cripps Esq CBE DSO TD QC: b.13.xii.1913; educated, Eton College and Christ Church, Oxford University and Combined RAF and Army Staff College; three sons. Barrister; Deputy Senior Judge, British Sovereign Base Areas, Cyprus; Chairman, Milk Marketing Board, 1956-90; National Panel, ACMS, 1972-90; Legal Advisory Committee, RSPCA 1978; University of London Appeals Committee, 1980; member, Brooks's & Lansdowne Clubs. Fuellers: 1982-1997; d.1997.

1991/2 Geoffrey Stuart Stokes Esq: b.22.ix.1927; educated, Wyggeston Boys Grammar School; one son, one daughter. Chairman, Hercock Simpson Holdings; independent Chairman, ACMS; member, Farmers Club; Liveryman, Builders Merchants' Company. Fuellers: 1981-2001; d.2001.

1992/3 John Anthony Boddy Esq DL: b.27.xi.1939; educated, Stowe School. National Chairman, CTBA 1988; High Sheriff, Sth Yorkshire 1989-90; member, Sheffield Club. Fuellers: 1983-present.

1993/4 Dr Paul William Glover MA DPhil: b. 31.v.1926; educated, King Edward VII Grammar School and St Edmund Hall, Oxford University and University of Alabama; one son. Director General, Staff, NCB 197485; Companion, Institute of Management; Chartered Fellow, Institute of Personnel and Development; Trustee, CTBA 1977-2008, Chairman of Trustees 1987-2007; Chairman, Chiltern Open Air Museum 1994-9; Honorary member, Rotary Club, Great Missenden. Fuellers: 1985-present.

1994/5 William Michael Pybus Esq: b.7.v.1923; educated, New College, Oxford University; two sons, two daughters. Chairman, Homeowners Friendly Society, 1991; Chairman, Siebe PLC. Director: Cornhill Insurance PLC; Conservation Foundation & Westcountry Television Trust; Bradford & Bingley Building Society, 1982-94; Past Master, Pattenmakers' Company. Fuellers: 1984-2006; d.2006.

1995/6 Michael Richard Toraville Bryer Ash Esq: educated, Bryanston School; one son, one daughter. Managing Director of companies in retail coal distribution, transport, waste disposal, shipping, builders merchants, garden centres; former National Chairman & Trustee, CTBA; former National President, CMF of Great Britain; former Chairman, NFC. Governor, Godolphin School; Director, Prince's Youth Business Trust, Dorset; member, Army & Navy Club. Fuellers: 1981-present.

1996/7 Charles Edward Wilkinson Esq CBE TD DL: b.5.v.1932; educated, Repton School and Manchester Business School; one daughter, one son. Various NCB East Midlands appointments 1954-72: Director, Associated Heat Services, 1968-74, Thomas Black 1974-8; Director, Leigh Interests 1978-94; Chairman, CIS, 1969-70; Chairman, Park Environmental Services Ltd. NS 1950-2, 2/Lt The Sherwood Foresters, Honorary Colonel, 3 Worcester Foresters; Brig., TA 1982-85; Chairman, E. Midlands TAVRA, Vice Chairman, Council, TAVRAs. ADC to HM The Queen 1978-85. Councillor, W. Midlands region, CBI 1987-94; Governor, Repton School 1993-2007. DL for Derbyshire 1985 to date; Member, Court, Derby University; Director, Derbyshire Community Foundation; High Sheriff, Derbyshire 1996-7; Committee, Derbyshire CCC; Lay Canon, Derby Cathedral, 2001, Emeritus 2008; Director/Trustee, Derby Playhouse 2007+; Chairman, Derbyshire Crimebeat; Chairman, Derbyshire Army Benevolent Fund. Member Army & Navy Club, Royal Fowey Yacht Club, West Mersea Yacht Club. Freeman, City of London; Guild of Air Pilots & Navigators. Fuellers: 1982-present.

1997/8 Colin John MacLeod Esq: b.29.ii.1928; educated, Nicolson Institute, Stornoway; two sons; two daughters. Managing Director & Chairman, Caledonian Mining Company; Newark & Area Conservative Association; CTBA (past President, Notts Area) & National Chairman, 1987. Fuellers: 1988-present.

1998/9 David Rupert Tremayne Waring Esq JP: b. 21.vii.1931; one son. Chairman, ICF Group, past Chairman & past President, CIS; member, Caledonian Club. Fuellers: 1982-2009; d.2009.

1999/2000 Vaughan Martyn Floyer Williams Esq: b.23.iii.1944; educated, Rugby School and Exeter University; one son, one daughter. Career mainly in coal, principally with BHP Co. of Australia. Subsequently involved in farming, Oxon. Member, MCC, East India Club, Huntercombe Golf Club, Hardwick Real Tennis Club. Fuellers: 1990-present.

2000/1 Fred Brian Harrison Esq CBE FCA IPFA: b.6.iii.1927; educated, Burnley Grammar School; two sons. Former Finance Director, NCB/BC; Past Master, Chartered Accountants' Company, 1994-5; member, United Wards Club. Fuellers: 1985-present.

2001/2 Richard John Budge Esq: b.19.iv.1947; educated, Boston Grammar School; two sons. Chief Executive Officer, then Director, RJB Mining; acquired privatised coal industry, 1994, now CEO, Powerfuel plc; Chairman, CIS Welfare Organisation; Notts. Enterprises; Markets & Forward Studies, European Coal & Steel Consultative Committee; past President, Confederation of UK Coal Producers; Trustee, National Coal Mining Museum. Fuellers' Energy Lecture: 2009. Fuellers: 1994-present.

2002/3 Andrew Bainbridge Esq FID: b.16.viii.1934; educated Bede Grammar School, Sunderland; two daughters. Director General, Major Energy Users' Council; Chairman, Power Efficiency; Past Provost, Honourable Society of Masters; Fellow of the Institute of Directors; member Carlton Club. Fuellers: 1994-present.

2003/4 Douglas Gordon Fleming Barrow Esq: b.6.viii.1951; educated, Loughborough and Ashford Grammar Schools; School of Navigation, Southampton University; Crusader Marine Ltd – Director; Maritime London – Chief Executive; Marine One-Stop Technologies Ltd – Director; Horton International – Advisory Board; IBIA – founder Chairman; Energy Institute – Fellow; Nautical Institute – Associate Member; Worshipful Company of Shipwrights, Court of Assistants; Incorporation of Hammermen, Glasgow – Member; Anchorites – President. First Fueller to be elected a member of the Court of Common Council of the City of London, for the Ward of Aldgate, 2007: appointed Ward Deputy 2008. Fuellers: 1997-present.

2004/5 David Charles Port Esq FCMA FID: b.7.v.1947; educated, Barclay School and City of London College; Chairman, ATH Resources Plc, GNE Plc, Petrol Express Ltd and Leach Colour Ltd. Non-Executive director, WMT Ltd, Voller Energy Plc, TRS Developments Ltd, and Global Natural Gas Ltd; Past President and Chairman, CTBA & Past Deputy Chairman, Yorkshire Mencap Blue Skies appeal; member, Army & Navy Club. Fuellers: 1993-present.

2005/6 'Mac' McCombe Esq MBE: b.7.vi.1928; metallurgical apprenticeship, C.A. Parsons. One son, two daughters. Chief Metallurgist/Foundry Manager, Technical Journalist: Director, Industrial Newspapers Ltd: edited/launched 22 trade/scientific journals; currently Editor, *Aluminium Times*. Institute of British Foundrymen: National President 1992-3; Foundry Equipment & Supplies Association. President, 1993-4; Diecasting Society, founder member; past President, Foundry College Association, Institute of Cast Metal Engineers (Thames Valley section); Institute of British Foundrymen's Oliver Stubbs gold medal. Editor, *The Fueller* 1998-2008, Founders' Company. Liveryman. Fuellers: 1995-present.

2006/7 Nigel Draffin Esq MIMarEST: b.18.i.1949; two sons. Educated, Roger Manwood's Grammar School, Sandwich, Cannock House School, Chelsfield, Riversdale Marine Technical College, Liverpool; 1st class certificate, Engineer Steamships. Oil Broker, Technical Manager, LQM. Former Head, Operational Economics, Shell International Marine, 1995; Bunker Deputy Manager, E.A. Gibson Shipbrokers, 2005; Chairman, Wilfred Noyce Community Centre; former Governor, Busbridge Middle School, Godalming and Rodborough School, Milford; educational co-ordinator, International Bunker Industry Assocation; Shipwrights' Company, Liveryman. Fuellers: 2000-present.

2007/8 David Bell Esq: b, 22.ix.1935; two sons, one daughter. Educated, Acton Technical College, National Foundry College & Aston University, after five-year apprenticeship with W.R. Anderson & Sons. Following experience with Qualcast, and Westinghouse, General Manager, Iron Foundry Division, Brockhouse, Birmingham, 1970. 1973: Management Board, Birmid, 1973: General Manager, foundries at Glynwed, 1977: Dansk Industri Syndikat Ala, Copenhagen, i/c foundry project in Azerbaijan. In UK, General Manager, Company's UK operations. 1993: Managing Director, 1995: Managing Director, merged Georg Fischer, of Schaffhausen, up to retirement in 2002. Earlier interest in local politics; latterly President of local Rotary Club. Fuellers: 1999-present; first Almoner 1999-2007.

2008/9 Michael Phillip Husband Esq, Dip M: b.9.vii.1950; two sons, one daughter. Educated, Barton Peverill Grammar School. British Gas Southern, General Sales Management 1980-91; British Gas South Eastern, General Manager, East Kent 1991-94, BG Transco, Operational Manager, Kent & East Sussex 1994-98, BG Transco HQ, External Relations Manager, 2000-3, Energywatch, Director, 2003-5: first Master, Fuellers, to spend whole career in gas industry. Fuellers: 1999-present.

2009/10 John Philip Bainbridge Esq, FCA: b.28.viii.1946; two sons. Educated, Chislehurst & Sidcup Grammar School. Blakemore Elgar & Co., Chartered Accountants, 1964-73; Schroders plc, 1973-2003: Head of Investment Trusts & Offshore Funds 1973-99; Director, Schroder Unit Trusts Ltd, 1988-2000; Executive Director, Schroder Investment Management Ltd, 1999-2003; Chairman, Group Companies in Guernsey and Ireland; Group Companies in Japan and Luxembourg; Group Company Secretary, Schroders plc, 2000-2003; member, Army & Navy Club. Fuellers: 1998-present.

(B): CLERKS OF THE COMPANY

1981/7	Arthur Raymond Puttock Esq
1987/95	Wing Commander Henry Charles Frederick Squire OBE
1995/9	Simon Jeffrey Lee Esq
1999/2002	Ralph Alexander Riley Esq
2002-present	Sir Antony Reardon Smith Bt GCLJ

(C): Plate, Possessions and Presentations

Item:	Presented by:
Master's Badge	Charles Needham CBE, Coalite Group
Senior and Junior Warden's Badges	The Founder Master, Charles Stephenson Clarke
Master's Lady's Badge (now worn by Senior Warden's Lady)	Mrs Thérèse Stephenson Clarke
Mace & Staff	PM Peter Brewis CBE
Silver Loving Cup	PM Martyn Wakefield
Master's Silver Goblet	PM Michael Bryer Ash
Pair of Silver Candlesticks	Mrs Doreen McGechan and Friends in memory of PM George McGechan
Silver Cup: Men's Golf Competition Trophy	Trustees of the CTBA
Silver Loving Cup	PM Geoffrey Stokes
Silver Tumbler	PM Richard Horne JP
Pair of Silver Tumblers	Alec Ramsay on behalf of the London Coke Contractors' Associations
Master's Bonnet	PM John Pugh
Brass Plates for Mace Stand	Beadle Frank Keeble-Buckle Past Clerk Henry Squire OBE
Mansion House Print	The Lord Mayor Sir Christopher Leaver
Silver & Gold Trophy: The Fuellers Daedalus Prize	The Company and its Liverymen
Ship's Decanter: Ladies' Golf Competition Trophy	PM David Port
Master's Chain of Office	PM Brian Harrison CBE
Silver Loving Cup: The Fuellers 216 Squadron Prize	PM Richard Budge
Silver Loving Cup	PM John Boddy DL
Master's Lady's Jewel	PM Andrew Bainbridge, PM's Lady, Marianne Bainbridge and William Pybus
Silver Rose Bowl: The Fuellers RFA Prize	PM Michael Husband
Junior Warden's Lady's Badge	Master's Lady, Marilynne Bainbridge
Chauldron Coal Waggon, Newcastle, 1838	Permanent loan from the Coal Meters, gift of PM Charles Stephenson Clarke
The Masters' Book	PMs John Pugh. Geoffrey Stokes, John Boddy DL, Paul Glover, William Pybus, Edward Wilkinson CBE TD DL, Colin MacLeod, David Waring JP and Vaughan Williams

(D): Affiliated Military Service Links

(i) HMS *Sultan*, Gosport RN engineering training establishment

(ii) 216 Squadron, RAF Brize Norton (In-Flight Refuelling)

(iii) Defence Fuels Group, Wimborne, Dorset

(iv) RFA Fast Fleet Tankers *Wave Knight* and *Wave Ruler*.

(E): The Companies of the City of London: 2009

For 'Modern Companies', such as The Fuellers, it is more useful to break down the traditional categories of Companies into five. [NB: No. (e.g. 95) = official CoL, order of precedence: City Livery Companies: CoL, 2006).

(a) Livery Companies: the Great Twelve, the 'Ancients'

H = Companies with Halls, 21st-century

[H] = Companies sharing Halls

1. Mercers [1394]	H
2. Grocers [1345]	H
3. Drapers [1364]	H
4. Fishmongers [1272]	H
5. Goldsmiths [1327]	H
6/7. Merchant Taylors [1327] } (Alternate annually)	H
6/7. Skinners [1327]	H
8. Haberdashers [1371]	H
9. Salters [1394]	H
10. Ironmongers [1463]	H
11. Vintners [1364]	H
12. Clothworkers [1528]	H

(b) Remaining older Livery Companies

Apothecaries (58)	H
Armourers and Brasiers (22)	H
Bakers (19)	H
Barbers (17)	H
Basketmakers (72)	
Blacksmiths (40)	
Bowyers (38)	
Brewers (14)	H
Broderers (48)	
Butchers (24)	H
Carmen (77)	
Carpenters (26)	H
Clockmakers (61)	
Coachmakers and Coach Harness-Makers (72)	
Cooks (35)	
Coopers (36)	H
Cordwainers (27)	
Curriers (29)	
Cutlers (18)	H
Distillers (69)	
Dyers (13)	H

Fan Makers (76)	
Farriers (55)	
Feltmakers (63)	
Fletchers (39)	[H]
Founders (33)	H
Framework Knitters (64)	
Fruiterers (45)	
Gardeners (66)	
Girdlers (23)	H
Glass Sellers (71)	
Glaziers and Painters of Glass (53)	H
Glovers (62)	
Gold and Silver Wyre Drawers (74)	
Gunmakers (73)	
Horners (54)	
Innholders (32)	H
Joiners and Ceilers (41)	
Leathersellers (15)	H
Loriners (57)	
Makers of Playing Cards (75)	
Masons (30)	
Musicians (50)	
Needlemakers (65)	
Painter-Stainers (28)	H
Pattenmakers (70)	
Paviors (56)	
Pewterers (16)	H
Plaisterers (46)	H
Plumbers (31)	
Poulters (34)	
Saddlers (25)	H
Scriveners (44)	
Shipwrights (59)	
Spectacle Makers (60)	
Stationers and Newspaper Makers (47)	H
Tallow Chandlers (21)	H
Tin Plate Workers alias Wire Workers (67)	
Turners (51)	
Tylers and Bricklayers (37)	
Upholders (49)	
Wax Chandlers (20)	H
Weavers (42)	
Wheelwrights (68)	
Woolmen (43)	

(c) 'Modern' Livery Companies [i.e. formed after 1931]

Master Mariners [1926] (78)	H #

Solicitors [1944] (79)	
Farmers [1952] (80)	H
Air Pilots and Air Navigators [1929] (81)	
Tobacco Pipe Makers and Tobacco Blenders [1960] (82) *	
Furniture Makers [1963]: (83)	H
Scientific Instrument Makers [1955] (84)	[H]
Chartered Surveyors [1976] (85)	
Chartered Accountants [1977] (86)	
Chartered Secretaries and Administrators [1977] (87)	
Builders Merchants [1961] (88)	
Launderers [1960] (89)	[H]
Marketors [1977] (90)	
Actuaries [1979] (91)	
Insurers [1979] (92)	[H]
Arbitrators [1981] (93)	
Engineers [1983] (94)	
Fuellers [1984*] (95)	[H]
Lightmongers [1979] (96)	
Environmental Cleaners [1972] (97)	
Chartered Architects [1985] (98)	
Constructors [1976] (99)	
Information Technologists [1992] (100)	H
World Traders [2000] (101)	
Water Conservators [2000] (102)	
Firefighters [2001] (103)	
Hackney Carriage Drivers [2004] (104)	
Management Consultants [2004] (106)	
International Bankers [2001] (105)	
Tax Advisors [2005] (107)	
Security Professionals [2000] (108)	

[NB: # The sole 'Honourable' Company;
* Re first 'date' for Fuellers, and example of an allowed earlier 'lapsed date' for the Tobacco Pipe Makers, 1619, *see* Ch.IV]

(d) 'Working' Guilds electing to remain without Livery

Parish Clerks (no need for Livery, as already 'uniformed')
Watermen and Lightermen (possibly due to activities during the 'Fire of London')   H

(e) Companies awaiting Livery

Educators

(f) Recognised City Guilds

Guild of Public Relations Practitioners
Guild of Art Scholars, Dealers and Collectors

Appendix III

Historical Supplement

(A): The Fueller's London

Listed here are some of the older landmarks or territorial terms for Greater London that were familiar to earlier generations of 'Fuellers', be they woodmongers, carmen, factors or brokers, lightermen, shipmasters or coal merchants. Also listed are addresses associated with named woodmongers or 'seacoal sellers' (for example, through Trade Tokens: *see* Ch.II); today many have been lost or obscured by development. The final section covers the phenomenon of the 'Coal Posts' (*see* Ch.IV). Locations should be read in conjunction with Rocque's map (16th-century London) and medieval maps of M.D. Lobel, *Historic Towns Atlas*], v.III), *see* Ch.I. For background on 'car-rooms' (as both parking-lots, and licences) for medieval carts, *see* Ch.II.

'Above Bridge': Thames west of London Bridge.
Aldgate, Holy Trinity Priory, Duke's Hall, Duke's Place: Fratery/Woodmongers' Hall, corner Aldgate St/Fenchurch St) owned – D. of Norfolk, sold> CoL 1603.
Aldgate Pump: one of many sites allocated in the 16th century as car-rooms for carmen, working with or under Woodmongers.
Arundel House Garden: site of former Meters' Office.
Barge-House, Woodmonger's: Thames frontage, near Waterloo Station.
Barkin/Barking: Coale Yard.
Billingsgate/Billings Gate: original fuel wharf.
Birchin Lane: car-room.
Botolph Lane: car-room.
Bridewell Dock: Robert Chapman; Gillis Ray.
Broad Street: car-room.
Broken Wharf: Robert Austin, woodmonger.
Cardinal Hat, the, without Newgate: car-room.
Castle Baynard Ward: possible site for woodmonger community.
Christ's Hospital: had oversight of the Woodmongers/ Carmen.
Coal Exchanges:
 (i) First, 1768, corner, Lwr Thames Street/Boss Alley.
 (ii) Second, 1805: Acquisition by CoL as a free, open market.
 (iii) Third, 'New', 1849.
Cornhulle: Cornhill, car-room.
Crutched Friars: car-room.
Dowgate, Cozen Lane & Conduit Lane: Dan Burry, woodmonger (733); Peter Tull, woodmonger.
Dudman's Dock: Coal Meters' work-station.
Duke's Hall, Duke's Place: *see* Aldgate.
Durham House Yard: site of former Meters' Office (now RSA).
Eastcheap: car-room.
Fen Church (Fenchurch Street): car-room.
Fleet Ditch: the old Fleet river, outside the City boundaries, arising as a spring at Hampstead Ponds, formerly a wharf for unloading seacoals, etc, from smaller ships that could go under London Bridge; now covered as Farringdon Street; (*see* Sea Coal Lane). Many unsavoury references in *Cal.Ltr.Bks/Liber Albus*.
Gracechurch: car-room.
Gravesend Office: Coal Meters' outpost.
Green's Street, Strand: home of Sir Edmund Berry Godfrey.
Hambro Coffee House: site of meeting, 3 January 1832, to set up Society of Coal Factors.
Harp Lane: site of former Carmen's Hall.
Haymarket, Pickadilla: Nathaniel Robins, Sea Coal Seller.
High Timber Street: near timberwharf, Queenhithe.
Hobart House: former NCB HQ; CTBA, also final HQ of Coal Meters.
King James' Stairs: coal-whippers' office, opened in the 18th century.
Leadenhall; Lime Street; Little Eastcheap: car-rooms.
Limehouse Hole (= Basin): Coal Meters' work-station.
Lower Thames Street: main thoroughfare from riverside wharves.
Mark Lane: car-rooms.
Milbank/Mill Bank: Ralph Fancott, woodmonger; Richard Fisher, woodmonger.
Milford Lane, Strand: John Burgesse, coalman, 1666 (1898); Robert Farmer, coleman, 1668 (1899); former Meters' Office.
Mincing Lane: penultimate Office of Coal Meters.

Monument Yard, near Billingsgate: alternative meeting place for the London coal trade.

Newgate Market: car-room.

Nightinga(le) Lane: Coale Yarde.

Paul's Wharf Hill: site of (second?) Woodmongers' Hall, 1580: 'a capital house called Woodmongers' Hall, at the west end of Poor Widdows' Alley, adjoining the College of Harrolds [Heralds] on the north, opening to Paul's Wharf Hill on the west, with ingress and egress to St Peter's Hill' [an *Inquisitio post mortem*, 1587]; 'to the east of Paul's Wharf Hill'. Site was 114 St Benet's Hill, swept away by the creation of Queen Victoria St' … 'Both St Peter's Hill and Paul's Wharf Hill were described by Stow as 'lanes ascending out of Thames Street to Knightrider's St'. Dale, *RSA*, p.819: 'Woodmongers' Hall not rebuilt after the fire, as it was settled to have a broad quay, 40ft wide, all the way from the Tower to the Temple, raised 3ft to avoid inundation … existed for a 100 years'. [*p.5].

Peter h(H)ill Lane: 'at the v(u)pper end of this lane, the corner there be called Peters Key … Then is Powles wharfe hill, on the East side wherof is Woodmongers Hall'. [Stow (1603), Kingsford edn (1908), p.14 v.2].

Philpot Lane: car-room.

Poor Widows' Alley: (*see* Paul's Wharf Hill).

Port of London: N. Foreland, & the Naze, west to London Bridge.

Pykardislane: John Ferrour's stock of wood, near Queenhythe.

Queenhithe: site of one of four main woodwharves.

Room Land/Romeland: 'at the head of Billingsgate-Dock is a square plot of ground encompassed by posts … which with the adjacent part of the street, hath been the usual place where the Shipmasters, Coal-Merchants, Woodmongers, Lightermen and Labourers, do meet every morning in order to be buying, selling, delivering, and taking-up of sea-coals and Scotch coals. This coal market was kept on Great Tower Hill in the time of the City's late desolation' by the Great Fire. It was moved back to Billingsgate … 1669-70'. p.101, see Delaune, *Angliae Metropolis* (new edn, 1690).

St Andrew Hubbard, Eastcheap: several woodmongers lived in this Ward; a contender as fraternity church for the Woodmongers.

St Benetes Bill, no 14/St Bennet's/St Benedict del Wodewharf; alternative site of a Woodmongers' Hall; listed, GH/L MSS., also ref to 'the Wodehawe there' (14 Edward II = 1320/1321): (*see* Paul's Wharf Hill).

St Dunstan in the East: site of Coal Meters' office, N. side.

St Magnus Corner: detail from Agas map, infamous for uproar due to carters (St Magnus Church, by [new] London Bridge).

Sea Coal Lane: street name still extant, off Farringdon Street, reminder of medieval role of the Fleet Ditch, one of four main wood and coal wharves.

Somerset House: site of former Meters' Office.

Southwark: William Longe, woodmonger (61, Southwark).

Stanton's Wharf: Coal Meters' work-station.

Strand Bridge: Thomas Williams, coal seller.

Thames Street: 'home of London's Carmen': site of 1805 coal market; [*History of Watermen*, v.2, p.311] John Clarke, woodmonger; 'Red Bull', Cold Harbour: house of woodmonger set in pillory near Cheapside Cross for false marking of (wood) billets: [*Machin's Diary*, 17 September 1561].

Tilbury Signal Station/hut/box/office: successor to Gravesend station (i) 1867: probably on a 'dummy' ('dumb' barge, decked over) at London, Tilbury & Southend Railway Station; (ii) 1884: Old Ferry Causeway, near 'World's End' near public house; (iii) 1923: concrete, Tilbury Fort, to *c*.1960.

Tower Street: car-room.

Trigg Lane: woodwharves ('ancient site, 29 Edward I' = 1300/1301).

Water Lane: site of former Meters' Office.

Westminster, Ye Brvrs (Brewers), Brutts Yard, King Street: John Hudson, woodmonger (Westminster; 1605).

White Fryars/Friars: John Clay, woodmonger; Govin Gooldegay, woodmonger.

White Hart Yard: Humphrey Vaughan.

Whitehall Place, No.5: office moved from Gravesend, 1852, closed 1867, as 'Telegraphic Communication from Tilbury Pier' opened.

Wood Market: east bank of Fleet River, north of Bridewell Dock.

Woodwharf: 1377 ref., in parish of St Peter the Less

Coal Posts

Ch.IV, Fig. 58 shows a typical coal post, with map showing post locations around London, measured at *c*.25 miles from St Martin's le Grand, detailed in 1861 London District map. There were *c*.217/219 such locations, according to definition. [M. Nail, *Coal Duties …*] (1972).

Sources:

Birch, Clive, *Carr*; Boyne, William, *Trade Tokens*; Dale, H.B., *Woodmongers*, pp.56-61; *RSA*, p.820; Delaune, T., *The Present State of London* (1681), p.342; *Angliae Metropolis* (1690) GH: Guildhall Library, CoL; Holmes, M., *Elizabethan London*; Humpherus, H., *History of Watermen*; Lobel, M.D., *Street Atlas, v.3: London*; Machin, H., *Diary* (1561); Nail, M., *Coal Duties of the City of London*, Smith, R., *Sea Coal*.

(B): Meters, Factors and the Market

Three of the Fueller antecedents identified during the History, and particularly in the final chapter, are still inter-related today: the Coal Merchants – linked with the Coal Factors – and the Coal 'Meters' (*see* Glossary). Under the law, these historic bodies largely determined how the shape of the London fuel market developed over the centuries. Their emergence has been touched on at the relevant periods: the Meters from the 14th century, the Factors from the 16th, and the Coal and Fuel Merchants from the 17th through to the present. All three in their very different ways experienced first an ascent to power, influence and varying degrees of wealth, then a decline due to 19th-century commercial trends. Only the Fuel Merchants still exist in a full sense as market participants, albeit many are no longer solely concerned with coal, or even with solid fuel. The Coal Meters are also in a technical sense now traders, in that their Committee trades in the investments they accumulated from their 19th-century activities. All three now maintain a predominantly ceremonial, social and charitable existence, albeit still exercising residual rights over their acquired artifacts, records and funds: these they have to guard from falling as *bona vacantia* into uncaring public hands unconnected with their past. All three have played important roles in the re-formation of their shared heritage – The Fuellers.

The main text has emphasised the Merchants, but space limitation has precluded examination of the market itself, and the ways in which the Factors and the Meters helped to shape the progress of that market, before it too was overtaken by direct wholesaling (e.g. Stephenson Clarke as both coal-factor and ship-broker). This Appendix corrects that perspective.

Although the full complexity of the 19th-century systems for regulating the sea-borne solid fuel trade in the Pool and the River Thames, and for operating a public market, far exceed the ambit of the Fuellers' History, a summary of those procedures can at least be offered. Price, the fundamental element in the mix, was governed by six variables: (i) the Vend price at the coal-owners'; (ii) weather; (iii) the timing of the tide in the Thames; (iv) the consequent time of arrival in the River; (v) the berths available; (vi) speed of unloading (the 'turn'). In the 17th century, a seventh variable had been the Dutch war.

Ch.III recorded Mayhew's estimate of the Fueller predecessors involved by the mid-19th century. Smith reported 19 Factors' houses employing some 38 individuals; some 15 Principal and 158 Deputy/'works' Meters – Sea Coal Meters and Land Coal Meters, with an appointed Chairman. When the supply of 'public' Meters ran out, private officials could be appointed, a dubious practice. There were up to 200 Coal Merchants; of these, eight to 20 could be the main buyers, many still lightermen and some still even woodmongers. [S p.181]

There can be no fixed number for the Shipmasters also involved, but estimates of the number of coal-carrying sail lying in the river at one time varied from 800 to 1,400. Supporting them were sundry officials, now to be seen as on the margins of the Fueller lineage: 'boys'/coast waiters, collectors of the Coal Duty, the Clerk of the Coal Market, a Clerk of the 'Night Office' (at Gravesend – initially the 'front door'), the Clerk and Registrar of the Coal Market, Trinity House men, Harbour-Masters and an Inspector of Colliers. Mayhew identified several other figures: the Coal Commissioners, who were often drawn from the coal merchants; trimmers, trouncers, backcoalmen, waggoners. Legally overseeing the trade – Parliament, and the City Aldermen: all making the cumbersome system work – by

law and agreed convention, and indeed by word of honour. Ancient regulations were continually re-formulated to control this growing activity – *see* List below, pp.175-6.

The history focuses first on the Meters (the weighers), many of them true Londoners: one Samuel Bamford met in prison 'an old coal-meter and his son … whose conversation and manners were of the most perfect Cockney cast': [J. White, *London*, p.111]. The following key events of their history also provide an overview of the main events in the development of the London coal trade. The account cannot do justice to all aspects of the Meters; e.g., the use and employment of 'colemeters' from 1497 onwards by the Ironmongers: Elizabeth Glover, *History of the Ironmongers' Company* (1991), p.22. (For this data, and many other inputs, I am indebted to current Master John Bainbridge.)

[Key (i) sources: D = Dale booklet; R = Dale lecture to RSA; CC = Court of Common Council, CoL; GH = Guildhall Library; TNA = The National Archive; S = Smith, *op. cit.*; F = *The Fueller*; DW = D. Wedderburn; M = Mayhew, *London Life*; (ii) Other: HoC = House of Commons; LM = Lord Mayor of London; Ws = Woodmongers; LCM = Land Coal Meters; CM = Coal Meters; SCM = Sea Coal Meters; SOCC = Society of Owners of Coal Craft; SCF = Society of Coal Factors; FA = Fuellers' Archive.]

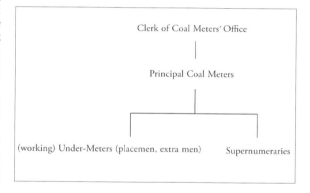

Date	Formative Event	Source
1330	CMs first recorded: only operated in the CoL on the River Thames	D2,82; R817
1444	Patrick Thobyn proposed as Billingsgate seacoal meter	S79
1599	24 Oct: Jrnls of CC: sworn Seacoal Meters' sacks to be used	D130; CC
1604	28 Sept: James I summons LM and Aldermen to appear, for interfering with the right of the Crown by disposing of the Office of Measurer of Coals …	D15

1604	27 Oct: letter to LCJ to hear claim of LM to exclusive privilege of measuring coals brought by water from Newcastle, and the duties levied thereon …	D16
1606	19 Apr: the revenue 'farmed out': four 'farmers' allowed deduction from their rent	D14
1611	13 Jy: grant confirmed by Lord High Admiral, regarding Office of Measuring Coals	D16
1614	15 Sept: grant to LM of Office of Coal Meting	D14
1618	20 Jy: King's orders to Customs Officers: quality of coal at Newcastle, Sunderland and Blyth must be approved	D16
1619	16 Jy: Surveyors of Seacoals appointed in NE	D16
1620	5 Oct: ACT of CC: 'Master' CMs must appoint Deputy CMs from 'Fellowship Porters'	D115
1622	29 Aug: CC write to Mayor of Newcastle, requesting certificate of search by the Customs' searchers	D17
1623	1 Sept: King Charles I renews request for appointment of two additional CMs	D17
1635	18 May: King Charles I refers to Queen Elizabeth I's edict for six CMs to add to existing four; recommends two more	D18
1635	17 Oct: King Charles I renews request	D18
1638	Wharfingers and Ws purport that their charges for 'metage', lighterage, wharfage and carriage 'stand' them 2s. the chaldron	D20
1648	CM's place is estimated to be worth £200 p.a.	D18
1664	14 Jan: HoC Committee on sale of wood, coals and other fuel	D36
1664	20 Jan: CCC: CMs unable to assist unloading at Smarts Quay, due to abuse by Ws	D38-42
	2 March: ACT; Assize and Measure of Wood and Coal	D36

1665	21 Jun: ACT of CC: (i) Ws win government of Cars and of the Carmen; (ii) Use of sacks mandatory; (iii) Ws not to own cars	D45; R818; CC
1667	Apr 20: (ADDITIONAL BUILDING ACT): CM91 Offices at Durham House Yard, Arundel House, Milford Lane & Water Lane (see Appendix III(A))	R820
1680	CoL Committee for the Markets makes new ACT: Woodmongers must use public carts, with sealed bushel for measuring, coal only to be in SCMs' sacks	R820
1694	Metage charge up from 4d. to 8d. per sack	R821
1695	'When duty laid on coals', ld per chaldron to be paid to Principal Ms, appropriating 3/4d. for themselves	D113
1696	CMs now to be instituted by CoL	D135
1703	1 Sept: Coal & Corn Meters propose to [the Committee for Improving the City Revenues] that Meters' Offices be set up, paid for and become assignable; similar proposals made later, by 13 Coal Meters: Samuel Ongley, Robert Lancashire, John Nicholson, Joseph Speed, John Child, David Gansell, Thomas Walker, William Sheppard, Edmond Sheppard, Samuel Skinner, Thomas Skinner, Hugh Sweetapple & Nathaniel Iles	D111-3
1712	5 Aug: Samuel Dodd signs statement that Principal CMs concealed from UMs their legislated farthing retention by HM Treasury	D113-4
1714	'Complaint and Address' by Under CMs to LM: names Stephen Wickins as Corrupt Clerk of the Coal Meters' Office: '15 SCMs paid £80 rent p.a.; UMs into four classes, others as Supernumeraries; abuses; the Principal Ms, the 'farmers of the City duty on coal', only allowed 25 per cent to UMs, who really did the work [Fig. App III (B), p.173]	D113
1724	London Gazette: 15 CMs working in CoL	D18
1734	Fleet River covered over from the Fleet to Holborn Bridges the rest remaining open until 1765	R820

1734	LCMs introduced into London: first duties include working hours 0500-2100, with no meal breaks. Mar: ACT creates new LCMs' Office in Westminster CMs' Office in Church Alley, St Dunstan's Hill	R822
1746	Mar: ACT creates new LCMs' office in Westminster.	D78
1756	CMs' Office in Church Alley, St Dunstan's Hill	D78
1766	(John Entick): 15 CMs now each had four deputies	D18
1767	22 Jan: Coal Merchants secure ACT to 'establish' LCMs; charges for measuring sacks; includes barges; extends sway from Tower to Limehouse Hole (= Basin)	D82; R821
1771	Coal Exchange offices include: Factors – Wm.King, Horne & Kemp, Biggin & Ward: Merchants – Rd. Wood & Sns, Wm. Hurford & Sns, Walter & Slade	S86
1775	The Watermen's *History*: importance of the Coal Meters in the evolution of the 'market'. The coal meter's office was on the N side of St Dunstan in the East … the market was held on a piece of ground next to Billingsgate market, called the Room Land, nearly opposite St Mary-at-hill	
1786	COAL BUYERS INDEMNITY ACT reconstitutes LCMs; duty to weigh coal moves from coal merchants to LCMs	R822, D51
1787	2 May: SOCC Chairman writes to SCMs Office	R822
1800	Chelsea and canal basin still excluded from LCM sway	F14
1803	Coal trade placed under care of a CoL Committee	D91
1807	ACT: Second 'CMs' Regulations'	D91-3
1826-8	City Companies enquiry: no Woodmonger answered summons	R823
1827	Coal Merchants write to HoC: CMs 'unsatisfactory'	D90
1829-30	HoC sets up London Coal Trade Enquiry Committee	R822
1831	5 Oct: ACT: abolishes SCMs 'for 7 years, LCMs for ever'; CMs' sacks must be used (for 1 cwt, 2 cwt or bulk); (*see* Ch.III, Fig. 52, p.107): opens CM Office	R822
1831	22 December: meeting of *c*.70 parties at the London Tavern, convened by the 'Woodmongers and Coal Wharfingers'	
1832	CMs form Protection Branch, for merchant and recipient	FA
1832	ACT: HoC Commission: move from measure to weight DV	F21
1834	Consequently SOCC and SCF form Society of Coal Meters	F14
1836	SOCC becomes Society of Coal Merchants (SCM)	
1840	Jn: [Second] 'SMs' Regulations – Coal, Culm or Cinders: 22 Rules, incl. 4: 'Ms are empowered to work from sunrise to sunset'; 3: not to absent themselves from the ship during [these] hours; 12: Ms must exhibit the Turn Paper to the Master/ Mate of the ship they are to deliver … and return same to the [Mrs'] Office with their account of the delivery	GH
1845	Turning point for coal arrivals – from ship to rail	F13
1849	30 Oct: royal opening by Prince Albert of new Coal Exchange, opposite Custom House Quay	GH
1860/2	Cory's 'Atlas' derrick for mid-river unloading: caused consternation in Coal Factors' Society, who managed the Coal-Whippers Office: innovation proved success	F13, 15
1861	55 per cent of sea-coal discharged in Thames handled by Ms	F14
1863	1 Jan: [Third] 18 'CMs' Regulations: ['Coal' vice 'Ship']: 3: duty 'to note the state of the cargo, whether full, short or apparently broken into'; 16: Ms shall not be engaged in any branch of the Coal Trade, or be concerned in any Public House, Wine, Spirit or Beer business or have any interest in any Ship, Vessel or Barge'	GH
1866	'Atlas No.2' ordered	F13

1892	5 May: [Fourth] 'Ms' Regulations, booklet with 30 Rules: incls: 4: Any M who shall ask or receive any money except through the Office shall be instantly dismissed'	FA
1895	Feb: Great Frost makes hydraulic machinery inoperable	F13
1897	24 June: address, Queen Victoria's Jubilee: Coal Factors Soc./Soc. of Coal Merchants/Inland Coal Owners Assoctn	GH
1899	30 Oct: 50th celebration of opening of Coal Exchange, 500-600 merchants and dealers present	GH
1900	Only nine per cent of coal discharged in Thames now handled by Ms	F14
1904	Floating HM Coal Depot No.1 at Portsmouth, to bunker RN warships	F15
1915	'Atlas No.3' under tow for France, sunk by torpedo	
1917	Only 0.2 per cent of coal discharged in Thames now used Ms	
1960s	Ms still in use at Newhaven, Deptford	
1980s	Ms' Protection Branch closed	

The Factors: this short Appendix amplifies the evolving role of the Factors. 'Any person could become a factor; no freedom of the City was necessary, nor any fee, oath or qualification'. He supplied needed capital, to become 'a vital component in the distributive process'. 'They were men of honour and strict integrity', paying the City dues on coal, liaising with the Corporation's Coal, Corn and Finance Committee, always at arm's length to the product. Eddington wrote in 1813, 'it was strange that the metropolis depended on about 30 Factors for one of the necessities of life (numbers varied from 19 to 30). Initially 'the [factor] made advances in money to ship owners and paid bills for them; he sold cargoes for the owners, his employers [as agent] – shippers or coalowners'. There was a body of factors by at least 1819, and by 1825 they had a Chairman. They became large-scale wholesalers: James Duke, later Secretary and Treasurer of the Society, declared in 1813 that he was authorised to buy coals for the Imperial Gas, Light and Coke Company. The Society of Coal Factors' *Minute Book* records that by 1839 there were 21 factors' 'houses'. End of the limitation of the 'vend' squeezed out the ship-owner as middleman, to become simply a carrier: 'a new era started – the factor as merchant', 'a merchants' merchant'; 'only a little more aristocratic name for a coal merchant'. (*see* Smith, Chs. 14-27).

The Market: the coal market went through at least four phases:

(i) selling out of any lighters on the river; caused debris, traffic confusion (17th century);
(ii) selling only from vessels bringing coals within the port;
(iii) selling on open spaces at the riverside: 'Roomland';
(iv) movement from open spaces to a building; movement from a floor of a building (open) to a reserved room (closed market).

The last three phases evolved over four centuries, through 12 physical/conceptual stages:

(i) Roomland, at head of Billingsgate Dock;
(ii) 1666, post-Great Fire: at Tower Hill, 1669-70;
(iii) 1681: back at Billingsgate: 'A square plot of land compassed with Posts';
(iv) 1682; Market also held at Monument Yard, Fish Street Hill;
(v) 1720: Stow: 'Billingsgate – Exchange for the Coal Trade';
(vi) 1768: first Coal Exchange built by private subscription: 'a good and very neat building [48ft long, 22ft deep] … [Through the porch was the Merchants' Area, nearly 54ft square and 15ft high] … handsome front leading to a large quadrangular room … coved roof supported by 12 Ionic columns … in the centre [under] a lantern light 30ft by 24ft … a large circular desk [*see* the old British Museum Reading Room design] … around the Area were small rooms … at the rear, 20 offices, the coffee room [*see* Lloyd's Insurance original] and the bar';
(vii) 1776: market days: Monday, Wednesday, Friday, 1200-1400;
(viii) 1793: Report to City Lands Committee of the Corporation: 'In 1769, the most opulent Coal Merchants and Coal Factors began to create the Coal Exchange': [14 Factors, 75 Coal Buyers] … Corporation considers take-over;
(ix) 1801: decision to enlarge the market, with a closed room;
(x) 1805: 1803 Act (43 Geo III) comes into force, empowers Corporation to establish free and open market for coals arriving in Port of London, creating second Coal Exchange;
(xi) 1849: national Coal Exchange No.3 built, royal opening;
(XII) 1950 Coal Exchange (No.3) closed; demolished 1963.

[NB: for above data *see* Dale, *op. cit.*, Smith, *op. cit.*, passim]

Procedures: Fueller predecessors of the 18th and 19th centuries performed tasks of great complexity, quite apart from the various conventions for commissions, scorage, spoutage, turn, discount, etc. The transaction by a (heavily risk-bearing) Factor of a coal consignment at the Exchange point could only follow after a sequence of some 15 links:

(i) Basis: LM had right to search and survey, and also to meter (weigh) all coals, etc: (his perquisite of 6 bushels per load passed down to Under-Meters by 1714);

(ii) At the Custom House by Thames Street there were a Controller and a Collector of Coal Duty. Factors and/ or Ships' Masters entered into prior agreement with them for the regular discharge of all future bonds/ debts;

(iii) Coast waiters at Gravesend sent daily lists of passing colliers to the Collector in the Custom House Long Room;

(iv) Factor took the Newcastle Custom House's 'Cocket of loading' from Ship Master to the London Customs House;

(v) Factor entered the ship's particulars at the Collector's Office within four days of the ship passing Gravesend;

(vi) Factor deposited money as security for the Duties, or he or the Ship's Master gave a bond for their payment;

(vii) warrant signed by the Collector and the Controller to obtain a Meter, sworn to act for both 'King and City';

(viii) Factors paid coast-light duty and Trinity House duties;

(ix) cocket was taken by hand to the coast-office for a LM's bill to be filled up;

(x) coal-office warrant and bill from the coast-office were carried to the coal-meter's office (the 'Crown' behind St Dunstan's Church, Thames Street);

(xi) officer despatched Meter for the delivery of the ship;

(xii) Meter exercised his control (initially by convention, subsequently by law) over measurement of all coal once it reached the merchants' wharf: provided a vat for discharging/measuring all loads from ship to barge;

(xiii) Factor paid metage money to Meters' Office, and returned warrant to the Collector;

(xiv) Duties re-computed by Collector, then by Controller;

(xv) Duties finally settled by Factor: load could at last be legally offered on Exchange, before whole procedure repeated for next incoming shipments.

[NB: for further detail, see Smith, op. cit., Chs.10 to 15.]

(C): Dale's Researches:
An Epitome of the Trade

In 1921/2 Hylton B. Dale wrote that he had never even heard of the Woodmongers before he started to research and write his pioneering little booklet – The Fellowship of the Woodmongers: Six Centuries of the London Coal Trade. The author of this History has to make the same confession, despite having served the energy industry in a consultative capacity for much of his working life, with family links to North-East collier owners, Prince Lithgoe, and to the management of the 19th-century London docks. This research has completed his education.

Hylton B. Dale was the son of Hylton Burleigh Dale (1857-1912). Partner by 1920 in Charrington, Dale & Co., the merged Company descended from three historic 18th-century merchanting firms – Charrington; Sells; and Dale. That Company itself further merged in what must be considered a portentous year for Fueller history, 1922, to form the giant Charrington, Gardner, Locket & Co., Ltd, embracing five further flag-carriers of the coal merchants' past: Locket; Judkins; Gardner; Hinton; and, from a foundation of at least 1719, the oldest of them all – the firm of Benjamin Horne (1698-1766) at Bankside, London.

As the Charrington 'family tree' demonstrates, in its corporate history, Two Hundred Years in the Coal Trade: 1731-1931, with the death in 1994 of Michael Locket, only one of those names now survives, in the 'Father' of today's Fuellers, Past Master Richard Horne [F5]. If space allowed, that tree, with a spread of some 50 businesses, could serve to embody on its own the great days of the London coal trade as whole.

The younger Hylton found he had 'spare time' during the 1921 Miners' Strike (precursor to the General Strike of 1926). He decided to devote it to the then unknown topic of the earlier history of his trade. Initially, he presented his findings as a lecture to the Society of Coal Merchants, and later on 20 October 1922 to the [Royal] Society of Arts, with whom he was also in correspondence on other energy topics. Through the generosity of his Chairman, Col W.F. Cheesewright, he was able to reproduce his lectures in the 'Coal Merchant and Shipper', and then to publish them in the form of a 152-page booklet, in 1922. At least one Fueller, that same Richard Horne, still has a cherished copy of the original booklet, handed down to him by his father, yet another traditional 'coal-man'. The booklet was later reprinted in its original – albeit quite hard-to-read format; that work, and subsequently the RSA lecture, have been essential starting points for this History.

Tribute is paid elsewhere to Dale's researches, notwithstanding the inherent limitations on much historical research at that time, for example the complete lack of Notes, which means that any subsequent researcher has to define where the sources might be found.

The work suffers too from having additional later material bolted on to it as Appendices, rather than have these items welded into the text at the appropriate point. It also reproduces pages of obscurely detailed 17th-century public Posters and Complaints in their entirety; their syntax alone makes them nearly unreadable, although they do now of course form part of the archival record to the Fuellers' History.

Ch.IV highlighted some of the gaps in Dale's work, but also emphasised how much of his narrative still merits attention today. It is fortunate that the 87 intervening years have made it possible to stretch the Fuellers' History to their full ten centuries rather than merely six: the record still stands as proud as it stood in those early days.

Appendix IV

Background Data

(A): Rulers of England: Regnal Years

Henry III	1216-72
Edward I	1272-1307
Edward II	1307-27
Edward III	1327-77
Richard II	1377-99
Henry IV	1399-1413
Henry V	1413-22
Henry VI	1422-61
Edward IV	1470-1
Edward V	1461-83
Richard III	1483-5
Henry VII	1485-1509
Henry VIII	1509-47
Edward VI	1547-53
Jane	1553
Mary	1554
Philip/Mary	1554-8
Elizabeth I	1558-1603
James I	1603-25
Charles I	1625-49
Protector	1649-60
Charles II	1660-85
James II	1685-8
William/Mary	1689-94
William	1694-1702
Anne	1702-14
George I	1714-27
George II	1727-60
George III	1760-1820
George IV	1820-30
William IV	1830-7
Victoria	1837-1901
Edward VII	1901-10
George V	1910-36
Edward VIII	1936
George VI	1936-52
Elizabeth II	1952-

Source: *A Handbook of Dates,* Royal Historical Society, [(ed.), C.R. Cheney: revised, M. Jones]

(B): Money Values

These two statistical excerpts are only intended as a rough guide to changes in the value of money over The Fuellers' 10 centuries. To be interpreted with extreme caution, they are taken partly from data once published by the Bank of England (1807-1997); these figures were derived from the Retail Prices Index, based at January 1987 = 100. Data in the period 1260-1914 has been taken from the source 'Phelps Brown, E.H. and Hopkins S.V. (1981), Seven Centuries of the Prices of Consumables, compared with Builders' Wage-rates'; [for explanation, see JSTOR: Economical Economics New Series v.23, no.92 (Nov. 1956), pp.296-314)]; publ Blackwells/Wiley]. The year 1807* provides a point of comparison between the two series; a 'composite unit' is the artificial compound of prices used in the original paper.

(i) Years and Prices of a 'composite unit' [*sic*]:

1264: 83	1447: 100	1697: 693	1897: 963	1937: 1,275
1297: 93	1497: 101	1797: 1,045	1907: 1,031	1947: 2,580
1397: 116	1597: 85	1807: 1,427	1917: 1,965	1954: 1,825

(ii) Changes in value of £1 in years 1807-1997

£1 in 1807 = £38.51*	£1 in 1937 = £33.14	£1 in 1987 = £1.73
£1 in 1857 = £42.70	£1 in 1947 = £24.96	£1 in 1997 = £1.17
£1 in 1907 = £53.31	£1 in 1951 = £15.51	[series ends 1997]

Appendix V

OPERCULA

Opercula – the legendary cast-iron 'London Coal Plates', the Victorian coal-hole covers for shooting coal from pavements down into the cellar – still decorate the streets of London. They form part of the local colour – albeit in black-and-white – for any study of the coal trade. The designs have been used by art colleges for generations as a source of ideas, ever since Shepherd Taylor first sketched – and named – them as a medical student, in 1863. An *operculum* is Latin for a cover, also used as a botanical term.

Their inclusion in this History derives from the library of a Past Master, 'Mac' McCombe: he kindly made his source book available: *Opercula – London Coal Plates*: sketched by Aesculapius Junior [Dr Shepherd Taylor]; revised edition, Golden Head Press, Cambridge, 1965: *see* also F10.

A selection of these designs forms a Leitmotiv for the History.

OPERCULA	POSITION
INTRODUCTION	
	Title Page: Wardour Street and Chancery Lane
	Endpage: Regent Street
CHAPTER I	
	Title Page: Cornhill and Regent Street
	s.i: Goswell Road
	s.ii: Newgate Street
	s.iii: Portland Place
	Endpage: Newgate Street and Lincolns Inn Fields
CHAPTER II	
	Title Page: Hunter Street and Trafalgar Square
	s.i: Tottenham Court Road
	s.ii: Doughty Street
	s.iii: Russell Square

Endnotes

INTRODUCTION, pp.XXI-XXVI

1. 'Our Energy Challenge: securing clean, affordable energy for the long term: A submission to the Department of Trade and Industry, On behalf of the Worshipful Company of Fuellers': 2006.
   Annual Energy Lecture series, founded by Lord Ezra, former Chairman, NCB (*see* Appendix I, p.165).

2. The residual Coal Meters' Committee, although, with the Coal Merchants Federation (Great Britain), a funder for this History, has a place as of right in this evolutionary story, as one of the many-faceted aspects of the activity embraced by the trade title 'fueller': (*see* Appendix III(B)).
   Of the new terms introduced here, by 1423, 'Tymbermonger(e) and 'Timber Merchant' were initially synonyms for 'Woodmonger'; Chambers & Daunt, *London English 1384-1425, see* Porland, *Brewers' First Book (1423)*, pp.154, 159; Dale asserted that these terms indicated a separate trade by the end of the 16th century: *Woodmongers*, p.119.
   Where Dale does identify sources, these will be covered in the Endnotes. Where possible, manuscript sources have been used. Dale devotes, for example, only three of his 150 pages to the whole medieval period, Ch.1.
   If what Dale has called the 'dodgy Latin' of the 1667 Charter surrender document (*see* Ch.II) is also counted, then the list of terms embraced by the 'Fueller' concept also includes the *Lignarii* of the *Societias Lignariorum*: Dale, *op. cit.*, p.53.
   As titles, the terms 'Coal Sellers'/'Sellers of Coal' have to be read with caution, despite repetition in various recent Fueller papers; although Dale (1922) (p.1) refers to a vanished 'Broadside' (poster) of 1730 (p.70), the terms are not otherwise recorded: (*see* Ch.II).

3. (i) Well after the first drafting for this book, the Chaucerian metaphor was also discovered in J.K. Melling's *Discovering London's Guilds and Liveries* (6th edn, 2003), p.5 et seq, essential reading for any deeper history of the guild idea, from the time of the Romans and even back to the Silversmiths of the Biblical era. They arose as far apart as China and Norway, and in the British Isles from Edinburgh to Bodmin.
   (ii) All individuals reappear in their appropriate places in the text. A 'Mayor' represented the Cities of both London (Henry le Waleys and Sir Richard Browne) and Westminster (Sir Edmund Godfrey: *see* Ch.II).

4. 'Carbon fuels' is used here in preference to the former 'fossil fuels' (*see* Prof. P. Odell, *Why Carbon Fuels*, Bibliography s.8.). Reference environmental issues, this History echoes the impartial approach of The Fuellers, balancing both the Al Gore 'Inconvenient Truth' lobby, and other scientific views that have been expressed.

5. Birch, *Carr & Carman*, p.7.

6. Briggs, *Social History*, p.7: my indebtedness to three great social historians, G.M. Trevelyan, Asa Briggs and today's Caroline Barron is hereby gratefully recorded. As apposite to this history of a London Livery as to Trevelyan's own work is Briggs' quotation from Mandell Creighton's *The English National Character* (1896): 'No nation has carried its whole past so completely into the present. With us historical associations are not matters of rhetorical reference on great occasions: they surround the Englishman in everything he does and affect his conception of rights and duties on which national life is built'. Writing in 1983, Asa Briggs added: 'social history was in the past often thought of as more trivial than constitutional, political or military history ... In recent years, however, all this has changed. Social history has now become a favourite kind of history ... social history is the history of society'.

7. Power, *Medieval People*, p.73; Ackroyd, *Chaucer*, p.39: 'One of the guarantees of virtue and sincerity in a medieval text – it derived from a greater authority'.

8. Trevelyan, G.M., *English Social History – A Survey of Six Centuries – Chaucer to Queen Victoria*, Chs I, II.

9. I attribute this useful metaphor to the military historian, and one-time graduate employee of one of Britain's great fuel industries, Corelli Barnett.

10. Fuellers' Submission to DTI, 2006, p.3; Sampson, *Changing Anatomy of Britain*, p.296; S. Friar, *Heraldry* (2004), p.216.

11. Weinreb & Hibbert, *London Encyclopaedia*, p.162. The interrelationship of the guilds with everyday life is also demonstrated in the many sayings that originate from various guild practices: 'a baker's dozen'; 'once in a blue moon'; 'under-and over-the-counter'; 'sent to Coventry'; etc: see Kennedy Melling, *op. cit.*, pp.5, 8, et seq.

12. *See* Nef, *Coal Industry*; Smith, *Sea-Coal*; Hatcher etc, *History ... British Coal Industry*, Ch.I; also Gwen Seaborne, *Royal Regulation of Loans and Sales in Medieval England*, II, Ch 3, Price Regulation; Ch 4, Laws against Forestalling and Regrating. Journal of the Royal Society of Arts, 20/x/1922, pp.816-23; Hylton B. Dale, 'The Worshipful Company of the Woodmongers and the Coal Trade of London'.

13. The varied designs of the traditional 'coal-hole cover' the *operculum* – serve as a Leitmotiv throughout the History: (*see* Ch.IV, and Appendix V). Its use here derives from botany –

'organ of a plant or animal that acts as a lid': *Schott's Original Miscellany*.

CHAPTER I, pp.1-27

[NB: short titles are used here: for full data, *see* Bibliography]

1. The traditional toast is: 'The Worshipful Company of Fuellers – root and branch – may it flourish for ever': it symbolises both origins and evolution. H. Dale, RSA Lecture, J. Adam Street, London (site of medieval Coal Meters' Office), 20.x.1922. The discovery of this paper during the research for this History, confirmed the final dating for his *History of the ... Woodmongers*, which preceded it in the pages of *The Coal Merchant and Shipper*, as 1922. *See* Appendix III(C).

2. *Liber Albus*, 'The White Book', a 'Repertory' compiled by Richard Whittington's Clerk in 1419, 'an unbroken record of all transactions and events ... in which the City in its corporate character has been interested': Introduction; Dyer, *Standards of Living ...*, pp.73, 189; M. McKisack, *The Fourteenth Century* (OUP), p.313.

3. The author records the debt he owes to many eminent medievalist historians, and in particular to those who have brought a new approach to the medieval guilds. Principal sources are listed in the Bibliography, but these names merit mention: George Unwin, Sylvia Thrupp, Elspeth Veale, Pamela Nightingale, Ian Archer, Matthew Davies, Sir John Clapham, D.W. Robertson, Rev. W. Cunningham, Clive Burgess, Marc Fitch, Eileen Power; above all Prof. Caroline Barron.

4. Ackroyd, *Chaucer*, p.xv; S. Friar, *Heraldry* (2004), p.216: '*livrée*' ex Latin *liberare*: 'bestow food etc to retainers'.

5. Ibid., p.6; Myers, *Chaucer's London*, p.23; McKisack, *op. cit.*, p.529.

6. For background on medieval 'carting', the author wishes to acknowledge his debt to the thesis by Dr Claire Martin, *Transport for London 1250-1550*; without their horse-drawn carts, two- or four-wheeled – owned, or hired from carters – the woodmongers could not have plied their trade. *Liber Albus*; *Cal. Ltr. Bks A-I*; 'car' as in report of Wellington's funeral: 'the last sight of the car as it passed Piccadilly': for further illumination, *see* H. Garlick, *The Final Curtain: State Funerals* (1999).

7. Dyer, *Middle Ages*, p.119: Power, *Medieval People*, p.177, *see* Langland, *Piers Plowman*: 'in the Middle Ages care of the roads was a matter for ... charity ... all except the great highways were ... indifferently kept'. Dyer, *Standards of Living*, pp.6, 73, 189.

8. *Liber Albus*, p.636.

9. Myers, *op. cit.*, p.16; Hatcher, *Coal Industry*, p.24.

10. Ackroyd, *op. cit.*, pp.xv, 152.

11. Ibid., p.56; Hatcher, *op. cit.*, p.35.

12. Dale, *Woodmongers*, pp.2-5; (*see also* Ch.II).

13. Ackroyd, *op. cit.*, p.158.

14. Timbermongers: Hovland, *Apprentices*, 'Crafts & Trades in Four London Parishes, 1376-1499', Appendix III, p.276. Dale, *op. cit.*, p.123, *see* Jnl of Common Council, 20 November 1529: 'the Master & Wardens of The Fuellers were Richard Sheppard, John Caille and John Perle'. Also *op. cit.*, p.5; also Lithgow, *Travels*); Murray, *op. cit.* (1908) v.IV, i, p.583: Wr. Wuelcker, 688/32, '*hic focarius*'; 1483 *Cath. Angl.*, 145/1. Murray, *op. cit.*, p.583; Ibid. (1908 edn) v.VI, i, p.606.

15. Thrupp, *Merchant Class*, p.xii; Power & Postan, *English Trade, 15th century*, pp.140-6.

16. Galloway etc, *EconHR*, 'Fuelling the city', pp.447-72. A prime source for this data is the Brewers' Book of 1418-41 (though clerk William Porland noted that the 'Woodmongers' were not among

the 17 crafts that 'dedn hyren owr halle'). From Tymbermonger John Stok, the Brewers bought 'dyuerse tymber' for their Almshouses. From lye Tymbermonger(e) of [appropriately] wodstrete', they bought 'vj bordes to dyuerse dores, and to an pipe of ye previe'; naills'; 'xvi j quarters of tymber', and sundry other items. Although Liza Picard, *Elizabeth's London* (2003), p.231, asserts that 'The Carpenters regulated all dealing in timber ...', her clear emphasis is on housing, not on the fuel trade, continuing '... and the construction of timber-framed buildings'. For detailed background on trades using wood, *see* Jessica Lutkin, *The Craft of Joiners*: this work identifies two more Woodmongers – Wm. Clapham and Wm. Jow.

17. Ibid., pp.452-3.

18. Ibid., p.452 (for fraternity/Ward sites, *see* n.22 infra).

19. Ibid., pp.452-3.

20. Prof. Caroline Barron, letter to author, 5.xi.06.

21. Galloway, *op. cit.*, p.452.

22. [A] Fitch, M., *Testamentary Records in the Commissary Court of London, v.1, 1374-1488* (1979): this evidence suggests: (a) that St Andrew Baynard parish ['St And Bn'] is the likely site for a Woodmongers' fraternity (10/31 mentions); (b) that the lower incidence of 'Timbermonger' attributions might imply that, being so much fewer, they probably needed to be members of the Woodmongers guild; (c) however, the parishes of St Andrew Hubbard/Eastcheap ['St And Hub']; St Benet, Paul's Wharf ['St Ben P.W.']; and St Peter, Cornhill ['St Pet Cor'] are 'possibles' too. All would accord with the probable location in Rocque's map of the second Woodmongers' Hall (*see* Ch.II, Fig. 23. p.41). Source also Lobel (ed.), *Historic Towns Atlas: The City of London from Prehistoric Times to c.1520* (Oxford, 1989). The Wills listed show name; parish; date will drawn up:

(i) '*citizen and woodmonger*':

p.6　Ashford, Tho.; All Hallows, Barking (A.H. Bark)/St Olave, Hart St (St O.Ha.); 1486

p.9　Avon, Walter; St O.Ha; 1488

p.10　Baldwin, Rich.; St And Bn; 1438

p.12　Barnard, John; St And Bn; 1454

p.13　Bartholomew, John; St And Bn; 1418

p.19　Beverley, Rich.; St Michael, Queenhythe (St Mich, Qh) 1453

p.44　Clapham, William St Mich Qh; 1479

p.50　Coke, Henry; St And Bn; 1432

p.74　Freke, John; St And Bn; 1427
　　　Freke, Thomas; St And Bn; St Marg, Westm, nr Charyngcrose, St Martin Fields?; 1415

p.90　Harness, Robert; St And Bn; 1440

p.95　Henxteworth, William; St And Bn; (1446)

p.105　Jennings, Thomas; St Bnt P.W.) 1452

p.106　Keene, William; St Sepulchre, Newgate; 1484

p.107　Kenmerton, William; St Bnt P.W. 1408

p.110　Kirsoppe, Richard; St Mich. de Queenhyhe; 1486

p.137　Overton, William; [London]; 1439

p.148　Potenhal, Robert; [London]; 1398

p.151　Quyntyn, Robert; St Nicholas, Shambles; 1436

p.176　Stokes, William; All Hallows, The Great; 1424

p.179　Talworth, John; St And Bn; 1427

p.194　Ware, Roger de; St Bnt P.W., St And Bn; 1418

p.197　Westbury, David; St And Hub; 1488 (* see n.29, infra)

p.198　Wettenhale, John; A.H. Bark; 1427

'*citizen and timbermonger*':

p.8　Attwood, John; St Bot, Ald; 1393

p.54　Cressing, – ; St Pet, Cor; 1413

p.77　Garoun, John; St Pet, Wp; 1392

p.130 Moysaunt, John; St Pet, Cor.; (1448)
p.141 Peert, Thomas; St Michael, Wood Street; 1486
p.152 Randolff, John; St Pet, Cor.; 1414
p.171 Sunnyng, William; St Mich, Cor; 1383

[B]: Fitch, M., *Testamentary Records in the Archdeaconry Court of London v.1 (1363)-1649* (1969): these list one 'Timbermonger', will of 1375/6 (Wm. Kyng); and only 12 'woodmongers': Wm. Bonet; Jn. Boyden; Anth. Clarke; Tho. Cowper; Wm. Davys (also a carpenter); Anth. Eddis; Jn Fromley; Wm. Newman; Wm. Starkey (sole 'St And Bn' reference); Jn. Whitehead; Tho. Yates; & Roger Yoxhale. Further search might clarify, but cannot be conclusive.

23. Murray, *Dictionary* (1928 edn), v.X, pt II, ii, pp.269-70.
24. Lyon, *English Nation*, p.181 (N.B: 'le' in a name became common usage, not automatically proving Norman ancestry).
25. *Cal. of Wills*, Roll 100 (87).
26. Murray, *op. cit.*, pp.269-70.
27. Riley, *Memorials*, p.383; Dale, *op. cit.*, pp.1-2, suggesting Boveney Lock, Eton); pp.3, 118: 28 June 1375: names of Woodmongers making agreement with John Baddeby: John Joudelayn, Robert Potenhale, John Lyghtefoote, Robert Parys, Walter Potenhale, Wm. Shrympelmersche, John Asshurst Thomas Herte, John Asshelee & Thomas Freke. Some names recur one year later as the Woodmongers' deputies to form a Common Council: Herte, Asshellee, Freke.

Thomas West of Wallingford, and London's Woodmongers:
A later epitome of post-medieval fuel trading along the Thames was corn and general merchant – and shop-owner – Thomas West of Wallingford, who exploited the opportunity created by the gradual opening-up of the river for trade navigation, after the long 14th-century decay induced by the plague. In the 16th century he would carry wood and timber in his horse-drawn part-owned barges one-way from Oxfordshire to London and even Deptford, bringing back the other way a wide variety of goods for his local customers – the blacksmiths as well as his shop trade – in Marlow, Reading, Pangbourne, Culham and Burcot: 40% of those loads was in wood, 20% in 'Newcastle coals', bought from London wholesaling 'woodmongerres' such as 'Masters' Bruckines and Spyerls and Henry Storie: [Mary Prior, *Oxoniensia*, xlvi (1981), pp.73-94: 'The Accounts of Thomas West of Wallingford, a Sixteenth-Century Trader on the Thames'].

28. Galloway, *op. cit.*, p.150, fn.25 (*see* Surtz E. & Hexter, J.H. (eds), *The Complete Works of Thomas More*, 4 (1965) p.179); Galloway, *op. cit.*, p.465: ('locative bynames of London woodmongers link them with Ham, Tolworth and Merton, all near Kingston, Portnall, near Egham, and perhaps Cobham and Godstone [woodmongers' database]').
29. Burgess, *Church Records of St Andrew Hubbard*: 240, p.222; Geoffrey Bell; 276, p.256, David Westbury; 283, p.261, Roger Grave; Barron, *Middle Ages*, pp.3, 440; *see also* Fitch, *op. cit.*, passim (also Note 22, supra). With no pretence as being the Woodmongers' fraternity church, St Michael is 'shared' with the Bakers, Water Conservators, Merchant Taylors, Woolmen, Upholders, Master Mariners, and Air Pilots & Air Navigators: F28, February 2007.
30. Seabourne, *Royal Regulation of Loans and Sales*, pp.73-124. Much price regulation was aimed at basic necessities, e.g. victuals, but fuel, including peat, was also included in several instances. Note: (i) Nottingham, 1395: 119 people amerced simultaneously as 'common forestallers and gatherers' of coal, selling it excessively high': Seabourne, *op. cit.*, p.136, n.79;

(ii) London civic courts, as early as 1300: 'wood & coal forestalled': Seabourne, *op. cit.*, p.131, n.47.
31. Barron, *op. cit.*, pp.v, 130-1, 218-22; Table 9.1.
32. Ibid., List of Mayors & Sheriffs, A. Lancashire, as App. I, p.308 et seq.
33. *Liber Albus*, H, p.44 *Cal. of Wills*, p.215, Roll 108 (33).
34. *Cal. of Wills*, p.215, Roll 108 (33).
35. *Letter book*, I, p.207.
36. Barron, *op. cit.*, pp.44-6, 263.
37. Barron, *op. cit.*, p.265: 'the city was still able to secure firewood' (thus not rely on imported coal as in the 17th century). Smith, *Sea-Coal*, p.3; *see Annals of Coal Mining*: 'Sea-coal in the Forest of Macclesfield'. 'Bygone Industries of the Peak', *Peak Advertiser*, 11.ix.2006.
28. Barron, *op. cit.*, pp.45, 204, 237-8.
39. Ibid., p.47, q Stenton, *Road System* … pp.1-21.
40. Ackroyd, *op. cit.*, p.7; Myers, *op. cit.*, pp.20, 200.
41. Barron. *op. cit.*, p.10; Nightingale, *Grocers* …, p.49; Thrupp, *op. cit.*, pp.1, 75. The tumultuous world in which London's 14th-century woodmongers and their fellow tradesmen carried on trade within hard-fought freedoms is well conveyed in such classic historic novels as Anya Seton's *Katherine* (1954), *see* Ch XIX, p.332: 'That pack of baseborn tradesmen – what right have they to liberties?'; Bennett, *Richard II* …, p.49.
42. Round, *Commune of London*, p.223.
43. Barron, *op. cit.*, pp.130-1.
44. Ibid., pp.15, 83; Longworth, P., *The Rise and Fall of Venice* (1974), pp.73-4. (Cannon Street Station lies on the site of the ancient Steelyard.)
45. Axworthy, R., London U, PhD thesis, 2000: 'London Merchant Community and its relations with Edward III …' (2 vols.).
46. Nightingale, *op. cit.*, p.50.
47. Ackroyd, *op. cit.*, p.2.
48. Ibid., p.7.
49. Bragg, *Adventure* …, p.66.
50. Galloway, *op. cit.*, pp.448-9, 459.
51. Hatcher, *op. cit.*, p.31.
52. Dyer, *op. cit.*, p.96.
53. Hatcher, *op. cit.*, p.18.
54. Dyer, *op. cit.*, p.119.
55. Power & Postan, *op. cit.*, pp.140-1, 187-8, 198; McKisack, *op. cit.*, p.349, q, L.F. Salzman, *English Trade in the Middle Ages* (1931), pp 281-2.
56. Myers, *op. cit.*, p.147.
57. Veale, *Fur Trade*, pp.4-5.
58. Hatcher, *op. cit.*, pp.19-20.
59. Dale, *op. cit.*, p.9.
60. Barron, *op. cit.*, p.48; Ackroyd, P., *Thames, Sacred River*, p.192: 'the dry land to which the docks gave access was known for many centuries as 'Romeland' although the origin of the word is not clear'.
61. Hatcher, *op. cit.*, p.25.
62. Ibid., *op. cit.*, p.1, see Gray, *Chorographia*.
63. Ibid., *op. cit.*, p.22.
64. Dale, *op. cit.*, p.11; also Robertson, *London*, p.45.
65. Barron, *op. cit.*, p.56.
66. Dale, *op. cit.*, pp.14-19; Smith, *op. cit.*, p.248.
67. Smith, *op. cit.*, p.2, see Riley, H.T., *Memorials of London & London Life*, 1868, pp.338-9. The names of the Meters were John Wirhale, Roger Cook, Henry Cornewaille & Geoffrey Prudhomme, *see Cal. Ltr Bks*.
68. Ibid., pp.2-3.
69. Ackroyd, *op. cit.*, pp.xiii, 8.
70. Barron, *op. cit.*, pp.130-1, see CPMR 1364-8.

71. Nightingale, *op. cit.*, p.177.
72. Cunningham, *Formation*, p.179.
73. Seabourne, *Royal Regulation ...*, p.131; Dale, *op. cit.*, p.3; Reade, *The Cloister & the Hearth*.
74. Dale, *op. cit.*, p.2; also Briggs, *Social History*, p.81.
75. Robertson, *op. cit.*, p.4.
76. Nightingale, *op. cit.*, Ch.III, passim.
77. Barron, *op. cit.*, pp.199-200.
78. Ibid., p.214.
79. Veale, *op. cit.*, p.101.
80. Briggs, *op. cit.*, p.99. The distinction was real: a historian of the guilds goes further: 'merchant guilds whose members' mercantile interests may be in direct opposition to those of the craft guilds': K. Melling, *op. cit.*, p.5.
81. Power & Postan, *op. cit.*, pp.145-6. Concepts of wholesaling/retailing are still an anachronism at this time: *see* Ch.II. BL MSS: 101.h.38.: Lawrence, Mayor, Tracts re Trade (1674).
82. Briggs, *op. cit.*, p.81.
83. Veale, *op. cit.*, p.102.
84. Nightingale, *op. cit.*, p.48.
85. Veale, *op. cit.*, p.103.
86. Power & Postan, *op. cit.*, pp.146, 284.
87. Veale, *op. cit.*, p.103 (*see Cal Letter Bk* G, p.74).
88. Ibid., p.103 (*see* Kingsland, *Prejudice*, pp.141-2).
89. Ibid., p.104 (*see Cal Letter Bk* E, pp.232-4).
90. Barron, *op. cit.*, p.206.
91. Thrupp, *op. cit.*, p.4; W. Carew Hazlett, *The Livery Companies of the City of London* (1892), pp.151-3.
92. Unwin, *Gilds*, p.353.
93. Unwin, *op. cit.*, pp.370-1; Dale, *op. cit.*, p.3.
94. Smith, *op. cit.*, pp.7-14; Power, *op. cit.*, p.149.
95. Further Hostmen research was done in Newcastle, 2006/7, by David Wedderburn, through good offices of PM C. McCombe; Ch.III covers the topic more fully. The main sources are:
Publications of the Surtees Society, v.105 (1901);
Remembrancia of the City of London;
Baillie, J., *An Impartial History of the Town & County of Newcastle-upon-Tyne and its Vicinity* (1801);
Middlebrook, S., *Newcastle-upon-Tyne: Its Growth & Achievement* (Newcastle, 1950).
96. Smith, *op. cit.*, p.23, *see* Nef, J., *Power, op. cit.*, p.157.
97. Oldland, J., *LJ* v.31, 2 November 2006: 'Wealth of Trades in Early Tudor London', pp.135-6, *see* Devon Record Office, ms. 312/fy 64: Broke 'left an inventory in excess of £1,000'. (For history of the Coal Merchants, *see* Ch.IV.)
   The relationship between England's North-East and the River Meuse (today's Belgium), where coal was produced from at least 1195 onwards, although marginal to this History, is of interest: there was both coal trade and competition, and a similar producers' guild, the *métier de Houillères*: P. Spufford, *Power and Profit, The Merchant in Medieval Europe* (2002), pp.321-2.
98. Museum of London; *see also* Brown, Michelle, *The Luttrell Psalter* (BL, 2006): (note misspelling as 'Louterell' elsewhere).

Chapter II, pp.29-67

1. Even if used colloquially as a synonym for 'Woodmongers', and it is quoted by Dale (*op. cit.*, p.1), the would-be formal trade title 'Coal-Sellers' does not appear in the Index nor in the manuscripts at the BL: (21.h.5; 816.m.12; 101.h.38; 816.m.12; 712.m.1; 8229.c.30). Nor, as can be seen in the text, does it surface in the Bodleian MSS, nor in the GH MSS, all illustrated here.

THE CARTERS

The early relationship between the Woodmongers and the newly founded 'Fraternity of St Katherine the Virgin and Martyr of Carters' is now revealed for the first time in Claire Martin's thesis of 2008, *Transport for London 1250-1550*, pp.240-55: 'the regulation of the carting industry would be shared between the fraternity, the mayor and aldermen, and ... the woodmongers. [The 15] carters who founded the fraternity in 1517 [included] Robert Hammond, woodmonger.' (CLRO, MS Letter Book N, ff. 38v-40). 'The next phase in the history of the Fraternity ... began in March 1528 when John Scotte and other woodmongers promised to see to providing the king with carriage' [one of the pressures on the carters at that time], This is the first reference to the involvement of the woodmongers with the Carters ... Two weeks later Hugh Church [of Broken Wharf], who was given the right to operate a car ... for the ... Duke of Norfolk, agreed to become a member of the Woodmongers but was not also compelled to join the Fraternity of St Katherine' (CLRO, MS Repertory 7, f.244, f.248v; Journal 12, f.37).

WOODMONGERS' HALL

A Hall is clearly evident by the time of *The Woodmongers' Remonstrance* of 1649 (BL: 8229.c.30).

'FUELLER'

Evidence for 'fueller' starting to be used as an alternative to, and in the same document as, 'woodmonger', occurs in Martin, *op. cit.*, p.248: 'new regulations ... were put forward by three founder members of the fraternity ... and other 'colliers [= coal-merchants?] vitellers and fuellars' [*sic*]. Also in a 'Memorial' from the Carrmen in would-be refutation of the Woodmongers' Case (BL:816.m.12: dated 1680), after surrender of the Letters Patent in 1667.

2. Evelyn, *Fumifugium* (1661) (a briquette of coal and lime) passim; *see* in Burton, *Jacobeans at Home*, pp.250, 133; *see also* B. Freese, *Coal*, p.34, q, Hugh Platt, *A new, cheap, and delicate Fire of Cole-balles* (1603) (coal and soil) based on even earlier Continental practice.
3. Defoe, *A Journal of the Plague Year*, passim.
4. Pepys, *Diary & Correspondence of Samuel Pepys Esq* (Bickers & Son, 1877).
5. Fuller, *The Worthies of England*.
6. Burton, *Jacobeans*, p.132.
7. Shakespeare (Globe edn, 1911), *King Henry V*, Act III, Sc. 2. 1.50; and Act V, Sc.1, 1.69.
8. Harrison, G.B., *Introducing Shakespeare* (Penguin NY, 1947), p.76.
9. Burgess, [C.], 'London Parishioners in Times of Change: St Andrew Hubbard, Eastcheap, c.1450-1570', JEcc1H, 53 (2002) pp.38-65.
10. Date of first 'Woodmongers' corporate reference is hereby confirmed to be 1376 as in Dale, not 1375 as in *History of British Coal Industry*, thence GL ref, at 2006; Letter from Stephen Freeth, Keeper of Manuscripts, GL, City of London, to author, 3/vii/2006.
11. Bodleian MS, Rawl.D.725b. Chartaceus, In folio, saec, xvii. ff.76; (*see* Catalogi, codicum manuscriptorum, Bibl, Bodl. pt.v, fasc. III, Ricardi Rawlinson, R.R. 65a (Oxon, 1893). This 76-page MS forms a vital Fuellers' document, touching on a variety of events during the years 1602-59; it is the nearest we get to any early Woodmongers' archival papers. It is notable for its illuminated section-headings (*see* Fig. 17, p.28); for James I's title as King of England, France, Ireland & Scotland; for an early official usage of the word 'Fueller', and of the term 'Coal

Trade'. The members of the first Woodmongers' Court were: 'Master, Thomas Hunt; Wardens, Mark Snelling, Cuthbert Coleman; Assistants, John Bryan, Simon Lee, William Cory, Richard Wootton, Lewis Gardiner, Thomas Selby, Ephraim Andrews, Edmund Dawson, Thomas Mills & Robert Hill: Smith, R., *op. cit.*, p.26. Ref Protestant estates, *see* n.22 infra; also Dale, *op. cit.*, pp.11-13; also Adams, A., *Blacksmiths*, pp.50-1, which also notes one of two other minor inter-Livery 'brushes' (allegiance of W. Stephens, 1609-10); also, Jupp, E.B., *Carpenters*, pp.264-5 (apparent attempt to persuade Carpenters to join the Woodmongers: 30/x/1605).

12. Neale, *Elizabeth*, p.241: '[Elizabeth in 1579] issued a long proclamation which the authorities were told to read to the City Companies …'; Stow, *London*, list of those attending Ld Mayor's feast 1531/2; also Dale, *op. cit.*, p.3.

13. Barron, *op. cit.*, pp.12, 210-1, *see* Unwin, *Gilds* …, p.171.

14. Dale, *op. cit.*, pp.22-6 [use of 'Coal Merchant' in 'SP'].

15. TNA/PRO: State Papers, Chas II, PC/2 59, p.327, 5 March 1666/'7': 'to which Order the said Woodmongers not having yielded Obedience, the said Attorny G[e]neral do proceed against the said Charter'; 17 April 1667, p.371: 'the Master, Wardens & Felowship [*sic*] of Woodmongers of London do forthwith attend His Maj's Att. Genrl with their Bookes & Entries of their Bye-Laws or Orders which they have made as a Company at their Company Hall … by 4 May … for the publique Good'; 16 September 1667, p.584: 11 … the Woodmongers [to] attend the Board to. to give their positive Answer whether they will surrender their Charter or not.' 20 September 1667, p.591: 'Att. Genrl. do proceed by a Quo Warranto against the Charter whereby the Woodmongers as Incorporated … denial of said Charter'. Also *see* Birch, *op. cit.*, Chs 3-4. These papers also raise another Fueller name – John Bromfield, yeoman of the woodwharf: Dale, *op. cit.*, p.55.

16. *See* Bodleian ref, n.11 supra, p.73v.

17. Humpherus, *Watermen*, v.2, p.137; Dale, *op. cit.*, pp.70, 90, 97.

18. Dale, *op. cit.*, p.3.

19. *The Woodmongers' Remonstrance, or, the Carmen's Controversie rightly stated* …: 1649; (BL: 8229.c.30). *See also* Note 15, supra; also Dale, *op. cit.*, pp.2-4.

20. Stow, *op. cit.*, v.2, pp.190-1; Smith, *op. cit.*, p.26, *see* Nef. In 1558 and again in 1607 fishmongers, haberdashers, leather-sellers, grocers, ironmongers and wharfingers were listed among those turning their hand to coal-wholesaling. Neale, *op. cit.*, pp.68, 300-1: 'following Sunday the Queen came in procession to St Paul's, such another spectacle as at her Coronation, with the City companies in their liveries, and waits over Temple Bar to make fine music.'

21. L: *Calendar of Wills* proved in Ct. of Hustings 1258-1688 (ed.), R.R. Sharpe (1890): pp.704/5: Will of William Heron, gentleman, of Clerkenwell, 1580. For data on carters, *see* Martin, *op. cit.*, p.211, *see* CLRO, MS Repertory 1. f.94.

22. Young, *Plumbers*, p.107; several of these sums appear, surprisingly, shorn of any context, in the Bodleian MS. already identified, *see* n.11, pp.76/7 recto.

23. Power & Postan, *Studies in English Trade*, pp.146, 285.

24. Ibid., p.262.

25. Stubbes, *Anatomie of Abuses* (puritanical sermons against the stage), 1583, passim.

26. BL: Tracts relating to Trade, 1674: 'An Act of Common Council for the Government of Carts, Carrooms, Carters & Carmen, & for the Prevention of Fraud in the Buying & Selling of Coal': Some Memorials 1664: 'to encourage the multiplicity of Traders in Victuals & Fuel … also in Wood'. For legal background,

see Maitland, *Forms of Action at Common Law*; Pollock & Maitland, *History of English Law*. (Another Fueller name at around 1673 was that of John Veere, a member of the City's Common Council, yet convicted several times for 'abusing the people in their measure of coals': Dale, *op. cit.*, p.61.)

27. *See* Ch.IV, ii.

28. An example of the creation of new guilds is that of the Witney Blanket Weavers Company in 1711: *A Walk Round Witney* (Witney & District Historical & Archaeological Soc., 1979).

29. Barron, *op. cit.*, p.4.

30. Thrupp, *Merchant Class*, p.32 and passim; *Remembrancia of the City of London*, p.282 (pages never before cut until this research): 'Letter from the Court of Aldermen to the Lord Chancellor … recommending Leonard Courson for the grant of keeping the poor man's wharf of coal and wood … where there was a great portion of the poor's stock in coal and wood': 3/iii/1590. On 3/xi/1608, pp.57/8, reference to 'Woodmongers and carmen, under the control of Christ's Hospital' … and to 'the keepers of Woodwharves and the Company of Woodmongers' (no mention of 'Coal-Sellers').

31. Fisher, F.J., 'The Development of London as a Centre of Conspicuous Consumption in the 16th & 17th centuries', *TRHS* 30 (1948), pp.37-50; *London in the English Economy 1500-1700* (eds) F.J. Corfield & N.B. Harte (London, 1990), pp.105-18; *see* in Hope, Birch, Torry, *Freedom*, p.71.

32. Cooper, *A More Beautiful City … Robert Hooke* …, p.98.

33. Seabourne, *op. cit.*, p.109, *see* Wren's Report to Charles II.

34. Reddaway, *Rebuilding of London*, p.285.

35. For topographical background to London, *see* Holmes, *Elizabethan London*, pp.7, 61, 109; and Earle, *A City Full of People*, passim.

36. Oldland, 'Tudor London', *LJ*, pp.127-50: Tower Ward is ranked 6th & 7th by Oldland from two separate assessments, with such Wards as Cripplegate and Cordwainer above them, and Vintry and Bridge below, out of a total of 26 Wards.

37. Galloway, Keene, Murphy, 'Fuelling the City', *EconHR*, p.452.

38. Veale, *Fur Trade*, pp.94-5, q, S.C., Appr., i, ff. 1-67 (five came from fathers who were weavers, 10 from tailors, 30 who were generically husbandmen, 24 who were yeomen).

39. Thrupp, *op. cit.*, pp.44-51.

40. Oldland, *op. cit.*, p.146.

41. Dale, *op. cit.*, pp.131-2; Bodleian, MS: Rawlinson, D725b.

42. Dale, *op. cit.*, p.2; Birch, *op. cit.*, p.32; Knightrider Street and Paul's Hill are today's pointers to Woodmongers' Hall.

43. *Unravelling a Woodmongers' Hall* The drawing in the *Panorama* (1544) by A. van den Wyngaerde (ed.), H. Colvin & Susan Foister, LTS 151 (1996), does not indicate a Woodmongers' Hall: this is meaningfully four years after the 1540 cut-off date in the C.M. Barron Table 9.1. Even by 1570+, the time of completion (attributed to Ralph Agas) of the famous woodcut 'bird's-eye view' of London (based on the earlier 'Copperplate') no Hall was yet depicted at its authenticated site in Poor Widdowes' Lane, Paul's Wharf Hill, let alone any putative first site at Duke's Place, Aldgate. Although as the authors of *The A to Z of Elizabethan London* point out, the 'Agas' map is not 100 per cent accurate, nevertheless a building as important as one of the Livery Halls would surely have been shown if it existed. Thus, despite Dale's assertion of 1922 of a (first) Hall at Duke's Place, it can at least be confirmed that a (probably one and only) Hall existed after 1570 at the location detailed in John Stow's *Survey* in 1597. This sole site was equally speculatively portrayed by artist J. Gilkes in 2003 (Liza Picard, *Elizabeth's London*, at roughly the Stow location, but without

any new visual MSS corroboration. [Stow, *Survey of London* (1598; Kingsford edn, 1908), v.2, p.16; also Dale, *Woodmongers*, pp.2-4, 49: map of Holy Trinity Priory Aldgate: W.R. Lethaby, 'The priory of Holy Trinity, Aldgate', *Home Counties Magazine*, 2 (1900), pp.45-53: Guildhall Library, City of London: (original deemed possessed by Marquess of Salisbury); Dale's brave surmise might have been supported by the history of the Glass-sellers, who abandoned Joyners Hall and then met at a tavern). Bell, W.G., *The Great Fire of London in 1666* (2003 edn), Appendix III, *see* Hollar, *Exact Surveigh within the Ruins* (LTS, 1667); *see also* a will of David Smith (aka Smythe) who founded the six 'Embroiderers' tenements' (almshouses) to the east: 'a capital messuage called Woodmongers' Hall at the west end of the alley opening on to Paul's Wharf hill on the west': *c.*1587. *See* Harben, H.A., *A Dictionary of London* (1918) p.218: he added that the site had by then been covered by the building of Queen Victoria Street *See also* J. Rocque's *Plan of the Cities of London and Westminster* (1746): (Guildhall Library, City of London: Ms 13813): *see* Fig. 23, p.41. Ball, *op. cit.*, p.337: 44 Halls were burnt, not 50, or 53, as Strype wrote].

44. Holmes, *Elizabethan London*, et seq, pp.4-5, 19-20, 22-7.

45. Neale, *op. cit.*, Chs. 2, 3, 4; Martin, *op. cit.*, pp.223 et seq; p.255: 'Woodmongers continued to control the carters until 1582 but they did not destroy their corporate identity or swallow them up ... three carmen devised a scheme to escape the Woodmongers by replacing their control with that of Christ's Hospital ... The hospital retained dominance until 1605. Endless infighting ensued and it was another hundred years before the Carmen finally managed to rid themselves of the Woodmongers.' Kyle, C.R., 'Parliament and the Politics of Carting in Early Stuart London': *LJ*, 27 (2) 2002, pp.1-11: his account of the early Stuart years of the dispute is here preferred; for the Tudor background, and the later Stuart period, Birch, *op. cit.*, is the quoted source. Dale, *op. cit.*, although not used as prime source for this material, contains detail of the public articles, pp.36-44.

46. Lord Ezra, conversation with the author, November 2006; boundary disputes have inevitably characterised the long history of the Livery Companies, by reason of trade evolutions (e.g. most recently the resolution of a potential overlap between the ancient Painter-Stainers and the new Guild of Arts Scholars, Dealers & Collectors: conversation with Murray Craig, CoL, 3/iv/08).

47. For further background to this account, *see* Birch, *op. cit.*, pp.25, 27 & Chs. 3, 4, 5, passim.

48. Kyle, *op. cit.*, passim; for 'New Ice Age' reference, *see* 'The Independent', Climate Change bill, 14 March 2007, p.13. Previous accounts have come from the vantage points of Woodmongers and Carmen.

49. Birch, *op. cit.*, p.43, *see* poet John Taylor, & Ch.5.

50. The use of the two statutory royal prescriptive writs of *Quo Warranto* of 1290 ('by what authority?') and the *scire facias* (*sic*) ('act so that thou shalt discover') would have been taken to indicate the seriousness with which the Privy Council investigated apparent excesses of all Royal Charters, whether here for Livery Companies, or in Edward I's time for the nobility: '*Quo warranto* inquiries could be represented as stamping royal authority on the nobility and gentry by forcing them to submit their exercise of power to royal scrutiny': A. Musson, *Medieval Law in Context* ..., p.236; *see also* T. Plucknett, *Studies in English Legal History*, Essay II, p.790: 'the king himself was having difficulties in bringing *quo warranto* proceedings against usurpers of franchises'. *See also* Radcliffe & Cross, *The English Legal System*: 'proceedings against the

Crown as for instance by *scire facias* to cancel royal letters patent on the ground that they were made against the law ... were generally brought before the Chancellor' (in Chancery). *See also* D. Sutherland, *Quo Warranto Proceedings in the Reign of Edward I, 1278-1294*. TNA/PRO: Acts of The Privy Council, 1627-67, PC 2123-51.

51. *See* Note 15 supra; the detail of these events is also recorded in Birch, *op. cit.*, pp.47-8.

52. TNA/PRO as above, 1666/7; 1667/8; Dale, *op. cit.*, pp.53, 55: '... per idem nomen perpetuum habere successionem prout predictas literas patentes ... manifesto liquet et apparet – ... vos ... dedisse, concessisse et libere rursum reddidisse ac per presentem dare ... concedere et libere rursum Domino Nostro Carolo ... simul cum omnibus juribus privilegiis Franchesys, Jurisdictionibus et libertatibus ...; but see also* LMA, Jnl of Court of Common Council, Lawrence to Turner, JOR 46 1664-9, COL/CC/01/01.

53. Some of the problems facing the coal fleets are referred to in *The Plot Against Pepys*, p.253: 'The Newcastle coal boats heading for London used the 'colliers' route' [to avoid the Leman Bank and Ower sandbanks, which would cause the shipwreck involving Pepys himself] hugging the coast for some time, but more cautious sailors stayed well off-shore.'

Defoe, *op. cit.*, pp.228-30; locations of health fires: the Custom House, Billingsgate, Queenhithe, Three Cranes, Blackfriars, Bridewell, corner of Leadenhall Street & Gracechurch, north & south gate of Royal Exchange, Guild Hall, Blackwell Hall gate, Lord Mayor's door, St Helen's, west entrance to St Paul's, entrance into Bow Church, Bridge-foot, 'just by St Magnus Church'.

54. For above, *see* Pepys, *op. cit.*, vols. IV & V: entry, Sept 2 1666; pp.82-94; Tomalin, *Pepys*, Ch.15, passim.

55. Pepys, *op. cit.*, entries, 4-9 September; Tomalin, *op. cit.*, p.5, 231; Ball, *op. cit.*, p.86.

56. Reddaway, *op. cit.*, pp.26, 139.

57. Pepys, *op. cit.*, entry, 8 September.

58. Ibid., entry, 9 September.

59. Reddaway, *op. cit.*, p.185; Ackroyd, *Thames*, p.191.

60. Cooper, *op. cit.*, p.131; Seabourne, *op. cit.*, p.188.

61. Hope etc, *op. cit.*, p.57.

62. Reddaway, *op. cit.*, pp.183, 183-4, 190, 194, 301: Appendix B, p.313, speaks for itself (totals only given here):

PAYMENTS OUT OF THE COAL DUES

FROM THE CITY'S ACCOUNT		ACCOUNT OF THE PARISH CHURCHES	ACCOUNT OF ST PAUL'S CATHEDRAL
Yrs:	All, excl interest	Interest:	By Commissioners' Orders:
1667-87	£320,871+	£58,878+	£265,467+ £88,302+

63. TNA/PRO: Acts, Privy Council, 1666-7: (Bendish and Pope); Williamson, G.C. (ed.), Boyne, W., *Trade Tokens issued in the Seventeenth Century, by corporations, merchants and tradesmen*, 1889, v.I – London etc, v.II – Southwark etc; also Dale, *op. cit.*, pp.56-8. Grateful thanks for summaries of Museum of London deposits from John Clark, Deputy Head of Dept., Early London History.

64. Smith, *Seacoal*, p.29, *see* Dale, *op. cit.*, pp.33-4; also L. Stephen, *DNB* (1886). *See also* S. Pepys, trans J. Smith, *Diary ... Samuel Pepys*, v.1 (J.B. Lippincott, Philadelphia, 1855), pp.138-41.

65. Ibid., pp.30-2, see Dale, *op. cit.* pp.46-7, 49-51, 53-5, 66-7; I am also indebted to the Mayor of Westminster, through his Private Secretary, Kevin Taylor (letter, 12.ii.2009), and to Westminster City Archive, for data on Sir Edmund's status as contemporary 'First Citizen'.

66. Dale, *op. cit.*, pp.46-7, 51, 66-7; *see also* Long, J. & B., *The Plot against Pepys* (2007), Ch.4, & *Sunday Telegraph*, 19/viii/07, p.37. Re Godfrey Cup, *see* Bell, *op. cit.*, pp.352-3: the Earl of Lonsdale had two cups (one large, one small); Sudbury, Suffolk's cup was presented by its 17th-century MP, Sir Gervasse Elwes; a fourth was auctioned by Debenham, Storr in 1895; W.L. Lamplugh's family had a fifth (*Daily Telegraph*, 1895); Mrs Proctor, Aberdovey, a sixth; the Morgan Collection, a seventh; the Lushington family, an eighth. R. Lushington. [Bonham's?] Catalogue; also *Illustrated History of English Plate* (1911). Two ovals record both the visitations which form part of the Woodmonger-Fuellers' history; the Latin inscription reads: 'A man truly born for his country; when a terrible fire devastated the City, by the Providence of God, and his own merit, he was safe and illustrious in the midst of the flames. Afterwards, at the express desire of the King (but deservedly so) Edmund Berry [*sic*] Godfrey was created a knight, in September 1666. For the rest, let the public records speak'. 'John Berrie' was a cousin and godfather; 'Bury' aka 'Berry' came into common use as more familiar.

67. Ibid., p.35, *see* Edington, R., *Treatise on the abuses in the coal trade …* (1817); [*see* Ch.III, n.44]. The author gratefully acknowledges help from the Archivist of the Grenadier Guards, Maj. Wright, and Lance Sgt J.E. Tack.

68. Hollaender & Kellaway, *Studies in London History*: D.V. Glass, 'Socio-economic status & Occupations in London at the end of the 17th century': pp.382-3, Table 7: C.o.L within the Walls, 1692 Poll Tax sample: Category VII, Production & distribution (714 individuals/811 sampled): (1) All paying surtax: coachmaker 1; cakeman 1; diamond cutter 1; distiller 1; flaxman 1; haberdasher 33; hosier 6; merchant 88; needlemaker 1; packer 1; refiner 3; saddler 2; silkman 19; shopkeeper 1; skinner 5; smoker 4; soapboiler 1; steward 1; stocking presser 1; throwster 2; vintner 11; warehouseman 9; whaling master 1; wharfinger 3; winecooper 1; woodmonger 2: total 201 (out of 714). No trade was listed twice, i.e. under different headings.

That this is no isolated example of ongoing Woodmongering wealth can also be inferred from the Hearth Tax Loans of 1664-8 (article by C.A.F. Meekings in the same *Festschrift*, p.333): Woodmongers (with 54 subscriptions) are among 16 trades paying the top £2,000: others included clothworkers (60, 86); fishmongers (128); goldsmiths (67); mercers (59, 64); merchant taylors (55); or vintners (68). Prince's Meadows: Sir H. Roberts and W.H. Godfrey (eds), *Survey of London*, v.23 (English Heritage, 1951). After 1660, the Woodmongers' Company still had one of three barge-houses there, leased for 31 years. The names of Daniel Goodersay, Edward Smith and Thomas Shirley probably need to be recorded as early 'Fuellers'. [I am indebted for this information to Master John Bainbridge.]

CHAPTER III, pp. 69-107

1. The author is indebted to Prof Flinn's *History of The British Coal Industry*, v.II, as also to Prof J.U. Nef's *The Rise of the British Coal Industry* (1932) for much of this background. For political/Walpoleian corruption, *see* E. Pearce, *The Great Man: Sir Robert Walpole* (Cape, 2007).

2. Chesney, K., *Victorian Underworld* (1972), p.121.

3. Socio-economic setting, *see* Porter, R., *English Society in the Eighteenth Century* (1990); & George, D., *London Life in the 18th Century* (1966).

4. Flinn, *op. cit.*, p.451 et seq.; Smith, R., *Seacoal*, Ch.9.

5. Flinn, *op. cit.*, p.283, *see*, Adam Smith, *An Enquiry into the Nature and Causes of the Wealth of Nations* (ed.), Cannan, 1904, v.II, p.358.

6. Flinn, *op. cit.*, p.456.

7. Smith, R., *op. cit.*, Ch.I. Smith's pioneering research was well fulfilled in the *History of the British Coal Industry*.

8. Dickens, C., *Hard Times*.

9. Rackham, O., *English Countryside*, pp.49-50.

10. Smith, R., *op. cit.*, p.23.

11. Saint, A. and Darley, G., *Chronicles of London*, *see* Evelyn, J., p.121.

12. Freese, B., *Coal*; *see also* 'Sunday Times Magazine', 14/x/07, pp.80-91; R. Girling, 'Black to the Future'.

13. Dale, *op. cit.*, 69.

14. Sources for the Hostmen section (*see also* Bibliography):
    (a) desk research by David Wedderburn, Corbridge, in:
        (i) *Publications of the Surtees Society, Newcastle Hostmen*, v.105 (1901);
        (ii) Baillie, J., *Impartial History …* (1801);
        (iii) Middlebrook, S., *Newcastle …* (Newcastle, 1951);
    (b) Smith, R., *Seacoal*;
    (c) Brand, J., *History & Antiquities of the Town … of Newcastle upon Tyne, including an Account of the Coal Trade of that place* (1789) *pace* C. McCombe;
    (d) J.W.N. Petty, Senior Steward, The Company of Hostmen.
    Information has been also derived in part from:
        (i) *Liber Albus* (1861 transltn), p.629 et seq;
        (ii) Ashley, *Economic History*, v.i, pt.ii;
        (iii) Gregory (ed.), Gairdner, Camden Soc, n.122, *Chronicle of London*;
        (iv) Surtees Soc., 93, 101, '… Merchant Adventurers'.
        (v) Dendy, F.W., *Hostmen …*; Galloway, R.L., *Annals of Coal Mining*, Colliery Grdn C. (London, 1898-1904).

15. Middlebrook, *op. cit.*, p.71.

16. Re Keelmen and Keels, *see* Surtees, *Newcastle Hostmen*, Intro, pp.1-11; also Smith, R., *op. cit.*, pp.15-16; Thornton, C.E. (ed.), *Bound for the Tyne: Extracts from the diary of Ralph Jackson, Apprentice Hostman of Newcastle upon Tyne 1749-1756* (Company of Hostmen, Newcastle, 2000), p.1. Jackson, b. Richmond, Yks 1736, started seven-year apprenticeship with Quaker William Jefferson, 1749. Space in the Fuellers' History does not allow extensive quotation from the Diary, but a few items (with editorial commentary) deserve mention here [*see also* Glossary]:

    (p.2): 'The keelman's work in manually shovelling coal from the keel, up and over the side of a collier into its hold, was strenuous and dirty … Wm. Jefferson brewed his own ale, and maintained a regular supply to his keelmen to quench their thirsts. This had a parallel … in London, where the coal heavers … were employed by the landlords of public houses …'.

    (p.30): '1.iii.1753: After breakfast I … wrote some Receipts, ordered the fire Coal deliver'd to sundry people.' ['As well as supplying the collier vessels, Hostmen also supplied coal to domestic properties …'.]

    (p.35): '6.iii.1756: I went to ask Mr Aub. Surtees if he would take a bill for £160 0s. 0d. on Mr Richard Gaire, Merchant near Billingsgate, London …'.

17. Brand, J., *op. cit.*, pp.269, 657-9.

18. Smith, R., *op. cit.*, p.7 et seq.

19. Surtees Soc., *Hostmen*, p.76, *see* Welford, *Newcastle*, v.iii, p.326; also Smith, R., *op. cit.*, pp.13-14.

20. Ibid., pp.8-10.

21. Surtees, *Hostmen*, Ibid., p.xiv, *see* Murray, *Dictionary* (1901) v.V, p.314: first ref is in Surtees, *op. cit.*: 1518.

22. Surtees, *op. cit.*, p.124, *see* Hostmen, Orders & Minutes, 1600-1901; the relevant passage, 7 April 1662 reads (*pace* transliteration, Dr P. Taylor, Archivist, Girdlers' Company): 'Upon the reading of a letter from Mr John Rus(c)h(k)worth [probably not a Woodmonger] to the Governor(s) of this Company, intimating that the Woodmong[e]rs, Shipp Masters, and others are frameing a Peticon to p[re]sent to the Councell complaineing at/of the Hoastmen for vending bad coles and therefore desireing an Offic[e]r might be appointed to survey the Coles (.) It is Ordered that an answer thereunto be drawne and sent up by the Governor(s) to some p[erson], who in case any such Peticon be p[rse]nted to the Councell, may acquaint them that the Hoastmen are concerned therein and desire that they may have time to give in their reasons against it'.

23. Surtees, *Hostmen*, Intro., p.xxi, *see* Surtees, 'Newcastle Merchant Adventurers' 93, p.47; Ref Liège, *see Belgium Insight Guides*, 2005, p.249.

24. Surtees, *Hostmen*, Intro., pp.xxviii-xxix.

25. Smith, R., *op. cit.*, pp.7-8.

26. Middlebrook, *Newcastle*, p.41; Surtees, *Hostmen*, Intro., pp.xix-xxi; Smith, R., *op. cit.*, pp.15-16.

27. Surtees, *Hostmen*, p.xxix, *see* State Papers, Domestic, Elizabeth, v.105, n.30.

28. Surtees, *Hostmen*, Intro., pp.xxxiii-xxxiv; Gardiner, R., *England's Grievance Discovered* (1655).

29. Baillie, *op. cit.*, pp.463-5, *see* Gray, *Chorographia* (1649).

30. Ibid., pp.455-6.

31. Thornton, *op. cit.*, p.1.

32. Smith, R., *op. cit.*, p.xii.

33. Ibid., p.1. Some indication of one family's development in function from the wholesaling 'Coal Factor' (or 'Coal Distributor') to the retailing 'Coal Merchant' can be seen in the family history of one of the longest coal genealogies, spanning 10 generations of the Quaker Hornes of Bankside, London. From Richard (d.1766) to his son Thomas (d.1802), their wills describe them as 'citizen and clothworker, and coal factor' (*see* 'precedence', Ch.I). The first reference to 'coal merchant' comes with the will of grandson Anthony (d.1816). It must have been his son Thomas (b.1782, d.1864) who at the peak of his career, aged 57, was still in a position as a member of a Society of Coal Factors, to receive a medallion to commemorate the abolition of the 'Land Coal Factors' by Act of Parliament in 1831: [*see* Fig. 48, p.101]. This family of Freemen was also 'represented on the Livery' of the Clothworkers (with benefits, through the mediation of Lester Horne – b.1899, d.1984 – for the emergence of the Fuellers: *see* Ch.IV) in an unbroken line from the 18th to the 21st centuries, with no mention of allegiance to any Livery for the coal trade: this tradition only introduced with current member of the family, Lester's son Richard, Past Master of both Companies (b.1926). [Sources: G. Sherwood, *The Pedigree Register*, Mar. 1913, and discussions with Richard Horne, 17/iv/07.]

34. Ibid., p.14.

35. Ibid., Ch.6 passim; Defoe, *Tour of Great Britain* (1769), v.II, p.151; Murray, *Dictionary*, v.2, p.1,174.

36. Ibid., p.64.

37. Chesney, *op. cit.*, p.105.

38. George, *op. cit.*, p.18.

39. Smith, R., *op. cit.*, p.57, *see* 1620 *Jor.* 31, f.227 (1686); Riley, H.T., *Charters relating to metage dues* pp.176-7.

40. Ibid., pp.57-8.

41. Dale, *op. cit.*, pp.82-3, *see* 'Gentlemen's Magazine' (1768).

42. Ibid., pp.79-80; also Mayhew, *London Labour*, p.235.

43. Ibid., p.87; Colquhoun, *Treatise on Commerce* ..., pp.142-7.

44. TOW-ROW: Thanks to Maj Wright, Archivist, & L/Sgt Tack, RHQ Grenadier Guards, corr. of August 2007: ROs 1758-64, folios 121, 139, 142: an Act of 1750, and ROs of 11 August and 14 September 1759 forbade the three Regiments of Foot Guards from acting as Coal-Heavers; the CO at the Tower was ordered to 'Court Martial soldiers who had been confined in the Savoy' for disobeying these Orders.

   Plaque reads: 'The original Coal Hole was located in a cellar in Fountain Court, a few yards from our present establishment. Its name seems to have derived from the Coal Heavers who worked nearby on the River Thames. Edmund Keane, one of the biggest theatrical stars of his day, founded the Wolf Club at the Coal Hole. The story was that it was established for oppressed husbands who were not allowed to sing in the bath. The reality was an excuse forbade heavy drinking in the company of loose women. Keane collapsed on stage in 1838 and died later. The Coal Hole was demolished in 1889 and this building opened in 1904, briefly called The New Strand Wine Lodge.' P. Ackroyd adds to the background on the development of the embankment: 'where once the gardens of the noblemen had sloped down to the river, there were constructed wharves and jetties for the use of brewers and wood merchants': *Thames*, p.189.

45. Dale, *op. cit.*, p.87.

46. Smith, R., *op. cit.*, pp.166-7.

47. White, J., *London in the 19th Century* (2007) p.284: 'there were pubs that were labour exchanges for beggars, actors, street entertainers, even body-snatchers and most notoriously for the Thames coal-whippers'.

48. Dale, *op. cit.*, p.16 (6 April 1622: 'Petition by Woodmongers Chandlers and others ...'); p.17 (29 August 1622: Common Council to Mayor of Newcastle etc ref 'complaints of the Woodmongers, Brewers, Chandlers and other traders in sea coal in London ...'); p.20 (7 November 1638: Middlesex J.P.s' Report to Council, ref 'Chandlers and other retailers'); p.28 (27 January 1643, London contemporary pamphlet – 'Sea-coale', 'Char-coale' and 'Small-Coale' – 'They all accuse Sea-Coal's factors, the Wharfers, Woodmongers and Chandlers and the like ...'). Also p.75, *see* Swift, Jonathan, 'Tatler', 9, Will's Coffee-house, 28 April 1709), *Description ... Morning*; George, *op. cit.*, p.49. White, *op. cit.*, p.211: 'Others, like mackerel, lived on the furthest edge of a great industry to pick up what scraps of profit they could – like the trolleymen who might buy a sack of cheap coals and hawk them by the bagful to the city's poorest customers'. Two pictures were painted by Woolaston of the 'Musical Small-Coalman, Thomas Britton, in his blue frock[coat], with the small coal-measure in his hand ... he lived in Aylesbury Street Clerkenwell, at a cornerhouse of a passage leading by the Old Jerusalem Tavern into St John's Sq ... On the ground-floor were the coal stores and above them a long narrow room ... where he held musical reunions attended by the fashionable, including Handel. He was buried in Clerkenwell churchyard, Oct, 1 1714'. (Thanks to Past Master Fueller C. McCombe re data on T. Britton; *see also* his article in F, September 2008).

   'Trolleymen'/'Trolleyrounds' were still common in London's coal trade in the 1990s; a definitive TGWU-agreed sum was paid above the piecework rate. In E. Anglia/Beds. etc, the terms were 'Hawker'/'hawking rounds': I am indebted to C.B. Brinkman, former Charringtons director, for this data.

49. White, *op. cit.*, p.200: 'some [women] achieved immortality of a kind, Peggy Jones, who disappeared without trace in February 1805, waded at Blackfriars in short petticoats, searching for coals with her toes, filling a bag-like apron round her waist and selling then at 8d. a load to the coal merchants ... and Mary Casey, 25 and Irish, who was noted in the early 18609 by that

interesting *flaneuer*, Arthur Munby. He saw her 'naked from the thigh down', striding into the half-frozen Thames in search of coal, risking any danger or discomfort to win a crust.' Ackroyd, P., *Thames, Sacred River*, pp.181-2.

50. George, *op. cit.*, p.161.
51. Smith, R., *op. cit.*, p.xiii.
52. Ibid., p.33.
53. Ibid., pp.34-5, *see* [Anon] *Frauds and abuses of the coal-dealers detected* ..., 1743-4. pp.7-9.
54. Humpherus, *Watermen*.
55. Smith, R., *op. cit.*, Ch.5.
56. Ibid., pp.37-8.
57. Ibid., p.38.
58. Ibid., pp.43-4.
59. Ibid., p.45.
60. Ibid., p.47.
61. Ibid., p.48.
62. Humpherus, *op. cit.*, p.311, 'Lightermen had an office at the Dog Tavern, Billingsgate, with a Committee ... Wm. Ward, Mallory Pierson, John Gibson and Benjamin Horne (Coal Factors) and Joseph Merryman and James Hurston': Dale, *op. cit.*, p.77.
63. Ibid., p.397.
64. Ibid., p.430; Smith, *op. cit.*, p.79.
65. Pudney, J., *London's Docks* (1975): pp.18-19, and Ch.2; Colquhoun, *op. cit.*, pp.142-3, 181, 229.
66. Flinn, *op. cit.*, p.187.
67. Humpherus, *op. cit.*, pp.58-9.
68. Ibid., p.246.
69. Ibid., p.300.
70. Ibid., pp.294, 302, 322-3.
71. Dale, *op. cit.*, p.75.
72. Ibid., p.80; p.82 also yields names of Coal Merchants John Evans, Joseph Harrison, Joseph Coltman, and John Walter, who on 22/i/1767 'prayed Parliament for an Act to establish a Coal Meter's Office' (*see* Appendix III(B)).
73. Ibid., pp.70-1.
74. Ibid., pp.94-5.
75. Ibid., p.95.
76. Ibid., p.95; Mayhew, *London's Labour*, pp.257-8, gives these statistics for mid-19th-century coaltrade [* = other docks trades]:

Ships	2,177
Seamen*	21,000
Tons of coal entering PoL p.a.	3,418,140
Coalmeters	170
Coalwhippers	2,000
Coalporters	3,000
Coalfactors	25
Coalmerchants	502
Coaldealers	295
Coal-waggons	1,600
Horses for ditto	5,200
Waggoners*	1,600
Trimmers	800

77. Dale, *op. cit.*, pp.96-7. On 8 August 1703, Woodmongers & Carmen petition the Lord Mayor for re-incorporation 'all the unhappy differences between the partners now being reconciled: Thomas Mayo, Robert Marshall, John Toone, Abram Palmer, Roger Benfords, Wm. Lovell, Ed. Chancy, Daniel Peacock, Thomas Inwood, Wm. Franklyn, Rd, Avery, Thomas Arnott, Jn. Searle, Edwd. Highmore, Jn. Mawby, Wm, Wilcoks, Jn.

Smare, & Rd. Lilly': Dale, *op. cit.*, pp.138-9.
On 24 July 1733, another Petition surfaces, by 16 '"Woodmongers and Dealers in Coals" in the City of London on behalf of themselves and the Fellowship of Porters', about price practices, signed: Wm. Nose, Thos. Smith, Jn. Atkins, Jn, Mitchell, Rd, Hewitt, Christopher Beatty, Samuel Illing, Nath. Highmore [# family link], Philip Truchard, Robt. Dobson, Free. Cooper, Thos. Raynold, A. Ward, Chas. Hunt, Jn. Greaves & Martin Wardell': Dale, *op. cit.*, pp.142-3.

78. Ibid., pp.97-8, *see* Humpherus, *op. cit.*, p.389.
79. Ibid., pp.83-5.
80. Smith, R., *op. cit.*, p.78, *see* amending Dale, *op. cit.*, pp.100-1.
81. [Humpherus, *op. cit.*, pp ... *ILN*, ref Coal Exchange opening]
82. Peggy Hart, *The Magic of Coal* (Puffin Books, 1945)
83. Wordsworth, W., *Poems*, 'Composed upon Westminster Bridge'.
84. Dickens, C., *Hard Times*; Gaskell, Elizabeth, *North & South*; Zola, E., *Germinal*.
85. Church, *History, British Coal Industry*, v.III, p.582, *see* Bulman, *Coal Mining & the Coal Miner*: Other notable disasters were at New Hartley, Northumberland (1862), The Oaks, Yorkshire (1866), Blantyre, Lanarkshire (1877), Abercarn, Monmouthshire and Albion, Cilfyndd, Glamorgan (1894), and in the next century, the biggest losses of life of all at Hulton, Yorkshire (1910), and Universal, Senghenydd in Glamorgan (1913), when 344 and 439 men died respectively.
86. Mayhew, *op. cit.*, passim.
87. Orwell, G., *Down and Out in Paris and London* (Penguin, 1988), p.104.
88. Robinson, Jane, *Mary Seacoal, the charismatic black nurse who became a heroine of the Crimea* (2005).

CHAPTER IV, pp.109-43
(F = issue of *The Fueller*):

1. For coal industry statistics, *see* Church, *History of British Coal Industry*, v.3, Ch.1 ('Rise of the Coal Economy'), pp.18-23 and v.4, passim.
2. Ibid., v.3, pp.41-7, 75-80.
3. Ibid., v.3, pp.73-4.
4. R. Mercer, *Building on Sure Foundations, The South Eastern Gas Board 1949-1972* (Br.Gas, 1996); p.ix, 1, 39. Church, *op. cit.*, v.3, pp.80-1.
5. For further data on 19th-century gas industry, I am indebted to Dr F. Goodall, *Burning to Serve: Selling Gas in Competitive Markets*; also *Coal Industry*, v.3 passim.
6. GH, CoL, 19th-century Trade Cards collection.
7. *Coal Industry*, v.4, passim.
8. Ibid., v.5, p.5. *See* Minute Books of Railborne Coal Factors & Wholesale Merchants' Association, 26/ix/1924 – 7/x/1927; & of National Council of Coal Traders 14/x/1918 – 11/xii/1922: Fuellers' Archive, courtesy Archivist Rex Rose.
9. Ibid., v.4, Part B.
10. Ibid., [maps], v.5 p.4.
11. Dale, *op. cit.*, p.22, *see* 'Domestic State Papers', City of London to Inner Star Chamber, 15.v.1639.
12. Smith, *op. cit.*, pp.10, 20-1, *see* Nef, *British Coal Industry*.
13. Dale, *op. cit.*, p.73; p.25, 'Order in Council'; p.49: 'Journals of House of Commons, 5 January 1666/7; Pepys' *Diary* [prob. 15 January 1666]'.
14. Smith, *op. cit.*, pp.20-1.
15. Dale, *op. cit.*, p.65.
16. Ibid., p.78: Maitland, *History of London*, ref to Billingsgate: 'Here the Coalmen and Woodmongers meet every morning

about 8 or 9 o'clock, this place being their Exchange for the Coal Trade …'.

17. Ibid., pp.96-7: 'Woodmongers and Coal Wharfingers held a meeting at the London Tavern … 22 December 1831 …'.

18. Ibid., p.97.

19. Although space precludes full reference here, books by two eventual members of the House of Lords, Lord Ezra, *Coal and Energy: The need to exploit the world's most abundant fossil fuel*; and the autobiography of one of the more moderate NUM leaders, Lord (Joe) Gormley, *Battered Cherub*, set the scene for both these trends in the current demise of the UK coal industry. A contrary, brighter factor during the writing of the History has been a re-investment in a new deep mine by British Coal plc. For 'the moment of truth' *see The Independent*, 12/i/08.

20. *See* Appendix V.

21. *See* Appendix III(A).

22. Emile Zola, *Germinal*; D.H. Lawrence, *Coal Dust*; 'How Green Was My Valley' (directed by J. Ford), *13th Film Guide* (2005), p.316; an ironic and indeed prophetic questioning of the apparent inevitability of coal-mining came from George Orwell: 'People have a way of taking it for granted that all work is done for a sound purpose … coal-mining, for example, is hard work, but it is necessary, we must have coal': *Down and Out in Paris and London*, p.104.

23. The NCB commissioned many paintings by Josef Hermann, a coal-miner refugee from the 1956 Hungarian uprising; these were hung in the offices of Hobart House for many years.

24. Letters to the author from:

(i) Mrs Thérèse (Stephenson) Clarke: 'The Charringtons stay with us at Brightwell Grove the week-end of 8/12 January 1970. I think, the first time that the idea of recovering the Charter was aired between Jack [Charrington] and Charlie [Clarke] … Charlie and Jack leave together for work on Monday morning. Theresa, [Charrington] and I meet them for lunch at the Aperitif when the Charter was definitely talked about – if in vague terms … On 21 June 1973 we take the Ezras and the Charringtons to Glyndebourne – this could be about the time when Derek first became involved?': 20/i/08. (Charles Stephenson Clarke, Chairman, Stephenson Clarke Ltd.; Jack Charrington, Chairman, Charringtons Ltd; Sir Derek Ezra, Chairman, NCB.)

(ii) Peter Stafford: 21/iii/07. *See also* correspondence raised by Roger Cloke in pursuance of his creation of a complete Fuellers' database, notably e-mail from PM Brian Harrison of 9/xii/2006.

25. Dale, *op. cit.*, Preface. A retrospective insider's view (*see* Endnote 29) was that back in 1922, the Woodmongers would not necessarily have succeeded, due to the deep City conservatism of that era, well before the liberalisation of candidature, with the introduction of the Master Mariners, 1926: (Jim Sewell, discussion with author, 14/v/08.) C.B. Brinkman & R. Cloke, Hon Court Assistants, The Fuellers.

26. SCM Minute Book, 1976.

27. Discussion with Mrs Thérèse Stephenson Clarke, at Letcombe Regis, 11/i/08: Thérèse was not able to confirm any date for such a key meeting but believed the venue might well have been *The Cavendish Hotel*. Letter, Sir Derek Ezra, NCB Chairman, to George McGechan, Chairman, SCM, 25/iv/79, after Sir Derek had presented the SCM Chairman with a new Chain of Office, at the Plaisterers' Hall banquet on 24/iv/79 to celebrate the award by Colin Cole, CVO, TD, FSA, Garter Principal

King of Arms, of 'Letters Patent Granting and Assigning the Arms and Crest' [Armorial Bearings] to the Society: [Fuellers' Archive, collection of G.A. McGechan].

28. Birch, *Carr & Carman*, p.142.

29. Evidence of the skill with which the Society of Coal Merchants was accelerated to Livery status as a 'special case', from an assumed 10 years, lies in the letter for Linklaters to send to the sponsoring Alderman, draft by Arthur Puttock and John Pugh, 11.xii.1979: [Fuellers' Archive; acknowledgement to Thérèse Clarke.] The author is greatly indebted for guidance on aspects of the workings of the Court of Aldermen, to Jim Sewell, Clerk of the Chamberlain's Court from 1973 to 2003. *See* Master Paul Glover (F1), Autumn 1990; also letter from Stanley Heather to John Pugh, Fuellers' P/14 & Treasurer CMO, 7/v/1990: 'the old Company can be regarded as representing the distributive aspect of the contemporary fuel industry of the country as a whole'. 'Oklahoma' song. 'Woodmongers' Supper', Armourers' & Braziers' Hall, 11.xi.08.

30. Silverware (F8, 9, 16); *see* Appendix II(D).

31. Modern Companies: (F22).

32. Woodmongers' Supper: (F23).

33. Fuellers' response to 2007 Law Review Commission.

34. Correspondence, M. Bryer Ash to Duke of Westminster, 1994/5: (by kind permission of Michael Bryer Ash).

35. *See* issues of F, 1998-2009.

36. Fueller Prize holders: 1993: CPOAEA (M) Kevin Sargent (F2); 1994: Paula Price (F5); 1997 PO Stephen Heggie (F9); 1998: WO M. Sedgley (F12); 1999: CPOAEM Bailey; 2000: PO Wren Langdon, HMS *Sultan*; 2001: CPO AEA(M) A.E. Stancliffe (F16); 2002: POAEM(M) Andrew Claxton (F17/18); 2003: CPO AEA (L) David Harris (F20); 2004: POAE9M) Steve Mepsted, HMS *Sultan*; 2005: CPO AEA (E) Gareth Rees, HMS *Sultan* (F25): Cpl Gillian Doctor, 216 Sqd: Seth Treasure, City & Guilds U: Chris F. Jones, City U.; 2006: Wo2 Derek Harwood, HMS *Sultan*: Flt Lt James Osborne, 216 Sqd; 2007: Cpl Mike Durnford, 216 Sqd: Wo2 Martin J. Gosling, HMS *Sultan* (F29): Brian Soave, City & Guilds U.: Muhammed Khan, City U.; 2008: PO Ian Porter, HMS *Sultan*: Cpl Jemma Kerr, 216 Sqd: Colin Bissenden, City & Guilds U.: Chris Wilson, City U.: First Offr Scott Tait, RFA *Wave Knight*; 2009: David Mead, City U.: Janet Ricketts City & Guilds U.: Lt Paul Bastiens, HMS *Sultan* [NB: HMS *Daedalus* up to 1996; thereafter HMS *Sultan* (link shared with other Livery Companies: (F3)]; 2009: Chief Technician Steve Keating, RAF 216 Squadron; Third Officer Nicola Lutman, RFA, *Wave Ruler*.

37. Apprentice scheme; Charles Stephenson Clarke Memorial Prize; (F18, 19, 24).

38. Hannah Thomas, Elinor Moran (F21, 22); Stockwell Park High School (F28).

39. *See* Ch.II, Endnotes 1, 11.

40. Corporation of London, *City Livery Companies* (2006), p.37; F.

41. Hollaender, A.E.J. and Kellaway, W., *Studies in London History*, pp.197-216, nb p.215: Barron, C.M., 'Richard Whittington: The Man Behind the Myth'; *see* Brie, F.W.D., T*he Brut or the Chronicles of England* (EETS, 1908) pt ii, p.449. *See also* Mercers' Hall, Wardens' Accounts. F11, p.1.

42. DTI 2006 Review: 'Our Energy Challenge'.

43. John Hutton to Adam Smith Institute, March 2008: *The Independent*, 10.iii.08: 'Back to Black' … 'First coalfired power stations for a generation to be given green light'. *The Times*, 9/ix/08.

Glossary

In a History with multiple audiences, this Glossary has several purposes, and is designed to be read in conjunction with the text. Given that The Fuellers of the 21st century need to communicate with interests complementary to their own, it explains some of the slang or terms (a) which may be common ground to those closely involved with the coal and energy industries, but which will present problems of understanding to those outside these worlds; (b) terms which are *lingua franca* to members of Livery Companies, or to medievalists but unfamiliar to a wider readership; (c) technical terms/acronyms familiar to the 21st-century field of environmental science.

('…': *see* the Glossary). [Key: C = Colquehoun (*op. cit.*); 'CoL' = City of London; P = Pudney (*op. cit.*); S = Smith (*op. cit.*); M = Mayhew (*op. cit.*); H = *History of British Coal Industry*; G = Gwen Seabourne (*op. cit.*); D = Dale, RSA lecture]

(A) The wood, timber, coal and dockland trades

addit 'day-eye' pits: horizontal tunnels in hillsides.

Agent: officer working on behalf of a principal (*see* Fitter).

bag: transmission of details of arriving colliers, first at Gravesend, then Tilbury, by steamer/rail; later, telegraph.

bailage: duty imposed on non-freemen of the CoL in respect of goods imported into/exported from the 'Port of London'.   **S178**

ballast: essential to colliers' return journey to North-East.

Basis, the: calculation of an average 'vend' or production of coals from the various North-East coast collieries.   **S**

Basket/bowl/corf: containers of varying dimensions as between different collieries, used to convey coal from face to surface; units for calculating piece-rate agreements. **H**

Basket man: foreman of a gang of 'coal-whippers' whose duty it was to shoot into the 'vat' the contents of the 'basket' used to whip coals from the hold of a ship.   **S**

baulked days: days on which a 'Meter' assigned to a ship in 'Pool' was baulked or prevented from working.   **S**

bavin: small bundle of 'faggots', used in kilns etc.

'black': 'He's a black': a thorough-going coal industry person.

Blackwall clause: 18th-19th century: intended to prevent forwarding of ship's papers before she arrived at Blackwall; often evaded.

Body of Wharfingers: corporate association of Wharfingers, CoL, 18th/19th century.

Boy:

(i)   *c.*1811: member of ship's crew sent to London Custom House (out of hours to a Wm Topper at St Mary Hill, precursor of Meters' Night Office) with ship's papers on arrival at Nore or Yarmouth.   **S197, 201**

(ii)   As in 'coal boys', carrying coal in barrows, 20th century.

brocage: making or soliciting bargains/contracts by brokers between merchant and merchant or buyer and seller.   **S**

buscher: EX. lat. *buscarii*: woodmonger.

bushel: domestic coal measure.   **S**

caper: Dutch privateer, raiding Newcastle collier fleets.

car/carr/cart: carman is a man who drives a carr, a carrier or carter; place he plies for hire – a 'car-room'; a car was used by carmen to convey merchandise within London.   **B**

car-room:

(i) purchasable/alienable open public space for parking, hiring 'cars'/carrs/carts.

(ii) licence for same.

cats: aka 'hags' aka 'flyboats' aka 'hagboats'.   **S**

chaldron aka **chalder**:   **S168; H**

(a)   Newcastle chaldron, variable, late 17th century; *c.*1700 = 53 cwt; mid-18th century = 2.6 tons of coal (*Bound for the Tyne*).

(b)   London (or Winchester or Winton, or Imperial), usually half of a Newcastle chaldron, 26.5 cwt: Newcastle and London chaldrons – usual proportion: 15 to 8/25½ cwt.

(c)   Scottish chaldron, very variable, 1.5/5 tons.

Coal: many different classifications for varying purposes:
- (a) sea-coal: (i) outcrop from NE coast; (ii) carried by sea to London, from NE or Bristol/Forest of Dean mines; or (iii) minable inland e.g. 'Sea-coal in the Forest of Macclesfield': *Annals of Coal Mining*, 1382.
- (b) pit-coal, deep-mined: (anthracite, steam, lignite, etc).
- (c) charcoal, up to the 17th century.
- (d) Scotch-coals: sea coal from Scottish ports/mines. **S**
- (e) gift coal: an overweight bonus given by the 'Hostmen' to the shippers: abolished 1637. **S**
- (f) railway coal: mid-19th-century importation into London market. **S**
- (g) concessionary coal: 20th century, finally given to all employees.
- (h) stone coal: anthracite.
- (i) cannel coal: high quality, bituminous, Lothians/Lancs.

coal dues: taxes on coal entering CoL, nb 17th century.

Coal Factors' bag: ships' papers sent twice daily by steamer (forbidden to go by Post) from Gravesend (opened 1833) to the Factors' office at the Coal Exchange by 1800 hrs. **S212-3**

Coal Factors' Society: 1845 name for Society of Coal Factors; not all factors were member firms (16 in 1847). Did not regulate coal trade. Uniform factorage rate ended 1846. **S306**

Coal-heavers: by the 19th century = 'Coal-Whippers': gangs that raised or 'whipped up' coal from lighters in Thames, prior to introduction of cranes and derricks using steam/hydraulic power; see also **Porters**. **S291**

Coal Meters: weighers of coal (see also **Meters**).

Coal Trade Committee: Newcastle 1852-60; attempt to co-ordinate coal prices with other owners and with London factors, in face of depressed London market. **S281**

cocquet/cocket: certificate of loading given by the Collector of Customs in the Cocket Office at the Custom House, or at the port of loading, to a ship-master with a dutiable cargo; originally a seal. **S**

collier:
- (a) miner.
- (b) >17th century, charcoal-burners (e.g. 'of Croydon').
- (c) sea-going vessel carrying coal as cargo.
  - (i) sailing.
  - (ii) screw/steam from 1852-36 by 1854.
- (d) coalman, 19th century. **S205**

colouring/colour: selling unfreemen's coals, ostensibly in the name of the Hostman: 'Hostmen employed fitters or servants not free of the Society who "under Color of their masters … do buy and vend great quantities of coles of their own and other unfreemen's"'. **S**

colt: young new miner. **S**

combination: agreement between coal-fitters and others at Newcastle to restrain or cartelise coal trade. **S**

'commoner': a non-managerial member of the coal mine workforce (East Midlands Coalfield slang).

crimp: Dutch/Flemish origin = 'screwing/scrimping, measuring under rather than over':
- (a) small middle-man in London coal market, often no more than a contractor ('undertaker') of the labour of coal heavers or coal-'whippers' for unloading 'colliers'.
- (b) (i) 17th-century functions – both broker and 'undertaker'.
  - (ii) 18th-century broker is styled as the crimp or factor.
  - (iii) 1747+: wholesale dealers with/without sense of broker or factor.
  - (iv) outside coal trade, up to late 19th century, agent for procuring or impressing seamen. **S**

culm: small coal or 'stone coal' (= anthracite). **S**

customer, coal: By the 18th century, of five kinds:
- (i) 'loader on account'.
- (ii) dealer.
- (iii) retailer (kept a shed and sold by the bushel).
- (iv) consumer (large 'manufactories who took their supplies in bulk').
- (v) the housekeeper. **S**

del credere commission: further 10 per cent commission for 18th-century factor on top of standing 10 per cent, for guaranteeing and being responsible for the solvency of the persons to whom he sold. **S**

delph: early name for coal mine.

drops: ground in N. London, mid-19th century, let to coal-dealers/coal owners as storage selling-places for 'railway coal'. **S204**

engrossing: (i) to buy up wholesale; (ii) buy up as much as possible of a commodity for the purpose of 'regrating' it at a monopoly price: cornering by buying up large quantities. (*See* Note 'A' below) **G**

factor: (a) initially London agent of a NE coal-owner, who acted on commission as middleman between shipmasters and the principal coal-buyers; (b) later 19th century, buyer on Coal Exchange who was still a factor; often 'the factor was the actual 'exporter'/'partner'/'attorney'; merchant's merchant. **S345**

faggot: bundle of rods, sticks etc for kindling.

fighting aka **free trade**: mid-19th-century attempt by factors and coal owners to maintain price of coal in London, following ending of the limitation of the vend, 1845; coal-owners forced to charter own ships and take their coals to London. **S165**

first buyers: bought entire cargoes of coal from factors, to sell on to e.g. five 'customers'; next stage in distributive chain after factor mediated with coal-owner/shipper. **S**

Fitter aka **'Factor'**: (a) (N-E) a Newcastle shipping agent who arranged the sale of coal to shipmasters on behalf of a coal-owner, owned 'keels', employed keelmen; unofficial name for a Hostman (*Bound for the Tyne*); (b) fixed cargoes for owners with buyers from a distance and got coals delivered from staiths to ship. **S**

flyboats: *see* 'hags'.

forestalling: intercepting goods prior to the open market. **B**

fother: as much fuel as can be carried in cart with one horse.

Fueller: synonym for Woodmonger, obsolete usage.

'game' (docks slang): of a bribable customs officer.

gate: 18th-century Newcastle term for waggon.

Gear: implements used in unloading – baskets, shovels. **S314**

grindstones, whetstones, rubstones: alternative ballast for colliers from Newcastle: (spoils still visible on beaches).

groundage: duty on vessels entering port/lying on a shore, payable by every vessel-owner (*see* 'bailage'). **S**

hags/hagboats: small boats.

Harbourmasters: appointed by Corporation of CoL under Port Act 1799, to accommodate shipping/colliers in the Pool. **S198, 329**

'horsemen' (docks slang): 'light' or 'heavy': well-organised gangs of Coopers, Watermen, 'Lumpers' – plundering lighters.

Hostman/Hoastman/oastman: medieval intermediary in European trade: householders assigned to entertaining merchant non-'free' 'strangers'. For Newcastle, by a charter of 1600, right to trade in coal was limited to the guild of Hostmen. By end of the 17th century, Hostmen had become a fraternity not of [coal-]owners' officials but of fitters/agents.

husbands: one of many intermediaries acting for masters of coal-carrying ships. **S**

ingrain: allowance to the buyer of coals bought on board ship of one chaldron to every hundred: established trade practice by 1366. **S**

Inspector of Colliers: noted time of colliers' arrival at Gravesend, then Tilbury, reported to Secretary, 19th century. **S213**

keels aka **barges/**(also **shouts: Thames**):
- (i)   flat-bottomed vessel operated by keelmen, Tyne/Wear, for loading colliers;
- (ii) quantity of coals in a keel:
- (iii) also individual 'keelman'.

King's Duty: equivalent of H.M. Customs, distinct from payment of dues to the CoL; later mediated via 'crimps'. **S**

laystalls: areas in CoL, set aside for dumping of rubbish.

load: coal usually sold in loads, each of a specific number of corves/'baskets': could be horse-load, cart-load; wain load (often = a 'fother' or ton). **[H]** >

loader on account: first category of 'customer', loading coal into his own craft, but without capital to own a wharf at Billingsgate. **S**

'lumper' (docks slang): docker.

marking: 18th-century: 'if masters or their crimps did not sell to lightermen, their ships would be 'marked' [i.e. proscribed]. **S**

merchant: wholesale trader (also retail, 17th-century); 19th century *c.*150, 50 first buyers, often also in corn; 19 houses of factors, also later acted as merchants. **S172**

Meters: Official appointed to measure goods entering London for duty, e.g.
- (a)   Salt Meters, etc.
- (b)   Coal:
  - (i)   Sea-coal Meters for coal as it was unloaded from colliers' barges.
  - (ii) Land-Meters working on shore. [*see* Appendix III(B).]

mine: five main types:
- (a)   Deep mine.
- (b)   Drift mine.
- (c)   Opencast aka 'adit/day-eye' (coal near surface).
- (d)   Bell mine (earliest method).
- (e)   'Outcrop': surface coal.

monger: OED, from ON *mangari* (a) dealer, trader, trafficker; (b) 16th-19th century: 'nearly always implies one who carries on a contemptible or discreditable trade' (e.g. rumourmonger).

'mudlark' (docks slang): prowlers at low water, to take off goods illegally slung overboard by 'lumpers'. **P**

night-plunderers (docks slang): gangs of the most dissolute Watermen, preying on unprotected lighters. **P**

outcrop: *see* 'mine'.

Pool, The/Port of London: 'Upper Pool' – London Bridge to Tower Bridge: 'Lower' to Bermondsey: 'London River' – Westminster to Greenwich. Jurisdiction of the Coal Commissioners reached from the Arsenal at Woolwich to London Bridge; (Gravesend held to be within the 'Port of London'). **S**

porter/coalporter/coalbacker/coalheaver/coal-labourer: by the mid-19th century, London term 'coalheavers' out of use, divided into the 'coalwhipper', and the 'coalbacker' who 'carried coals on his back from ships to the waggons'. 'Coalporters' fill' the coal merchants' waggons at their wharfs, and deliver the coal at customers' residences. **S**

publicans: performed role of 'undertakers'; possibly 'relative of the northern shipowners'.

Purlmen: watermen who 'keep rowing all day about the coal fleet', licensed to carry liquor to the coal-whippers at work.

quarters: measure of coal; *see* 'quarterage', sect. (B) below, p.194.

raves: additional high sides for coal carts. **D830**

regrater aka **huckster**: one who 'regrates' (*see* Note 'A' below, p.194). **G**

regrating: 'buying goods in a licensed market and selling them to a third party at a higher price'. **G**

'river pirates' (docks slang): most desperate of 'nautical vagabonds, generally armed and equipped with boats'. **P**

rook: widely used measure of production/sales in Midlands' coalfields, e.g. to contain 18 'corve-fulls'. **H**

Room:
- (i)   a measure of coal: 'a weight of 7 tons of coal or 5¼ chaldrons' (*Mech. Mag.*); 'coal is sometimes bought by what is called the Room'. **C**
- (ii) 'Room/Rome/Roomland/Roomlands': open space of waste ground at London riverside used for landing and selling coal: [origins unknown: may have derived from coal jargon (room between uprights) or naval use (space between joists); *see* Harben, *Dictionary of London*; [or from former Roman market on the site].

Rotation Books/lists: pre-1843, documents for co-ordinating colliers' arrivals, metering and berthing in The Pool. **S217**

rutter: pilot book (15th-century). **S**

schute aka **schuyte/shout**: flat barge bringing in coal or wood.

scorage: ancient concession/rebate to buyers, long considered legitimate profit; e.g. due to paying 1s. per 'score' of coals, in lieu of ship-master offering dinner to buyers. **S**

'scuffle-hunters' (docks slang): shore thieves, assisting porters, with long aprons to conceal stolen goods. **P**

sections: allocation of queuing space in Thames, pre offload.

shipmaster aka 'Merchants Marryners': owners of 'colliers'. **S**

'shoot up' a mine: open it up.

spoutage: re spout = shoot for discharging coals from ships into barges; subject to additional charges. **S**

staithes: structure for discharging coals into keels, or collier brigs.

stranger; outsider to trade/mine.

tens: a North-Eastern measure of coal, of three kinds:
- (a)   getting tens: production of coal;
- (b)   led tens: coal carried from colliery to river;
- (c)   vending tens: sale and shipping of coal (=10 Newcastle sea 'chaldrons'). **H**

Tiers: system for mooring colliers in three lines in The Pool, maximum stay 15 days (1838). **S222**

trade tokens: 17th-century, supplementary unofficial coinage, produced by many traders, in default of Crown currency.

tret: allowance to coalbuyers in lieu of 'ingrain', e.g. £1 %. **S**

turbary: peat reserve.

Turn system: ACT 1807: Coal Buyers (Merchants) agree to work cargo according to the Turns set down by Lot in the Turn Paper: 19th-century system for regulating turn-round of a shift or day's unloading of coal; at one time embraced meter-turn (as lynchpin), sales turn and entryturn, with berthing. **S170, 229**

undertaker: from 'crimp', organised 'whippers'. **S**

vat/fat/fatt: coal container/measure. **S**

Vend: (N-E) quantity of coal marketed either by individual collieries or by all sea-sale collieries through coastal shipment. From 1771, quantity was regulated by agreement with coal-owner. Limitation system collapsed, 1845. **S**

waggoner/carman/shooter; accompanied by a 'trimmer', 'trouncer'/'pullback'; also by 'scurf'/'sifter': (all part of complex 19th-century dock jargon, class system). **M262**

Waterage: conveyance from the vessels to the shore. **M239**

weynescote: form of wood (also Ryghholt = Riga Wood).

wharfinger aka **Warfinger/wharfenger**: owner of wharf on river.

whipping-up/coal-whipper: cargoes delivered by teams of c.nine whippers (four in hold, four to whip up on deck by ropes over pulley, one at basket) usually provided by 'undertakers' licensed by CoL. Managed by Factors Society to 1886, handed to Meters' Society. Formed Society of Coal Whippers, Tankmen & Winchmen 1878, 1,000 men … Extinct by 1900. S. Ch.24, p.316.

white wall: face of non-coal-bearing rock, encountered when geology causes seams to rise vertically, not horizontally.

'winning a long five': bribing the 'meters' to make five chaldrons out of six – equivalent to a 20 per cent fraud. **H**

woodmonger/timbermonger, OED, 1260+:
(a) dealer in wood, timber merchant, seller of wood/fuel;
(b) Shakespearian Glossary (1607): a dealer in wood;
(c) Woodmonger: fuel merchant, member of guild.

(Note A: Engrossing, Forestalling (crime of forestal: originally with violence i.e. ambush: ref by 1268), Regrating/regraters: ref by 1353): the variations and evolution of these medieval legalisms are too complex for this History; for details *see* G, *Royal Regulation*, Ch.4, Laws against Forestalling, Regrating and Related Conduct, pp.125-33).

(B) Liveries and medieval terms (CoL)

Aldermen: elder man or senior counsellor. Twenty-five Aldermen now constitute the upper Court, chosen by the residents and certain other business owners or tenants in his ward, retiring at seventy. **D**

(Apprenticeship: *see* 'Servitude')

Assistants: the Court of Assistants make up the governing body of a 'Livery Company', elected or co-opted from the Liverymen; the Skinners first made up a court of assistants to the 'wardens' from 16 of the 'worshipful'. **D**

Bachelor: the composite sections of a merchant Company – former liverymen, business failures, aka 'yeomanry'. **S13**

baillage and **'groundage'**: duties imposed on non-freemen of the CoL in respect of goods imported into/exported from the 'Port of London'. **S**

Beadles: Livery Company officials responsible for ceremonial duties; guard Company's wicket [gate] at Common Hall meetings at Guildhall; has own CoL Beadles Guild.

brotherhood: concept of fellowship within a Livery.

Clerk: 'Learned Clerk': chief executive of the Livery.

clothing: upon admission to a Company a new member is 'clothed of the livery' in a company gown (by the 'Beadle')

Common Council: elected members from the wards, separate from the Aldermanic Court.

Court: 'Past Masters', 'Master', 'Wardens' and 'Assistants' (below the chair). All members are known collectively as the Court of 'Assistants': committee of management.

craft: in 1328 a list of 25 'Mysteries' was drawn up consisting mainly of mercantile and wealthy manufacturing crafts.

custom of London: freemen of a buying and selling guild were 'free' of [i.e. to join] any other.

fines: dues paid on admission and election to office in Livery Company.

Fraternity: religious origin of many guilds.

Freeman: citizen of the CoL, reached in four ways 'honorary', 'patrimony', 'apprenticeship', 'redemption'. A potential Liveryman is admitted as Freeman of the Company, then of the City, before being admitted as a Liveryman. **A/D**

guild/gild: medieval body of workers or traders, usually with a religious foundation, associating for mutual benefit and protection of their trade/craft. Still a category of City Companies.

husbands: guild jargon: *see* (A)

incorporation: formation of a legal or political body; e.g. a 'guild' sponsored by an Alderman and agreed by the Court of Aldermen, A guild may subsequently become a 'Company without Livery' requiring a charitable fund of *c.*£300,000 before applying for Livery status to be granted by the Lord Mayor.

in utero: unborn child, with rights to CoL freedom.

journeymen: qualified workmen serving a guild master.

Letters Patent: legal document establishing an exclusive right, by ancient legal device, from College of Arms (Heralds).

liberty: areas of London outside the City's jurisdiction, e.g. medieval Blackfriars, Southwark, Farringdon Without.

Livery:
(a) bishop's/nobleman's allowance of food/clothing to his household; (b) 'provision to support an office'.
(c) 'payment for services rendered'.
(d) distinctive clothing.
(e) uniform with badges worn by guilds/fraternities.
(f) a guild (synonym).
(g) collective body of Liverymen.

Liverymen: freemen who on election/payment of fee become entitled to wear the Livery/clothing of their Company. Collectively they constitute the City's Livery.

Lord Mayor: Corporation's chief magistrate and ceremonial head. When an Alderman has served as Lord Mayor, he is 'past the chair'.

Mark: German coin introduced into London, 12th century. = 13s. 4d.

Master: originally referred to Master of an apprentice; 'In merchant companies it became the custom to address veteran wardens as Master not only while they were presiding but for life. The title was still a genuine distinction, no other citizen enjoying it except a few in special occupations, such as doctors and lawyers and the chief masons and carpenters'. Also Prime Warden or Upper Bailiff.   **S23**

Master and Wardens: *cursus honorarium* of Livery Company.

'Modern' Livery Companies: *see* Appendix II(E).

mortmain: under posthumous legal control.   **OED**

Mystery: OED, med, Latin *misterium*:
(a) handicraft, craft, trade, profession or calling.
(b) trade guild or company; (attributed elsewhere to Italian *misterio*).

Past Masters: former Masters of Livery Company; immediate Past Master is the most senior Past Master, representing the Master as required (PM).

patrimony: son/daughter can claim to enter if father was freemen of the company at the time of applicant's birth. **A**

quarterage: levy/subscription p.a., once quarterly.

redemption: membership of Livery by payment of a fee.

Renter aka **Junior Warden:** formerly responsible for collecting 'rents'; now chairman of Company finance committee.

rent: ancient charges to Liverymen.

scot and lot: man who was in 'scot and lot' could vote in his 'wardmote': 'if a merchant had any property in the City, it was to his interest to remain continuously in scot and lot, that is, to bear his share of City taxes'.

scutage: 'money paid to king instead of personal military service'.

servitude: entry to Livery when an apprenticeship has been satisfactorily completed.

Sheriff: shire reeve – oldest royal [up to 1191, leading] official; two elected p.a. by 'Common Hall'. An Alderman cannot become Lord Mayor without having served as Sheriff.

The Staple: (fr. *étape* = dump; a location, as at Calais.

Upper Warden: senior warden, chairman of social committee, whose members are 'stewards' who serve for seven years.

wardmote: (Sax. Folkesmote, lat. '*plebiscita*') communal meeting.

wards: each of 25 wards represented by an 'Alderman' and a certain number of Common Councilmen.

'Worshipful': prefix designation of all guilds (except Master Mariners) poss. denotes religious 'Fraternity' origins.

yeoman: 'originally a young man, a rank below gentleman; a small farmer, very occasionally the rank between freeman and liveryman'.

(C) ENERGY POLICY AND CONSERVATION TERMS

ATM: advanced technology mining.

carbon aka fossil fuel: term applied to coal, oil and natural gas.

carbon sequestration: process for reducing carbon emissions to zero.

CCGT: Combined Cycle Gas Turbine.

CCS: Carbon-Capture-and-Sequestration; also Carbon capture and storage.

CCT: Clean Coal Technology,

CV: calorific value: measure of the amount of heat obtained from a fuel, expressed in British Thermal Units (BTU), therms, joules.

ELSIE: Electronic Signalling & Indicating Equipment.

GW: Gigawatt = 10[9] Watts.

IEA: International Energy Authority.

Manufactured (or 'town') gas: coal as main UK source for gas prior to use of oil as feedstock.

mb/d: production of million barrels (of oil) a day.

MRDE: Mining Research and Development Establishment (NCB).

M.t.c.e.: million tons of coal equivalent.

NCB: National Coal Board (1947-82).

OPEC: Organisation of Petroleum Exporting Countries (Algeria, Ecuador, Gabon, Indonesia, Iran, Iraq, Kuwait, Libya, Nigeria, Qatar, Saudi Arabia, United Arab Emirates, Venezuela).

PF: primary fuel – usable in the basic form in which it is obtained, such an coal, petroleum, natural gas, nuclear and hydro-electricity.

reserves of fuel, estimates: levels of accuracy: (a) 'proven'; (b) 'probable'; (c) 'possible'.

smog: cloud of sulphur dioxide and smoke formed in London and other cities prior to the Clean Air Act 1956.

SNG: substitute natural gas (from coal).

strip mining: opencast (= surface) mining.

t.c.e.: tons of coal equivalent.

Tons of coal, different measurements:
  (a) 'long ton': UK: 1,015 kilograms.
  (b) short ton: US: 907 kilograms.
  (c) metric ton: 1,000 kilograms.
  (d) 'tonnes' of 'standard' coal: EEC.

UCG: Underground Coal Gasification

Information for the Glossary is gratefully acknowledged from:

BR   J.J. Bagley/P.B. Rowley, *Documentary History of England*, v.1 (1066-1540)
D   I.G. Doolittle, *City of London*
E   Derek Ezra, *Coal and Energy*
F   V.Hope/C. Birch/G.Torry, *Freedom*
B   Gwen Seaborne, *Royal Regulation*
K   J. Kennedy Melling, *Discovering London's Guilds*
M   Mayhew, *London Labour*
S   F.R.S. Smith, *Sea Coal*
H   M.W. Flinn, & [H] J. Hatcher, *British Coal Industry*, vs.1, 2
RSA   Hylton Dale, *Woodmongers*; lecture to RSA
PM   Alan Woollaston, The Plumbers.

Also: The Fuellers' own 2006 Report to the DTI Energy Review;
OED The original O.E.D. of Sir James Murray.

Select Bibliography and Sources

WITH ABBREVIATIONS

Published books/pamphlets are printed in italics; articles in 'inverted commas'; unpublished matter/theses, in plain roman type. If no place of publication given, it is London.

ABBREVIATIONS

BL: British Library, London
CLRO: Corporation of London Records Office
CoL: City of London
CPMR: *Calendar of Plea & Memoranda Rolls* of the CoL
EconHR: *Economic History Review*
EHR: *English Historical Review*
FA: Fuellers' Archive
GH: Guildhall Library, City of London
HT: *History Today*
IHR: Institute of Historical Research, London University
ILN: *Illustrated London News*
LJ: *London Journal*
LMA: London Metropolitan Archives (frmr Record Office, CoL)
LRS: London Record Society
MiD: Museum in Docklands
MoL: Museum of London
NMeM: National Media Museum, Bradford
R/C: Reform Club Library
RSA: Royal Society of Arts, Archive
TNA/PRO: (former Public Records Office) The National Archives
TRHS: *Transactions* of Royal Historical Society
U: University

PRIMARY SOURCES

(i): UNPUBLISHED ORIGINAL SOURCES

BL:

i. 'Ad session Oier et Terminer ... tent' pro Civitat' London ... decimo septimo die Junii ii [order for the prevention of the 'great disorders and rudeness of Carrmen, Colliers, Woodmongers, Draymen, Carriers and brick and tylers' etc; 17 June 1667.

ii. 'By the Company of Woodmongers [orders for the regulation of their trade]: 1657.

iii. Free Carmen: 'The Case of the antient free Carmen of London [in reference to the conduct of the Woodmongers' Company] humbly offer'd to the consideration of the Honourable House of Commons': 1690.

iv. 'Lawrence, Mayor. Com Concil. tent. vecesimo septimo die Januarii ... 1664 [acts of Common Council, other documents, for rectifying abuses ... by the Woodmongers in the price and weight of coals; the latest dated May 19 1674].

v. Christ's Hospital: 'Reasons offered by the Governours of Christ's Hospital against the Woodmongers' Bill': 1685.

vi. 'Some Memorials of the Controversie with the Wood-Mongers or traders in fuel, from ... 1664 to this day [October 8 1680] as it lieth before a Committee of the Common Council'.

vii. Wood-Mongers, London: 'The Wood-Mongers remonstrance, or, the Carmen's controversie rightly stated ... By W.L.': 1649 Harleian MS, 6482, f.265. Mercurius Politicus Redivivus, Add. MSS 10116-10117.

BODLEIAN LIBRARY, OXFORD UNIVERSITY:

Royal Charter of 1605 for Woodmongers and Carmen: MS Rawlinson, D725b; (for summary of contents, see *Catalogi Codicum Manuscriptorum Bibl. Bodl. pt.v, fasc. III, Ricardi Rawlinson, Oxon, MDCCCXCIII* (1893).

GH:

David Smith's Gift: correspondence & other papers, relating to 14, St Benet's Hill site: GL Ms 13820.
Company of Watermen & Lightermen; papers re Admiralty 1855: GL Ms 1079.
The Case of the Watermen & Lightermen working on the river of Thames 1730: GL B.side 16.38.
To the worthy citizens of London, but especially to the Common-Councilmen of the said City: The Case of the Woodmongers within this City in relation to Cars, [etc]: 1680: GL PB, B.side 12.40.
Worshipful Company of Watermen & Lightermen: Extracts of orders and regulations relating to the Company in their dispute [with the Woodmongers] 1675: GL PB, A2A2 no.44.

LMA:

Journals of the Common Council, 1666-7
Letter Books: 0 142-5; P 71; Q 258; T 188; X 392; Z 381

TNA/PRO:

C.49 Charles I, Parliamentary & Council Proceedings
Acts of the Privy Council: 1623-1671: PC 2 ser, vs II-XVII
State Papers Domestic: SP/441/23/p.128

(ii): ORIGINAL SOURCES: THESES

IHR/SENATE HOUSE, UoL:

Axworthy, R., *London Merchant Community and its relations with Edward III*, PhD Thesis, U of London (2000)
Hovland, Stephanie, *Apprenticeship in Later Medieval London*, c.1300-c.1530 (RHUL Hist, 2006): Appendices 3, 4, 5, 8.
Lutkin, Jessica, *The Craft of Joiners of London, 1200-1550*, MA Dsstn, Royal Holloway, U of London (2004)
Martin, Clare Anne, *Transport for London 1250-1550*, PhD Thesis, Royal Holloway, U of London (2008)

(iii): OTHER PRIMARY SOURCES

(A) MSS: FA – FUELLERS' ARCHIVES:

The Masters' Book; Minute Books 1984-2008

(B) PRINTED MATERIALS:

Burgess, C., *Church Records of St Andrew, Eastcheap* c.1450-c.1570 (LRS, 1999)
Campbell, R., *The London tradesman ...* (1747), pp.327-8
Carpenter, J. (ed.), Riley, H.T., *Liber Albus (The White Book of the City of London)* (1419, transltn from Latin, 1861)
Chambers R.W. and Daunt M. (eds), *A Book of London English 1384-1425* (Oxford, 1931)
Colquhoun, P., *Treatise on the Commerce and Police of the River Thames ...* (1800)
Descriptive Catalogue of Ancient Deeds in the [PRO] 1890-1915
Fitch, M., *Trades & Occupations in Medieval London (...)* (Incl. index of wills, London Archdeaconry & the Commissary)
Fitzstephen, W., *A Description of London* (1772)
Gardiner, R. of Cheriton, Northumberland, *Englands grievance discovered, in relation to the coal trade ...* (Ibbitson & Stent, 1655: CUL, EEBO)
Gray, W., *Chorographia: A Survey of Newcastle upon Tine* (Newcastle, 1649) new Harleian Miscellany, p.189
Hearsey, J.E.N., *London & the Great Fire* (John Murray, 1965)
Humpherus, H., *History of the Origin & Progress of the Company of Watermen and Lightermen of the River Thames ... 1514-1859* (1874, repub. Wakefield E.P., Mcrfrm, 1981) v.I, pp.98, 303, 324, 392, 400; v.II p.6
Kahl, William F., *A Guildhall Miscellany: A Checklist of Books, Pamphlets & Broadsides on the London Livery Companies* (1962) Woodmongers: London, Corporation: An act for licensing carts, to be used by the freemen, woodmongers, or traders in fuel ... within this City ... fol CLRO (1727)
Nicholas N.H. and Tyrrell E. (eds), *A Chronicle of London 1089-1483* (1827)
Nichols, J.G. (ed.), *The Diary of Henry Machyn, Citizen & Mercant Taylor of London, 1550-1563* (Camden Soc., 1848)
Remembrancia of the City of London, 1579-1664 (1868)
Riley H.T. (ed.), *Memorials of London & London Life in the XIIIth, XIVth & XVth Centuries* (1868)
Sharpe R.R., *Calendars of the Letter-Books of the City of London, Letter-Books 'A' – 'L' 1275-1498 I-XI* (1899-1912)
Sharpe, R.R., *Calendar of Wills Proved and Enrolled in the Court of Husting, London, pt. II, AD 1258-1688* (1890)
Thomas, A.H. and Jones, P.E. (eds), *Calendar of Plea & Memoranda Rolls ... City of London* (Cambridge, 1926-43)
Thomas, A.H. (ed.), *Calendar of Early Mayor's Court Rolls of the City of London*: 1208-1307, 1323-64, 1364-81, 1381-1412, 1413-37, 1437-57, 1458-1582? (Cambridge, 1924)

(C) TRHS, CAMBRIDGE UNIVERSITY PRESS:

Bazeley, Margaret, 'The Extent of the English Forest in the 13th Century', v.4, pp.140-59 (1921)

Cunningham, Rev. W., 'The Formation & Decay of the Craft Guilds'; new ser. v.III, pp.371-90 (1886)

Dunham, Frances H., 'The Relations of the Crown to Trade under James V; new ser., v.XIII, pp.199-247 (1899)

Fisher, F.J., 'The Development of London as a Centre of Conspicuous Consumption in the 16th and 17th centuries'; 4th ser., v.XXX, pp.37-50 (1948)

Giuseppi, M., 'Alien Merchants in England in the 15th century'; new ser., v.IX, pp.75-98 (1895)

Harris, G., 'Domestic Everyday Life, Manners & Customs in the country …: From the Commencement of the 16th century to the Commencement of the 18th century'; old ser., v.IX, pp.224-51 (1881)

(D) MiD:

Box 1: Parliamentary Papers, Official Reports: 1945-8

Box 2: Parliamentary Debates, 1947-9

Box 3: Parliamentary Debates & Pamphlets on Coal: Debates 1946-54; Pamphlets on Coal: 1729-1839; Regulations ref Coal Meters 1892; 26 Pamphlets 1786-1843+

Box 4: Records of Coal Factors Society, 3 Vols., 1761-1885

Box 5: Misc documents

Box 6: Acts of Parliament (incl. J. Hall Case) 1677-1923

Box 7: Books: Willis & Greenhill, *Coastal Trade … 900-1900*

R. Smith, *The Living City*

Carmichael and Lambert, *Views on the Tyne*

W. Eden Hooper, *The London Coal Exchange* (1907)

E. Fraser-Stephen, *Two Centuries in the London Coal Trade, The Story of Charringtons*

Sir W. Runciman, *Collier Brigs & their Sailors*

Sir G. Nott-Bower/R.H. Walkerdine, *National Coal Board – The First Ten Years*

A Link with Tradition: The Story of Stephenson Clarke Shipping Ltd 1730-1980

Box 9: Misc Reports 1799-1851

Box 10: Misc material

Box 11: Reports on the Coal Trade 1800-1838

Box 12: Misc Material ('C.F.S.') 1854-1959

Box 13: Papers ref Coal Meters' Protection Branch 1860-1991

iv: Secondary Sources

(A): Publications/Journals:

BIHR: Veale, E.M., '"Great Twelve": Mistery & Fraternity in 13th Century Lndn': BIHR LXIV No 156 (Oct 1991) pp.237-63

City Recorder, 25 Oct 1984

Economic History: M.D. George, 'London Coalheavers' (1927)

EconHR: vi, 1935: P.E. Jones & A.V. Judges, 'London population in late 17th century'; 2nd ser. x, no.3 (1958), pp.381-94

J.R. Kellett, 'The breakdown of gild and corporation control over the handicraft and retail trade in London'.

EconHR: xlix, 3 (1996), pp.447-72: Galloway, J.A., Keene, D. & Murphy, M., 'Fuelling the city: production & distribution of firewood & fuel in London's region, 1290-1400'.

Home Counties Magazine, 2 1900 pp.45-53 (Holy Trinity Priory)

Illustrated London News: 8.xi.1849

LJ, v.27, no.2 (2002): Chris Kyle, 'Parliament & the Politics of Carting in Early Stuart London'

RSA Journal (Jnl of the RSA), 20 October 1922

(B): Printed Books

(*see also* MiD Archives)

1. Woodmongers and related trades

Bennett, E., *The Worshipful Company of Carmen* (1952, 1982)

Birch, C., *Carr & Carmen, The Fellowship of St Katherine the Virgin & Martyr of Carters* (Buckingham, 1999)

Brown, R.S., *Digging For History – in the Coal Merchants' Archives* (Seaford, 1988)

Dale, H.B., *The Fellowship of Woodmongers: Six Centuries of the London Coal Trade* ('Coal Merchant & Shipper', 1922)

Puttock. A.R., *Livery Company of Woodmongers & Coalsellers & The Society of Coal Merchants, 1376-1979* (1979)

2. Other Guilds of the City of London

Adams, A., *History of the … Company of Blacksmiths* (1951)

Arnold, Caroline, *Sheep Over London Bridge, The Freedom of the City of London* (1995)

Blackham, R.J., *The Soul of the City of London's Livery Companies* (1931)

Corporation of London, *The Livery Companies of the City of London* (2005)

Davies, M. and Saunders, Ann, *History of the Merchant Taylors' Company* (Leeds, 2004)

Ditchfield, P.H., *The Story of the City Companies* (1926)

Doolittle, I.G., *The City of London & Its Livery Companies* (Dorchester, 1982)

Friar, S., *Heraldry* (Sutton, Stroud, 2004)

Hazlitt, W.C., *Livery Companies of the City of London* (1892)

Glover, E., *History of the Ironmongers' Company* (1991)

Hope, Valerie; Birch, C.; Torry, G., *The Freedom: The Past & Present of the Livery, Guilds, and City of London* (Buckingham, 1982)

Jupp, E.B., *Historical Account … Carpenters* (1887)

Kahl, W.F., *The Development of London Livery Companies* (Boston, Mass: 1960)

Kennedy Melling, J., *Discovering London's Guilds & Liveries* (Princes Risborough, 5th edn, 2003)

Nightingale, P., *A Medieval Mercantile Community: The Grocers, Company & The Politics & Trade of London 1080-1485* (New Haven, 1995)

Unwin, G., *The Gilds & Companies of London* (1966 edn)

Veale, E.M., *The English Fur Trade in the Later Middle Ages* (2nd edn, LRS, 2003)

Ward, J.P., *Metropolitan Communities; Trade Guilds, Identity & Change in Early Modern London* (1997)

Young, A.J., *History of the Worshipful Company of Plumbers 1365-2000* (pte, 2000)

3. Medieval London, The Thames and England

Ackroyd, P., *Brief Lives: Chaucer*, Chatto & Windus, permission of the Random House Group (2004)

Ackroyd, P., *Thames, Sacred River*, Chatto & Windus, permission of the Random House Group (2007)

Bagley, J.J./Rowley, P.B., *Documentary History of England*, v.1 (1066-1540) (1966)

Baker, T., *Medieval London* (1970)

Barron, C.M., *London in the Later Middle Ages, Government & People 1200-1500* (Oxford, 2004)

Birch, W. de Gray, *The Historical Charters & Constitutional Documents of the City of London* (1887)

Borer, M.C., *The City of London; a History* (1977)

Clapham, J., *Concise Economic History of Britain* (Cambridge, 1949)

Day J., *The Medieval Market Economy* (Oxford, 1987)

Dyer, C., *Making a Living in the Middle Ages: People of Britain 850-1520* (New Haven, 2002)

Ekwall E., *The Street-Names of the City of London* (Oxford, 1954)

Fitch, M., *Trades & occupations in Medieval London* (2003) (Incl. index of wills, London Archdeaconry & the Commissary)

Harben, H.A., *Dictionary of London* (1918)

Hollaender, A.E.J. and Kellaway, W. (eds), *Studies in London History* (1969):
C.M. Barron, 'Richard Whittington, Man Behind the Myth';
D.V. Glass, 'Socio-economic Status and Occupations in the City of London, End of the Seventeenth Century';
C.A.F. Meekings, 'City Loans ... Hearth Tax, 1664-1668';
S.L. Thrupp, 'Aliens in ... London in the 15th Century';
E.M. Veale, 'Craftsmen and the Economy of London in the Fourteenth Century'.

Jacobs, M.K., *The Fifteenth Century 1399-1485* (Oxford, 1961)

King, E., *Medieval England 1066-1485* (Oxford, 1988)

Kingsford, C.L. (ed.), *John Stow, Survey of London* (1603) 2 vs (Oxford, 1908)

Kingsford, C.L., *Prejudice & Promise in the Fifteenth Century* (Oxford, 1925)

Lobel, M.D. (ed.), *Historic Towns Atlas: The City of London from Prehistoric Times to c.1520* (Oxford, 1989)

Loyn, H.R., *Making of the English Nation* (1991)

McKisack, M., *The Fourteenth Century 1307-1399* (Oxford, 1959)

Power, Eileen, *Medieval People* (1924; 1954)

Power, Eileen and Postan, M.M., *Studies in English Trade in the Fifteenth Century* (1933)

Previté Orton, C.W., *Shorter Cambridge Medieval History* (Cambridge, 1952)

Robertson, D., *Chaucer's London* (1968)

Round, J.H., *The Commune of London* (1899)

Saint, A. and Darley, G., *Chronicles of London* (2003, Weidenfeld & Nicolson, division of Orion Publishing Group)

Seaborne, Gwen, *Royal Regulation of Loans and Sales in Medieval England* (Woodbridge, 2003)

Spencer, B., *Chaucer's London* (1972)

Stenton, F.M., *Anglo-Saxon England* (Oxford, 1943)

Surtz E. and Hexter, J.H. (eds), *The Complete Works of Thomas More*, 4 v.s (1965)

Thrupp, Sylvia L., *The Merchant Class of Medieval London, 1300-1500* (Michigan, 1948)

Trevelyan, G.M., *England in the Age of Wycliffe* (1946)

Weinreb, B. and Hibbert, C., *The London Encyclopaedia* (1983)

Wilkinson, B., *The Later Middle Ages in England 1216-1485* (1969)

4. Legal background

(also relevant to other periods):

Baker, J.H., *Introduction to English Legal History* (1971)

Holdsworth, W., *History of English Law* (1903)

Lewis, A., etc *Law in the City* (Dublin, 2007)

Maitland, F.W., *Forms of Action at Common Law* (Cambridge, 1909)

Musson, A., *Medieval Law in Context* (Manchester, 2001)

Plucknett, T.F.T., *Studies in English Legal History* (1983)

Pollock, F. and Maitland, F.W., *History of English Law* (1895)

Radcliffe, G.R.Y. and Cross, G., *The English Legal System* (1954)

5. 16th-Century London and England

Archer, I., *The Pursuit of Stability: Social Relations in Elizabethan London* (Cambridge, 1981)

Beier, A.L. and Finlay R. (eds), *London 1500-1700: The Making of the Metropolis* (1986)

Corfield P.J. and Harte N.B. (eds), *London & The English Economy 1500-1700* (1990)

Delaune, T., *The Present State of London* (1681), p.342 *Angliae Metropolis* (1690)

Finlay, R.A.P., *Population & Metropolis: the Demography of London, 1580-1650* (Cambridge, 1981)

Hearsey, J.E.N., *London & the Great Fire* (John Murray, 1965)

Holinshead, R., *Chronicles of England* (1577)
Holmes, M., *Elizabethan London* (1969)
Innes, A.D. and Henderson, J.M., *England Under the Tudors* (1953)
Nicholas N.H. and Tyrrell E. (eds), *A Chronicle of London, 1089-1483* (1827)
Neale, J.A., *Queen Elizabeth I* (1967 edn)
Outhwaite, R., *Inflation in Tudor & Stuart England* (1969)
Picard, Liza, *Elizabeth's London …* (2003)
Rappaport, S., *World within worlds: structures of life in 16th-century London* (1989)
Prockter, A. and Taylor, R., *The A to Z of Elizabethan London*, London Topographical Society No. 122 (1979)

6. 17TH-CENTURY LONDON AND THE TIME OF THE GREAT FIRE

Bell, W.G., *The Great Fire of London in 1666* (LTS, 2003 edn)
Boyne, W. (ed.), Williamson, G.W., *Trade Tokens Issued in the Seventeenth Century* (1889)
Burton, Elizabeth, *Jacobeans at Home* (1962)
Cooper, M., *A More Beautiful City: Robert Hooke & the Rebuilding of London after the Great Fire* (Stroud, 2003)
Earle, P., *A City Full of People, Men & Women of London 1650-1750* (1994)
Fuller, T., *The Worthies of England* (1622)
Glass, D.V., *London Inhabitants within the Walls, 1695* (LRS, ii. 1966)
Hearsey, J.E.N., *London & the Great Fire* (1965)
Hollaender, A.E.J. and Kellaway, W. (eds), *Studies in London History* (1969):
    D.V. Glass, 'Socio-economic Status and Occupations in the City of London, End of the Seventeenth Century';
    C.A.F. Meekings, 'City Loans … Hearth Tax, 1664-1668';
Hollar, W., *Exact Surveigh within the Ruins* (1667, LTS)
Reddaway, T., *Rebuilding of London after the Great Fire* (1940)
Saint, A. and Darley, Gillian, *The Chronicles of London* (1994)
Schofield, J., *The Building of London from the Conquest to the Great Fire* (1997)

7. 18TH-CENTURY ENGLISH ECONOMIC LIFE AND SOCIETY

Ashton, T.S., *Economic Fluctuations in England, 1700-1800* (1959)
Clark, G., *Wealth of England from 1496 to 1760* (1946)
George, M. Dorothy, *London Life in the Eighteenth Century* (1925)
Hardyment, C., *Housekeeping Book, Susanna Whatman* (NT, 2000)
Porter, R., *English Society in the Eighteenth Century* (1982)
Redford, A., *Economic History of England 1760-1860* (2nd edn 1960)

Rude, G., *Hanoverian London 1714-1808* (1971)
Summerson, J., *Georgian London* (1949)
Uffenbach, Z.C. von, *London in 1710* (1934)
Watson, J.S., *Reign of George III, 1760-1815* (Oxford, 1976)

8. 19TH-CENTURY ECONOMIC LIFE: ENGLAND AND LONDON

Booth, C., *Life & Labour of the People in London*, vii (Williams & Norgate, 1892-7), pp.367-84
Briggs, A., *The Age of Improvement 1783-1867* (1959)
Chesney, K., *Victorian Underworld* (1979)
Ensor, R.C.K., *England 1870-1914* (Oxford, 1975)
Halévy, Elie, *Victorian Years 1841-1895* (1970)
Mayhew, H., *London Labour and the London Poor* (1861)
Nail, M., *Coal Duties [CoL] and their Boundary Marks* (1972)
Pudney, J., *London's Docks* (1975)
Sheppard, F., *London 1808-1870: The Infernal Wen* (1971)
White, J., *London in the Nineteenth Century* (2007)
Woodward, L., *The Age of Reform* (Oxford UP, 1962)

9. THE HOSTMEN

Baillie, J., *An Impartial History of the Town & County of Newcastle upon Tyne and its Vicinity* (1801)
Brand, J., *History & Antiquities of the Town& County … of Newcastle upon Tyne*, v.II (London, 1789)
Dendy, F.W., *Extracts from the Records of the Company of Hostmen of Newcastle upon Tyne* (Publications of the Surtees Society, v.CV, Newcastle, 1901)
Middlebrook, S., *Newcastle upon Tyne: Its Growth & Achievement* (Newcastle, 1950)
Publications of the Surtees Society, v.105 (Newcastle, 1901)
Thornton, C.E., *Bound for the Tyne, Extracts from the diary – of Ralph Jackson, Apprentice Hostman of Newcastle upon Tyne 1749-1756* (Newcastle, 2000)

10. HISTORY OF ALL FUELS; ENERGY POLICY

Annals of Coal Mining and the Coal Trade (Galloway, 1898)
Ashton, T.S. and Sykes, J., *Coal Industry of the 18th Century* (1929)
Bulman, H.F., *Coal Mining & the Coal Miner* (1920)
Byatt, I.C.R., *The British Electrical Industry 1875-1914: The Economic Returns to a New Technology* (Oxford, 1979)
Dyer, A.D., 'Wood & Coal: a Change of Fuel', *History Today*, 26 (1976)
Ezra, D., *Coal and Energy: the need to exploit the world's most abundant fossil fuel* (1978)
Freese, Barbara, *Coal, A Human History* (2005)
Goodall, F.G., *Burning to Serve: Selling Gas in Competitive Markets* (Ashbourne, 1999)

The History of the British Coal Industry (Oxford, 1993):
- I   *Before 1700: Towards the Age of Coal*, J. Hatcher (1993)
- II   *1700-1830: Industrial Revolution*, M. Flinn (1984)
- III *1830-1913: Victorian Pre-Eminence*, R. Church (1986)
- IV   *1913-1946: Political Economy of Decline*, B. Supple (1987)
- V   *1946-1982: Nationalized Industry*, W. Ashworth (1986)

MacAvoy, P.W., *The Natural Gas Market: Sixty Years of Regulation & Deregulation* (New Haven, 2000)

Nef, J.U., *The Rise of the British Coal Industry* (2 vols, 1932)

Odell, P., *Why Carbon Fuels will Dominate the 21st Century's Global Energy Economy* (Brentwood, 2004)

Parliamentary Papers, 1867/8, xxx, pt. II; 1878/9, XI, Select Committee on Lighting by Electricity

Robens, A., *Ten Year Stint* (1972)

Sampson, A., *The Seven Sisters: The Great Oil Companies & The World They Made* (1975)

Smith, R., *Sea Coal for London – History of the Coal Factors …* (1961)

Society of Coal Merchants, *London Coal Exchange* (1950)

Williams, R., *The Nuclear Power Decisions – British Policies 1953-78* (1980)

Williams, T., *A History of the British Gas Industry* (Oxford, 1981)

11. General Social History

Bragg, M., *The Adventure of English – The Biography of a Language* (2003)

Braudel, F., *Capitalism & Material Life, 1400-1800* (1974)

Briggs, A., *A Social History of England …* (1985)

Heald, T., *Networks* (1973)

Sampson, A., *The Changing Anatomy of Britain* (1982)

Trevelyan, G.M., *English Social History A Survey of Six Centuries Chaucer to Queen Victoria* (1948)

V. Literary Sources

Chaucer, G., *The Canterbury Tales* (1374-8)

Defoe, D.A., Burgess (ed.), *A Journal of the Plague Year* (1722; Penguin, 1966)

Dickens, C., 'The True Story of a Coal Fire', *Household Words*, 1 (1850)

More, T., *Utopia* (1563)

Orwell, G., *Down & Out in Paris & London* (1933)

Pepys, S., R. Latham & W. Matthews (eds), *Diaries* (11 vs, 1970-83)

Reade, C., *The Cloister & the Hearth* (1861)

Index

Compiled by Howard Cooke

Please note: locators in *italics* refer to illustrations, photographs, maps and tables, including information in captions

[203]

M: M:Millan for Workhous

Every description of Grain
Lighter'd, Landed & Carted.

*To
Coal Me
Wh
N: 93,
& Hop*

To 5/4 Ch: Best Coals @

Shooting & M

Exm:d TH

COAL 'MARKETING': MERCHANTS AND PRODUCERS
*Trade cards were used to assist the sale of fuel by merchants such as T. Downing
(of Fenchurch Street and Hope Wharf, Wapping) in 1827. Downing still dealt in
the traditional mix of coal and corn, charging also for 'shooting' and 'metage'*